James G. Burnett

Of the Origin and Progress of Language

Volume IV.

James G. Burnett

Of the Origin and Progress of Language
Volume IV.

ISBN/EAN: 9783742808547

Manufactured in Europe, USA, Canada, Australia, Japa

Cover: Foto ©Andreas Hilbeck / pixelio.de

Manufactured and distributed by brebook publishing software (www.brebook.com)

James G. Burnett

Of the Origin and Progress of Language

OF THE

ORIGIN AND PROGRESS

OF

LANGUAGE.

*Graiis ingenium, Graiis dedit ore rotundo
Musa loqui.*———— HORAT.

VOL. IV.

———

EDINBURGH:
PRINTED FOR J. BELL, EDINBURGH.
AND
T. CADELL, IN THE STRAND, LONDON.
M.DCC.LXXXVII.

The CONTENTS.

BOOK I.

Of the different Excellencies and Defects of different Languages.

         Pag.
Introduction, - -   1

Ch.
1. *No beauty in any art without variety.—There must, therefore, in a perfect language, be a great variety of sounds.—The variety of the sound in the termination particularly to be*

Ch.	Pag.

attended to.—*Defect of the ancient Persian language in this respect.—Defect of the languages of the South Sea in point of variety of sound.—A perfect language must be sweet in the sound, as well as various, but not too sweet of sound.—The barbarous languages defective in this, being too vocal.—The words must not be too short.—The Barbarous languages go to another extreme.—The sound of a language much raised by the use of diphthongs.—The Barbarous languages defective in this.—The difference of spirits in pronunciation makes an agreeable variety.—This the Barbarous languages have.—The quantity of syllables, or the rhythm, makes another variety.—This some of the Barbarous languages have.—Of the melody of language.—Some languages of Savage nations have melody,* 4

2. *Words considered as significant.—In a language of art there must be of them a sufficient number to express all*

The CONTENTS.

Ch.   Pag.

the variety of things.—Defect of Barbarous languages in this respect.—There must not be a redundancy, any more than a defect of words.—This prevented by that art of language we call flection.—In this the Barbarous languages very defective.—The words of the language should convey the meaning fully and accurately,—also without obscurity or ambiguity.—In both these articles Barbarous languages are defective.—They supply the defect by tones of the voice.—Words, that have a connection in their meaning, connected together in their sound by derivation and composition.—The Barbarous languages want this art.—The want of words supplied by metaphors and other tropes.—In this the Barbarous languages are not deficient,—but most deficient of all in syntax.—Reasons for this.—All languages spoken by Barbarous nations not barbarous,   -   -   12

Ch.	Pag.
3. Greater variety both of sound and sense in composition than in single words.—The greater variety the greater beauty,—also the greater difficulty.—The wonderful variety of composition in the learned languages. Of composition in the Barbarous languages.—There must be more or less of the art of composition among such Barbarous nations as hold public assemblies, and therein make harangues. —A story to that purpose,	20
4. An account of the Greek language.— This the most perfect language the author knows.—Its resemblance to the Sanscrit language of India.—From the Greek language the author has formed his notion of what is most perfect in language.—Of the sound of the Greek language.—More sounds in it than we can pronounce.—Vowels in Homer frequently gaping upon one another.—Also rhymes, both of verses and of hemistics.—The words in Greek neither too short nor too long.	

| Ch. | Pag. |

—*The shortest words are those that occur the most frequently, such as Conjunctions and Prepositions.*—*The terminations of the Greek words most various and most pleasant to the ear.*—*None of their words terminate in mute consonants.*—*Difference of spirits in Greek.*—*This should not be confounded with* loud *and* low.—*No such distinction betwixt the syllables of the same word in Greek or Latin.* 24

5. *Of the music of the Greek language.*—*It consists, like other music, of* melody *and* rhythm.—*It has melody in succession, and may be considered as having music in parts.*—*Of the difference betwixt the melody of music and that of speech.*—*Of the* rhythm *of the Greek language, and the beauty it must have given to their pronunciations.*—*The music of language known even among some Barbarous nations.*—*The northern nations of Europe probably got their language from nations who spoke a musical language;*

Ch.   Pag.

but not having a genius for music, they lost that part of the language.—*The Greeks a most musical nation,—got the elements of music from Egypt, but improved it very much.*—Of the music of the Indians of North America, how they came to have music in their language accounted for.—*Conclusion of what is said upon the sound of the Greek language.*—Necessity of analysing it, as has been done, in order to form a right judgment of it.   34

6. *Of the words of the Greek language, considered as significant.*—The art of the Greek language most wonderful in this respect.—*Of the* noun, *and the various things denoted by its declension.*—Of the verb, *and the still greater variety of expression by it.*—*Of the words in Greek formed from the verb.*—The Greek verb, though expressing so many different things, not incumbered or overloaded.   43

7. *Of the* composition *in Greek.---The use of it in saving words, and making the*

The CONTENTS. ix

Ch. Pag.

*syſtem of the language more perfect.—
Of the variety of its compoſition with
verbs and prepoſitions.—Of* derivation
*in the Greek language.—The account,
given by the author, of the Greek derivation, makes the language a wonderful ſyſtem of art.—The ſame was
the ſyſtem of Hempſterhuſius.—Not
probable that both Hempſterhuſius and
the Author ſhould have fallen into the
ſame error, without communication
with one another.—Other arguments
in favour of this ſyſtem of etymology.
—The Greek, according to this ſyſtem,
reſembles very much the Sanſcrit language.—The language of Homer particularly has a wonderful reſemblance
to that language.* - 51

8. *Of* compoſition *in Greek—the greateſt beauty of all—requires variety as
much as any thing elſe belonging to
language.—The arrangement in Greek
wonderfully various.—By a proper
arrangement the ſenſe conveyed more*

b

Ch. Pag.

forcibly than it could be otherwise.—This composition, though difficult to be understood at first, becomes easy.—It appeared so beautiful to the scholars that flourished after the restoration of letters, that they disdained to write in their vernacular tongue.—Of the many particles used in Greek.—The use of these particles, both with respect to the sense and sound.—Of the wonderful beauty of the composition of Demosthenes, when pronounced by himself - 59

9. *Of the* Latin *language.—That language the oldest dialect of the Greek—liker therefore to the Oriental Languages.—It has tones, but not so accurately marked as in Greek.—But the quantity of syllables accurately observed in it.—As to spirits, much fewer aspirates than in Greek.—The Latin language defective in the elemental sounds, particularly in diphthongs.—These the Latins commonly resolve.—Examples of this.—*

The CONTENTS.

Ch.   Pag.

The greatest difference of all betwixt the sound of the two languages is, that the Latins terminate so many words in mute consonants, the Greeks none at all.—The terminations of -orum and -arum, in the Latin language, not pleasant. -   -   71

10. The words of the Latin language considered as significant.—In that respect inferior to the Greek more still than in sound—particularly in the verb.—Examples of the defect of the Latin language in that part of speech—inferior even to the English.—Defective also in participles.—The Latins want also the variety of two aorists and three futures.—Defective also in moods—wanting also a voice which the Greeks have in their verbs, and a dual number both in their verbs and their nouns.—The Latin wants one part of speech wholly, viz. the article.—The consequence of this defect is to make the expression of the

Ch. Pag.

language obscure and ambiguous.—
Examples of this. - 82

11. *Of Composition in Latin—not different in variety of arrangement from the Greek.—In some of the Latin poets greater variety of arrangement than in the Greek.--But in the prose authors a tedious sameness in the arrangement, by placing the verb last so often in the sentence.—The want of particles, such as the Greeks have, a great defect in the Latin composition.* 94

12. *The words of the modern Greek the same for the greater part with those of the ancient—different in the pronunciation and grammar.—Of the sound of the modern Greek—little variety in it.—Five letters sounded the same way.—No* diphthongs or aspirates—*no* melody or rhythm, *but only* accents, *such as ours.—They retain something of the grammatical art.—form some cases and tenses by flection—have genders and numbers in their*

nouns, and persons and numbers in their verbs—but their grammar cannot be reduced to any rule.—The English pronunciation of the ancient Greek very like to the pronunciation of the modern Greek—has all the faults that pronunciation can have—formerly it was still worse, as they neglected the quantity, and pronounced the accents as they do the accents in their own language.—A reformation may be made of the English pronunciation of the Greek, without much difficulty.—The advantage of the Scottish pronunciation.—The corruption and debasement of the Greek language should be a warning to other nations to preserve their language, by the study of the grammatical art in the ancient languages. - 97

13. *Of the sound of the English language.*—It consists chiefly of monosyllables.—The words crouded with consonants, and many terminated with the aspirated t.—This fault of the

Ch.   Pag.

*language aggrated by modern use.—
No melody or rhythm in the English language.—The words and syllables, at the same time pronounced with a great variety of* tones; *but these not reduced to any rule.—The wonderful art of the Greek language in this respect.—Of* accents *in English.—They give a variety to the pronunciation of the language, and make our versification more various and beautiful than that of other modern nations.—The abuse of our modern accents in our modern use of them.—Not to be compared, though ever so properly used, to the rhythm of Greek and Latin.—The words in English considered as significant.—In this respect, the language is still more inferior to the Greek and Latin, particularly in the verb.—The time of it not expressed, except by one flection of the word; nor the* numbers *except in one instance.—Defective also in the expression of* persons.—*We had once a* mood *expressed by the termination;*

Ch.	Pag.

but that is now lost.—Only two participles *expressed by termination.*—*The English more defective still in voices, than in tenses or moods.*—No middle voice.—*And no tense, mood, or participle in the* passive voice, *expressed by flection.*—*The clumsy circumlocutions that we are obliged to use to supply the defects of the passive voice.*—*As to* nouns in *English, they have no genders nor cases, and therefore may be reckoned indeclinable words.*—*The composition also of words very defective in English; and also the etymology, as it is not an original language.* - - - 110

14. *Of English composition of words in sentences.*—*The defect of it compared with the Greek and Latin composition.*—*The want of variety of arrangement in it.*—*Examples of this from Horace's ode to Pyrrha, translated by Milton.*—*Milton, in his prose stile as well as verse, has all the variety of arrangement that the language will*

Ch.	Pag.

admit.—*The present arrangement, like the French, in what is called the natural order.—Our composition cannot be sufficiently diversified, otherwise than by composition in periods. —Milton's Latin stile composed of very fine periods.—In his English prose, the language does not permit him to vary his stile so much; very different, however, from the fashionable stile at present.—An account of that stile.—It is of two different kinds,* 128

15. *The French language inferior to the English in sound, having neither accent nor quantity.—It is a fault in speaking French to mark any accent. —They have no perceptible difference in the quantity of their syllables.— This makes their versification very imperfect, compared with the English.—Their long verse particularly, most tiresomely uniform.—The French words not so much cronded with consonants as the English, but wanting*

| Ch. | Pag. |

aspirates too much.—The Grammar of the French language more complete than of ours, having much more flection,—but of this they do not avail themselves in their composition at present; but did so formerly, particularly in their verse. - - 135

16. *Of the Italian language.*—*The words of it long and full.*—*Of Vowels.*—*Few of their words terminated by Consonants.*—*Their pronunciation therefore more flowing than either that of English or French.*—*They have accents such as the English.*—*Make therefore poetry of blank verse.*—*Have long and short syllables, but no diphthongs, except one.*—*Their accents not so violent as those in English,—do not obscure the pronunciation of the other syllables.*—*It is a language better for music than any other now known.*—*The words not lost in their music.*—*It is more reconcilable to the rhythm of the language, than the mu-*

Ch. Pag.

sic even of the Greek Tragedy.—The grammar of their language more complete than that of the English, particularly in their verbs; but no declension of nouns.—This appears to be the most artificial part of language,—one part of speech it has more than the Latin, viz. the Article,—has greater variety in its accents, and therefore in its poetry, than the English.—Some observations upon language in general, arising from the Italian language.—The tone of different languages distinct from the pronunciation of the letters or words.—Very difficult to be acquired by a foreigner, - - 144

17. From the comparison of languages in the preceding chapters, it is evident that the Greek and Latin are much superior to the modern.—These are barbarous in the proper sense of the word.—The author, in this inquiry, has followed the ancient method of investigating things.—The ad-

Ch.	Pag.

vantage to be got from the comparison of different languages.—*Impossible that a man, who understands only one language, can know either its excellencies or defects.*—Not having the same materials as the ancients, it is impossible we can compose so well.—*All we can do, is to give as much variety as possible to our stile.*—This is to be done chiefly by composition in periods.—*Numbers in our prose, not to be affected.*—This the fault of some modern English writers.—*Of the degeneracy of all languages, the originals of which we know.*—The degeneracy most remarkable of the Greek language.—*The degeneracy of the English language in modern times, both in sound and signification of the words.*—Example of this last.—*Reason why the author has insisted so much upon the sound of the languages he has compared.*—Written language not spoken, may be called a dead language, whereas what is spoken, is a living language.—*The de-*

Ch.	Pag.

generacy *of language and other neceffary arts of life, cannot be accounted
for otherwife than by a degeneracy of
the people.—The want of an ear and
voice for mufic, makes the northern
nations incapable of pronouncing as the
ancient Greeks did.—Of the great difficulty of the invention of language,
both as to the* matter *and the* form.—
The matter *of language not furnifh-
ed, as that of other arts, by Nature,
but by man himfelf.—Of the defect of
the pronunciation even of vowels, in
fundry nations.—The* form *of language ftill more difficult than the* material *part of it.—Wonderful inventions for expreffing the infinity of
things, by a limited number of words.
—Language of fo difficult invention,
that it would not have been invented
by men, without fupernatural affiftance; but, being invented, it might
be cultivated and improved without
fuch affiftance.—Even for this certain
things neceffary which are not to be
found in this age.—The practice of*

Ch.	Pag.
language, *after it is invented, different from the practice of other arts,*	159

BOOK II.

Of Stile, and its Different Kinds.

Ch.	Pag.
1. Public speaking *an art—also* private conversation.—Writing *an art likewise.—The best orations could not please, if they were not first well written.—The art of writing different, according to the different subjects.—In writing upon certain sciences, such as mathematics, no art of stile is required.—Of the nature of that study, and how much it engrosses a man,*	189

Ch.   Pag.

2. *Writing, being an art, must be either invented or learned.*—*Was not invented among the northern nations, any more than any other liberal art.*—*Must be learned from the Greeks, as well as statuary and painting.*—*Good writing more difficult than either of these arts.*—*The comparison of them with the writing art, both as to the subject and the materials.*—*The best models of the writing art still extant* - - 197

3. *Variety the great beauty of stile, as well as of language.*—*Of the variety of single words.*—*There may be too great variety of these.*—*Examples of authors who exceed in that way, such as Plato, Cicero, and Lord Shaftesbury.*—*Demosthenes a model in that respect, as well as in others;*—*also Horace.*—*The rule to be followed in this matter,* - - 205

4. *Of the composition of words.*—*Of the variety, which the* rhythms *and ac-*

cents *of the Greek language gave to their pronunciation.—Those were a beauty of their prose, as well as of their verse composition.—No* melody or rhythm *in the pronunciation of English.—We have only what we call* accents.—*These measure our verse but not our prose.—The French have neither* quantity *nor* accent.—*The Italians have* accents.—*The modern Greeks have* accents *such as ours.— We want one of the greatest beauties of ancient composition, variety of arrangement of words.—Not easy to set bounds to that variety in the ancient languages.—That arrangement not so artificial in their conversation, and in their laws and decrees; very artificial in their poetry.—Examples of this from Horace's odes.—Not so much of it in his satires and epistles.—Virgil's versification distinguished in this way;—too much of it in him;—less of it in Homer, except in his similies. —Of the figure* Hyperbaton, *and of the difficulty of defining it.—Of the*

Ch. Pag.

singularity of the Latin arrangement of words, concluding the sentence so often with the verb:—Difference in this respect betwixt the Greek and Latin composition.—The only way of varying the stile of modern languages is by composition in periods.—Those who do not think periods beautiful, do not know what beauty is.—The disadvantages of composing in short sentences:—Weakens the comprehension of the hearers or readers:—Makes them unable to speak or read such composition.—The taste and the facility of composing in that way, only to be acquired by the study of the ancient authors, particularly Demosthenes.—A great orator in England formed by reciting his orations. - 211

5. *The beauty of the Greek composition perceived even by the people.—Of the difference betwixt a learned and an unlearned judge, in the matter of oratory and of popular writing.—The art of composition best learned from*

| Ch. | Pag. |

Dionyſius the Halicarnaſſian;—he divides the art into two branches, the choice of the words, and the joining them properly together.—This laſt, the moſt difficult of the two.—Two things required to make fine compoſition, that it ſhould be pleaſant, and that it ſhould be beautiful.—Theſe muſt depend upon the elements of ſpeech properly joined together.—Of the letters, the ſyllables, and the words in Greek.—Of the changes which their orators made upon their words.—The compoſition of words into periods, of great variety and beauty.—Four things required to make fine compoſition, melody, rhythm, variety, and what is ſuitable or proper to the ſubject.—Of the melody of the Greek language.—Different tones upon different words in other languages as well as the Greek, but not regulated by art. —Of the rhythm in Greek.—Shown that there is a rhythm in the proſe as well as the verſe.—A difference of rhythms suited to different stiles in prose.—Of the difference betwixt the rhythm of verse and of prose.—The mind much affected by rhythm as well as by other kinds of motion.—The greatest excellence of prose is to resemble verse, and of verse to resemble prose.—This explained.—Prose resembles verse by rhythm,—but it must not be the rhythm of verse.—Examples given in the Greek Lyric poetry, of rhythms that do not appear to be regular or measured.—Examples of such rhythms in Demosthenes.—That there are such rhythms in prose, attested by Aristotle as well as by the Halicarnassian.—Of poetry in English in which the verse is concealed.—Of prose in English resembling verse.—How verse is made to resemble prose.—Examples of this from Homer and from Milton.—Of variety in the prose stile.—That absolutely necessary to make it pleasant.—There must be a variety not only in the words, but of the rhythms and the melody.—Lit-

Ch.	Pag.

tle variety at present in our English prose.—Milton imitates the ancients in this as in other things.—Opinions of certain critics in the days of the Halicarnassian, that Demosthenes did not labour his words so much as the Halicarnassian supposes.—Answer to this objection.—The writing of numerous prose, though difficult at first, becomes easy by practice.—Examples of this from other arts.—The art of fine speaking and writing more difficult than the other arts;—requires greater labour to excell in it.—A great memory necessarily required in an ancient orator.—An art of memory among them, unknown in modern times.—The nature of this art.—If the moderns excell or equal the ancients in oratory, it must be by superiority of genius,—Commendation of the Halicarnassian's writings. - 246

6. In judging of what is proper in writing, the subject only to be considered.—Stile, divided according to the sub-

Ch.	Pag.

ject, is of six kinds,—1. Epistolary stile, should be concise, and without any thing like composition in periods. —The ancients excelled in that kind of writing as well as in every other. —2. Dialogue writing,—That nothing else but conversation written, —Of the stile of conversation,—few excell in it.—Bodily qualities necessary for that excellence.—Some so deficient in these, that it is impossible they can converse agreeably.—Speaking and moving distinguish a gentleman and lady more than any thing else.—Both studied more in France than in Britain.—Defects of pronunciation in private conversation may be corrected.—Of the fault of too fast speaking.—Of the contrary extreme. —Of speaking too slow and with an affected gravity.—Of too strong emphasis in speaking.—Too much study to speak well must not be shown in private conversation.—Provincial and professional dialects to be avoided.— Verses well repeated, an ornament of

Ch.

conversation.—Of politeness in conversation;—four things required in order to be polite, - - 289

6. Dialogue writing *is conversation upon the subject of some art or science.—Not a mere catechism, but of the poetic kind, having a fable with characters and manners;—not therefore real conversation, such as the Socratic conversations recorded by Xenophon.—Plato the great dialogist of antiquity.—His dialogues fictions even as to the matter.—Some of them admirable pieces of poetry;—but he does not succeed when he delivers whole systems of science in that way.—Aristotle's manner in such works much better.—The stile of dialogue should be simple.—Plato's stile not so in some of his dialogues.—A poetical arrangement of the words affected by him.—Cicero the next great dialogist of antiquity;—his manner quite different from Plato's:—Wherein that difference consists.—His stile also very*

Ch.	Pag.

different from Plato's;—great variety of matter in his philosophical dialogues.—The sect of philosophy, to which he was addicted, furnished arguments upon both sides of a question.—They are full also of examples from both Greek and Roman history.—The rhetoric of them better than of his orations,—his dialogues on the subject of eloquence, and in general his writings upon eloquence, the best part of his works.—Eloquence the delight and study of his life;—philosophy he only applied to when he could do nothing better.—Nothing therefore new or excellent in his philosophical works;—but his rhetorical, admirable of the kind.—Only two rhetorical dialogues;—of these the one De Oratore, the best thing that ever Cicero wrote;—it is perfect of the kind, having both fable and characters:—The personages in this dialogue;—not all the same the second day that they were the first:—The difference accounted for:—The time and place of the dialogues marked:—*The endurance of it also*:—*That more confiftent with probability, than the length of fome of Plato's difputations*:—*It is divided into two days.*—*The difputation of the firft contained in Cicero's* firft book.—*The fubject of that difputation.*—*The fecond day's difputation divided into two converfations; the one in the forenoon, the other in the afternoon.*—*The forenoon's converfation contained in the fecond book.*—Antonius *the fpeaker there, who goes thro' all the fubject matter*:—*The narration is agreeably diverfified by one of the perfonages explaining that part of eloquence, which confifts in pleafantry and facetioufnefs.*—*The* third *converfation in the afternoon of the fecond day.*—*This contained in Cicero's third book.*—*The fcene of it changed.* Craffus *the chief fpeaker there, who explains all the ornaments of fpeech.*—*The exordium of this third book very fine, and very pathetical, giving an account of the calamities,*

| Ch. | Pag. |

which after that befel the commonwealth, and in which most of the speakers in that dialogue perished.—Of the grand idea of an orator which Crassus had.—It comprehends, according to him, the knowledge of arts and sciences.—In ancient times, the knowledge of things and words was not divided.—This division first made in the schools of philosophers.—Answer to the objection that it is impossible to learn so many things.—A pause after this in the conversation, which is interrupted by Cotta putting Crassus in mind of the province he had undertaken, which was to explain the manner of an oration, as Antonius had done the matter;—Crassus accordingly explains the ornaments of single words;—of words in composition;—of rhythms;—of what is decent and proper; and, lastly, of pronunciation and accent.—Cicero concludes the dialogue, with a compliment to his friend Hortensius from the mouth of Crassus.—Of the decorum

Ch.	Pag.

observed in this last day's conversation with respect to those who speak.—*The speech of Crassus the most laboured part of the dialogue.*—Cicero there gives his own idea of the perfect orator.—*That idea a true idea;*—without that universal knowledge, an orator cannot be rich in the ornaments of speech, nor have that elevation of mind necessary for a great speaker.—*He cannot be such a speaker as Pericles.*—The dialogue upon the whole the finest part of Cicero's works.—*Of his treatise* De Senectute,—not a dialogue, but a most pleasant little composition.—*A translation of it into Greek by Theodorus Gaza.*—Another little treatise of Cicero upon Friendship.—*That comes nearer dialogue than the former.*—Some general observations upon Cicero's dialogues.—Cicero more happy in the choice of the personages of his dialogues than Plato.—*Also much greater politeness in Cicero's dialogues than in Plato's.*

Ch. Pag.

—*The best school of politeness to be found, is in Cicero's dialogues.—Cicero's dedication of his works to some friend, much to be approved of.—Those dedications show, that he had a heart capable of friendship.—The advantages of philosophy, friendship, and the society of such men as he lived with in those days, and in these,* 304

8. *Of Lord Shaftesbury's dialogue, entitled* The Moralists;—*this a complete dramatical piece in all its parts; —better divided as to time, than some dialogues of Plato.—Of the different characters in it.—The first day's conversation a proper introduction to what is principal in the piece, viz. the conversion of a sceptic to theism.—The second day's conversation is divided into four parts:—The first is of Philocles with Theocles in the morning, alone;—the second at dinner, when two new characters are introduced;—The third is in the fields, when Theocles, in a long dis-*

course, demonstrates the existence of God from his works.—Here the catastrophe of the piece begins.—The sequel of this conversation contains consequences from what had been before demonstrated.—The fourth conversation of the second day is upon the subject of miracles and prodigies.—This conversation agreeably varied with respect to the speakers as well as the subject.—Of the third day's conversation of Philocles with Theocles alone.—The scene the same as where they met the first day.—Of the Rhapsodies of Theocles in this conversation, and the stile of them;—not incredible to those who have heard the Italian rhapsodists.—Subject of the first rhapsody is an invocation of Divinity;—of the second, a description of that vivifying power, which pervades all Nature;—the third has for its subject the elements and minerals;—the fourth contains a description of the different countries of the earth, and the various appearances of Nature in

Ch.   Pag.

them.—*Betwixt some of the Rhapsodies, a great deal of cool reasoning and dialogue in the Socratic way of question and answer is interspersed.—Conclusion of the work suitable to the main design of it;—contains, 1mo, An account of Beauty, and the several kinds of it;—shows that all beauty is resolvable into the Supreme Beauty of the First Being.—Beauty produces admiration, and admiration enthusiasm. —Of the several kinds of enthusiasm. The sense of beauty shown to be innate in man, and not acquired.—2do, The conclusion also shows the necessity of philosophising; and that, in fact, every man does philosophise more or less.—Observations upon this dialogue: —The fable of it excellent, with greater variety than in Cicero's dialogue* De Oratore :—*The stile such as might be expected from a man like Lord Shaftesbury :—Politeness too, such as in Cicero's dialogues.—Observations on the philosophy of this piece. —The love, of which beauty is the*

| Ch. | Pag. |

object, made a fundamental principle both of virtue and religion.—This philosophy perfectly agreeable to Scripture.—From the same principle, Shaftesbury demonstrates the Being and Attributes of God.—This demonstration better than any demonstration of the same a priori.—Dr Clarke's demonstration examined, and shown not to be so complete as that of Shaftesbury.—Shaftesbury's philosophy, however, not perfect in this dialogue.—The distinction betwixt the animal and intellectual parts of our nature, not explicitly laid down.—The consequences of this distinction;—it demonstrates the beautiful to be good; —puts an end to the paradox of the Stoics concerning virtue;—their language more proper than that of the other philosophers.—Praise of Lord Shaftesbury's writings.--They are now out of fashion.—That the fate of other writings, which deserve it as little.—Of Mr Harris's dialogues upon art and happiness,—not properly dialogues, according to my definition.

Ch.	Pag.
—*They have, however, great merit, as all the writings of that author have,*	341

9. *Of the stile of* Hiftory.—*Of the difference betwixt* Hiftory *and* Biography.—*The subject of hiftory is narrative.—Whatever is not narrative in hiftory is epifodical —What epifodes are proper for hiftory,—not political or philofophical reflections upon human nature, fuch as thofe of Salluft in the beginning of* Cataline's *confpiracy, and of the* Jugurthine *war.— Explanation of particular cuftoms and manners of a nation, a proper epifode in hiftory.—Difference in this refpect betwixt the Greek hiftorians of Roman affairs, and their own.—Of the rhetorical ftile in hiftory.—Speeches in it, not digreffions or epifodes but matters of fact and parts of the ftory. —Speeches make political and philofophical reflections not improper in hiftory.—Hiftory therefore a moft pleafant and various compofition;—but the poetical ftile, a variety which hiftory*

does not admit.—*Of the peculiarities of the poetical stile which history does not admit, such as* Epithets, Similes, Metaphors, *and* Minute Descriptions. —*Of the* painting *in Homer, and the difference in that respect betwixt his stile, and the stile of history.*—*Of the choice of words in the historical stile.* —*Difference, in that respect, betwixt the stile of Homer and of history.*—*Of the* Composition *in history, by which the stile of it is chiefly to be distinguished from common speech;*—*not to be distinguished in that way by* variety of arrangement, *as in Greek and Latin, but only by* Periods.—*Of the great beauty of* Periods.—*Quotation upon that subject from Aristotle, showing, that he thought there could be no beauty, without a* System *and a* Whole.—*There is nothing that can be properly called* Composition *without periods.*—*Of the defect of Sallust and Tacitus in this respect.*—*The stile of Tacitus worse than that of Sallust.* —*One example of a Greek author,*

Ch.	Pag.
	who writes like Sallust.—Such compositions still more inexcusable in Greek than in Latin. - - 395

10. *The history of Herodotus most various both in matter and stile.—The matter takes in the whole history of the world, as far as it was known, before his time.—Yet there is an unity in his work, such as there is in Homer's poems.—He begins his work, as Homer does, with the cause of the wars betwixt the Greeks and Barbarians, which are the subject of his work.—Other things he has introduced as episodes.—Of the truth of the facts in Herodotus.—These not credible to a man, who believes that men have always been the same in all ages and nations.—No lies in Herodotus.—Of the variety of his stile.—Not poetical, though like the stile of Homer;—very much figured, and yet neither rhetorical nor poetical.—It is composed in periods, but not rhetorical periods.—Examples of the periods*

Ch.	Pag.

in Herodotus.—Cicero mistaken in saying, that there are no numbers in Herodotus.—Of the speeches in Herodotus;—there are but few, but these upon proper occasions;—the matter of them excellent.—Not many reflections, nor philosophical and political observations; but these to the purpose.—One example of them.—The dialect, in which he writes, Ionic.—He uses much the terminations of the datives plural in that dialect.—No epithets, similes, or picturesque descriptions in his stile, nor any of the strong figures used by Homer.—One figure of Homer, much used by him, viz. dialogue.—Examples of Herodotus's dialogue.—His stile distinguished in that way from that of every other historian.—Herodotus a religious historian.—All historians, as well as poets of the higher order, ought to be religious.—Herodotus not superstitious, or over credulous, in matters of religion, - 414

ERRATA.

P. 65. l. 20. and 21. For *German Professor Hoegenville*, Read *Dutch Professor Hoogeveen*.

—231.—26. For *for the Greek*, Read *for the Greeks*.

—293.—18. For *in the 10th book*, Read *in the 9th*.

——— For *Epist.* 9. Read *Epist.* 16.

PREFACE.

I Here prefent to the public the fourth volume OF THE ORIGIN AND PROGRESS OF LANGUAGE; and, in order to accomplish my plan, I have promifed a fifth. The reader will perceive, that in this and the preceding volumes of this work, and indeed in all that I have written, whether upon the fubject of Language or Philofophy, I have made much ufe of that great art, the greateft of all arts, as Cicero fays, by which we are taught *rem univerfam in partes tribuere, latentem definiendo explicare.* If therefore the reader be a man, who has never applied to any art or fcience, or, if he think that he has genius and natural parts fufficient to comprehend any art or fcience without fuch accurate definitions and minute divifions, he needs not give himfelf the trouble to read this work, or any other that I have publifhed,

PREFACE.

or shall publish; for by the study of the ancient philosophy I have got so much into the habit of treating every thing as a science, or system, that I can think, speak, or write, of no subject of art or science but in that way. He may therefore amuse himself by reading compilements of ancient or modern history, collections of facts of natural history, or some things upon the subjects of art or science, under the modest name of *Essays*; in which the authors think themselves confined to no order or method, but set down at a venture some loose thoughts that occur to them upon the subject.

Another thing the reader will observe, that I extol the ancient languages and literature above the modern; and maintain, that the works of the ancients must be our standard in the writing art, as well as in sculpture, painting, and architecture. Whoever therefore thinks that

Venimus ad summum fortunae,—

which, as Horace tells us, was the case of the Romans under Augustus Caesar, and

PREFACE. 3

that we have attained to the perfection of all arts*, him I would likewife advife not to read this work: For there are things in it which may ftumble him in his opinion of the excellency of this age; and, as every man partakes more or lefs of the glory of the age in which he lives, and he may perhaps think that he has a large fhare of it, this work muft have a tendency to leffen him in his own opinion, which I fhould be forry for; for, as I have faid elfewhere †, though I defire the praife of very few, I would not willingly give offence to any. He may therefore take the word of the reviewers, and believe the work to be of no value ‡.

---

* See what I have faid of the vanity of this age, Ant. Metaph. Vol. iii. p. 107.

† Preface to Vol. iii. of this work, p. 15.

‡ There is one of thefe writers, who, in the review of the fecond volume, as I remember, of this work, after finding a great many particular faults with the work, concludes with faying, that he knows very well the author will have no regard to his cenfures, tho' he thinks it a duty he owes to the public to let them know that the work is of no value. This, I take, as a great

PREFACE.

It may appear surprising, that an author, who publishes a work, should not desire as many readers as possible, but, on the contrary, should advise some persons not to read it. But, I do not write for profit; and as to reputation, I desire the applause of none but men of sense, knowledge, and good taste; for, I think, I am pretty free of that disease, which Mr Pope calls the *itch of vulgar praise*. Excepting therefore those few I have named, (for they must be few in every nation), I value the praise of the rest of mankind as little as their censure: And, if I had my choice, I would not wish to be praised by them, but rather censured; as people very seldom praise those whom they do not think like to themselves. Though I print therefore, it is not so much for the sake of publishing, as for the purpose of collecting and digesting what I have had lying by me for many years in loose sheets, which would have been lost even to myself, if I had not

compliment; and, if I knew who the reviewer was, I would give him more than I would have given him, if I had hired him to praise the work.

PREFACE

employed a printer to give me them in a fair character and good order *, and with such corrections and additions, as upon a second reading occur to me. I have, however, also made copies for the use of my friends; and, if others can be benefited by my works, there are copies also for them.

There is one other thing in this volume, which I would recommend to the attention of the reader; and that is the abuses which I have observed are creeping into the English language †. It is, I think, upon the whole, the best modern language, at least that I know; and, particularly, there is some of our poetry without the jingle of rhyme, or in blank verse, as we call it, which does more honour to modern times than any thing of the kind I know. Whatever, therefore, we have lost, or may further lose, I would have us preserve, if pof-

* See the Preface to Vol. iii. of Ant. Metaph. p. 79. and 80.

† See upon the subject of the English language, book i. chap. 13. and 14.

fible, our language; for, as all arts and
fciences began with language, fo the corruption of language muft neceffarily be attended with a degeneracy in thefe. In
the Greek nation we have a fad example
of a people, who fpoke the fineft language
that ever exifted, and excelled mankind in
arts *, lofing with their language all thofe
arts, and returning to a ftate of barbarity,
much worfe than the firft barbarity, from
which by arts and civility they were re-
claimed. For Savages are ftrong of body
and mind, and therefore are capable of
the higheft cultivation, and may be truly
faid to be the creatures of God and Nature;
whereas, thofe, who have degenerated into a ftate of barbarity from a ftate of civility and refined manners, are in a ftate
altogether unnatural, being fo worn out
by indolence and luxury, vice and difeafe, that they have not in them the materials, out of which the *human artifts* of
ancient times made men; and, therefore,
there is no example, nor will there ever

---

* See on the fubject of the modern Greek language,
chap. 12.

PREFACE.

be, of any nation, such as the Greek, recovering its ancient splendor.

There are, I know, who will think what I have said in the beginning of this volume, upon the subject of the elements of the grammatical art, I mean letters and syllables, trifling and frivolous. But for my part, the more I study language, the more I admire the art of it*, which cannot be understood, unless we know its elements and principles. It appears to the philosopher the most wonderful of all arts; nor does he think it the less wonderful, but rather more so, for being the art of most common use. One of the noblest studies of man is the history and philosophy of man. Now, I hold it to be impossible to know perfectly what man is, without knowing the nature of that art, the foundation of the civil and political life, and of all other arts and sciences, without which, man must have remained in the brute state, in which we know some

* See what I have said of the difficulty of the art, p. 49.—182. and following.

men were in ancient times, and some are still to be found. It is chiefly by means of language that man is so far recovered from his fallen state, as to be an intellectual creature, not only capable of intellect, but in the actual possession of it; for, that man is fallen from a higher state, I hold to be a truth of philosophy, as well as of religion, and will shew it to be so, if I shall live to finish the great work I have begun, THE HISTORY AND PHILOSOPHY OF MAN.

OF THE

ORIGIN AND PROGRESS

OF

LANGUAGE.

VOL. IV. BOOK I.

Of the different Excellencies and Defects of different Languages.

INTRODUCTION.

AS there can be no work of art perfect, of which the materials are not of the best kind, and language being the materials whereof style is compofed, it may not be an improper fupplement to

Vol. IV. A

Introduction.

what I have written on the subject of Stile, to present to the reader a comparative view of some languages, both antient and modern, in point of beauty and excellence, from whence he will be able to judge in what language, and for what reasons, the best composition, both in speaking and writing, may be made. He will also perceive how far in the rude and more imperfect languages the composition may be improved by imitation of languages more perfect.

Before I speak of particular languages, I will lay down the general and abstract principles by which we are to judge of the excellency of language, and then I will apply these principles to some particular languages.

Language being the expression of the ideas of the human mind by articulate sounds or words, it will be fully considered under two general heads, the sound of these words, and the sense of them; or, to express it in philosophical language, the ma-

INTRODUCTION.

terial and the formal part *. I will begin with the first.

---

* See this philosophical division of language explained in Vol. i. of this Work, page. 8. second edition, and Vol. ii. p. 23.

CHAP. I.

No beauty in any art without variety.—There must, therefore, in a perfect language, be a great variety of sounds.—The variety of the sound in the termination particularly to be attended to.—Defect of the antient Persian language in this respect.—Defect of the languages of the South Sea in point of variety of sound.—A perfect language must be sweet in the sound, as well as various, but not too sweet of sound.—The barbarous languages defective in this, being too vocal.—The words must not be too short.—The Barbarous languages go to another extreme. —The sound of a language much raised by the use of diphthongs.—The Barbarous languages defective in this.—The difference of spirits in pronunciation makes an agreeable variety.—This the Barbarous languages have.—The quantity of syllables, or the rhythm, *makes another variety.— This some of the Barbarous languages have.*

Chap. I. PROGRESS OF LANGUAGE. 5

—Of the melody of language.—Some languages of Savage nations have melody.

AS there can be no beauty in any art without variety, (for art is a syftem, and there can be no fyftem without variety, as well as order and regularity), the firft thing I require to make a language beautiful is, that it fhould have a variety of articulate founds *. Without variety to a certain degree, it would not anfwer the purpofe of expreffing all our conceptions even in the narroweft fphere of life ; but I require further, that a perfect language fhould have all the variety of founds that the human mouth can, with any degree of eafe and without grimace or diftortion, utter ; and, particularly, there fhould be a great variety in the termination of the words ; that being the part of the word which in pronunciation affects the ear moft. And I think there could not well be a greater defect in the found of a language than what Herodotus obferves of

---

* See what I have faid of the four things required to make a perfect language, Vol. ii. of this work, p. 6.

the Perfian, that it terminated all its words with the fame letter, *S* *. It would, I think, have been a great defect, if the letter *S* had been of the moſt pleaſant found: Whereas, the Halicarnaſſian ſays of it, that its ſound is more brutal than human; for which reaſon, the antients uſed it very ſparingly. And he ſays there were whole odes compoſed without one Σ in them†. And this, no doubt, is the reaſon that it is thrown out in many Greek words, when the analogy requires that it ſhould be there.

The want of this variety is ſeen in almoſt all the Barbarous languages, which are very defective, particularly in conſonants; (for, as to the five vowels, it appears that all languages have them ‡). The Barbarous languages of North America have neither the *V* conſonant nor the *F*. The Huron language wants all

---

* Lib. i. Cap. 139.
† Περι ευφωνιας. Sect. 14.
‡ Vol. i. of this work, p. 502. of the ſecond edition, where I think I have given a good reaſon why the firſt languages ſpoken by men are ſo vocal.

the labial confonants *; and it is for this reafon, that all thofe languages of North America are much more vocal than more perfect languages, and have words conconfifting wholly of vowels †. The languages of the South Sea are in the fame cafe. To fupply this defect of articulation, fuch languages are forced, in order to diftinguifh their words from one another, to repeat the fame letters and fyllables, fometimes more than once in the fame words ‡.

The *fecond* thing I require is, that the found of the language fhould be fweet and pleafant to the ear. But here again that great beauty of all the works of art, I mean variety, muft not be forgot. For, as in the fineft mufic there muft be difcords, fo in the moft perfect languages there muft be fome harfh founds; but thefe may be fo mixed with fweet and foft founds, that the found of the language fhall be upon the whole fweet, but not of a fweetnefs that is lufcious or cloying, but with fuch a mixture of

* Ibid. p. 560.
† Ibid. p. 506. and following.
‡ Ibid. p. 501.—508.

auftere and rough founds, as to make it manly and forcible, as well as pleafant. In this point alfo the Barbarous languages are defective, for they are much too vocal for the reafon above mentioned, having a great many vowels in their words, and often, as I have obferved, repeating the fame vowels, and wanting almoft altogether the afpirated confonants.

3*tio*, I require that the words fhould not be too fhort, but, for the greater part by far, words of feveral fyllables. For a language all of monofyllables, fuch as the Chinefe, or with very many monofyllables, fuch as ours, can never have a fweet or pleafant flow, as there muft neceffarily be a ftop, more or lefs, betwixt every two words. Here the Barbarous languages go to another extreme, for the words of them are unmeafureably long, for a reafon I have given elfewhere *; to which may be added, that I believe the want of an articulation fufficiently varied may have obliged them to lengthen their words, in order to diftinguifh them one from another.

* Vol. i. p. 500. fecond edition.

Chap. I. PROGRESS OF LANGUAGE.

4*to*, In order to swell and raise the sound of the language, vowels, that will coalesce together in the same sound, ought to be joined and enunciated together, producing what we call diphthongs, which I think may not be improperly compared to what the antients called symphony and we call harmony, that is, music in parts, in which, by the mixture of the grave and acute joined properly together, the note is swelled, and made much more pleasant to the ear. These double sounds may be also sometimes separated in the pronunciation, which will make an agreeable variety. And consonants may be also joined together, and separated sometimes for the same reason. In this point, the Barbarous languages are as defective as they are excessive in the other.

5*to*, Some vowels and syllables should be uttered with the breath thickened or condensed, while others are pronounced more smoothly, and with less force. This makes the difference of what is called the two *spirits*; the one being *aspirated* or thickened, as the Greeks call it, the other softened or smoothed *. This is carefully to be distinguished from *loud* or *low* in pronouncing letters or syllables. Many, indeed I believe all the barbarous languages, have this variety of spirits.

6*to*, Some of the vowels and syllables which they form should be pronounced short, others long. This is a most natural, as well as most agreeable variety, and is what is called the rythm of language, being a certain ratio which the ear perceives betwixt short and long sounds. This too is very well known in some of the barbarous languages †.

* It is to be observed, that the word *aspirated* does not properly express what the Greeks call Δασυς; for it seems to denote that the sound is made rough or harsh; whereas it is only enunciated with more breath: And the Greek grammarians have been so accurate, as to observe that there is a middle class of consonants betwixt the Δασυς and the ψιλοι or *tenues*, which are enunciated with a breath not so much thickened or condensed as when we pronounce the Δασυς, or not so slender or gentle as that with which the ψιλοι are enunciated. See Vol. ii p. 234. 235.

† See Vol. i. of this Work, p. 509. second edition.

Lastly, In a perfect language, there should be melody as well as rhythm; that is to say, the syllables should be varied and distinguished from one another by certain musical tones, with which they are pronounced. Of this I have treated fully in the Second Volume of this Work *. I shall only add here, that, though I believe there was melody originally in all or the greater part of languages, it is lost in all the European, but is preserved in some of the Barbarous languages spoken by certain tribes of Savages in North America, as I was well informed by a gentleman who was long there; and the Chinese, by giving different tones to the same monosyllable, make it signify seven or eight different things.

This is all the variety I can conceive in the sounds of single words. What further variety may be produced in their sound by composition will be afterwards observed.

* Book ii. chap. 4.

CHAP. II.

Words considered as significant.—In a language of art there must be of them a sufficient number to express all the variety of things.—Defect of Barbarous languages in this respect.—There must not be a redundancy, any more than a defect of words. —This prevented by that art of language we call flection.—*In this the Barbarous languages very defective.—The words of the language should convey the meaning fully and accurately—also without obscurity or ambiguity.—In both these articles Barbarous languages are defective.— They supply the defect by tones of the voice.—Words, that have a connection in their meaning, connected together in their sound by* derivation and composition. —*The Barbarous languages want this art.—The want of words supplied by* metaphors and other tropes.—*In this the Barbarous languages are not deficient,— but most deficient of all in* syntax.—*Rea-*

Chap. II. Progress of Language.

sons for this.—All languages spoken by barbarous nations are not barbarous.

I come now to speak of words as significant, first considering them single, and then in composition.

As to single words, there must be so many of them as to express all the variety of things; and, as things are divided into certain classes, so are words. The division of things was made by the antient philosophers into certain classes, called Categories, which I hold to be the ground-work of grammar, as well as of logic; and, accordingly, that division of words, which we call the parts of speech, takes in all the categories; the first part of speech, or the Noun, answering to the first Category, Substance; and the other parts of speech to the several Accidents of things comprehended under the other Categories.

In this manner, substances, and all their several qualities, are expressed, and in short all the variety of things. How defective the barbarous languages are in this respect,

I have shown in the First Volume of this Work [*].

2do, As a perfect language must be full and complete in words significant, so it must not be redundant, nor express by several words what can be expressed by one with some variations made upon it. For example, if certain accidents, or relations of words to one another, can be expressed by a change made upon the word, it would be superfluous and a defect in the language, if a new word was employed to express that accident or relation. The change made upon the word for that purpose is what we call *flection* or *inflection*; by which the cases of nouns, and tenses of verbs, are formed. But, as some words, by their nature, do not admit of such variation, hence comes a a distinction of great importance in language, into words declinable and indeclinable. In flection, the barbarous lan-

[*] Book iii. Chap. 9..where I have observed, that there are some of them which have not any adjective, nor any word denoting a quality abstracted from the subject. See also page 534. of the same Volume.

guages are more defective than in any thing elfe, few of them having any thing like cafes or tenfes; fo that their words are all, or by far the greater part, indeclinable *. And this too muft produce a difagreeable famenefs in the found of thofe languages; as, on the contrary, nothing varies the found of a language more than the different terminations, and different lengths of the words, which flexion produces.

3*tio*, In a language of art the words fhould exprefs every circumftance of the thing, and convey the meaning to the hearer as fully and accurately as poffible.

But, 4*to*, There fhould be no obfcurity or ambiguity in the words, otherwife the principal end of language cannot be anfwered, which is to convey the meaning to the hearer. In both thefe laft articles the barbarous languages are very deficient,

* See Vol. i. Book iii. Chap. 9. of this Work, p. 532. fecond edition.

and they fupply the defect, as we are told, by accents, or tones of the voice *, and no doubt by geſtures, or action of the body.

5*to*, The variety of things being fo great, that, if there were words entirely unconnected with one another to exprefs every particular thing, the language would be too bulky and cumberfome, and too great a load upon the memory; therefore the artificers of language have contrived a way of connecting words fignifying things that have a connection, by the means of what is called derivation and compofition: So that fome words are radical, fome derivative; fome words are fimple, and others compounded. In this too, the languages barbarous, that is, without art, are remarkably deficient; for they exprefs things having the neareſt connection by words quite different †.

And, *laſtly*, as, even with derivation and compofition, words are wanted to exprefs many things, this neceffity has introduced

* Vol. i. of this Work, p. 535. fecond edition.
† Ibidem.

the ufe of metaphors and other tropes, which I am perfuaded were at firft ufed from neceffity; fo that it was not till later times that they came to be ufed as an ornament of difcourfe.—In this figurative ftyle the barbarous languages abound exceedingly, more from want of proper words than for the fake of ornament.

Although a language were ever fo complete in its words, yet, if thofe words are not properly put together, they will exprefs no meaning. This part of the grammatical art is called *fyntax*; and it is the completion of the art of language. In this the barbarous languages are remarkably defective; for it is performed chiefly by the means of genders, numbers, and cafes, all which the barbarous languages want, and alfo by conjunctions and prepofitions, two parts of fpeech which are not to be found in thofe languages *.

But, when I fpeak of barbarous languages, I muft not be underftood to mean

* See what I have faid upon the fubject of *fyntax*, Vol. ii. Book iii. Chap. 1.

all the languages spoken by nations we call barbarous: For there are some of these nations that speak languages of very great art, such as that spoken by the *Garani* in the country of Paraguay, in South America; another, of greater art still, spoken in that great country, in the same continent of South America, known by the name of Patagonia. The Gothic too, (which, as we use the word, should denote a language altogether barbarous), was a language of much greater art than any of its descendants, such as the German, Swedish, or English. Even the languages of Lapland and Greenland are in some respects more artificial languages than any spoken by the civilized nations of Europe. And the language of the Algonkins, in North America, is, in some things, even too artificial. Of all these languages I have given a particular account in another part of this work *, where I have said, that I do not think it is possible that those nations, so little advanced in other arts of life, should have invented such

* Vol. i. Book iii. Chap. 10. of this Work.

artificial languages, but they muſt have learned them by intercourſe with ſome other nations more civilized: For that there have been ſtrange migrations and mixtures of people on this earth, is a fact that cannot be doubted of by thoſe who have ſtudied the hiſtory of man *.

* Vol. i. p. 546. of this Work, where I mention a very ſenſible obſervation of Herodotus, upon the ſubject of a colony of Medes being found in the middle of Scythia.

CHAP. III.

Greater variety both of sound and sense in composition than in single words.—The greater variety the greater beauty—also the greater difficulty.—The wonderful variety of composition in the learned languages.—Of composition in the barbarous languages.—There must be more or less of the art of composition among such barbarous nations as hold public assemblies, and therein make harangues.—A story to that purpose.

I come now to speak of words in composition, where there must of necessity be much greater variety, both of sound and sense, than of single words. And, where there is the greatest variety, if there be art and system at the same time, there also the greatest beauty must be. Thus, an Heroic poem, such as the Iliad or Odyssey, is a much finer thing than a tragedy, becaufe it is a whole, as well as a tragedy, but of much greater extent and variety, and containing many *peripeteias*, and furprifing changes of fortune; whereas tragedy has but one. And, for the fame reafon, a tragedy is a much finer thing than an epigram. And, accordingly, the mafters of the writing art tell us, that, as ftile confifts of two things, the choice of words, and the compofition of them, there is much greater difficulty, as well as beauty, in the latter, than in the former.

In compofition, there is indeed a wonderful variety. For, 1*mo*, in languages of art, which have cafes, tenfes, genders, and numbers, there is a variety of arrangement, to which it is difficult to fet bounds—Then there is the fyntax, or conftruction of the words, either plain and fimple, or figured—Then the figures of the fenfe, that is, rhetorical figures, by which the fenfe is expreffed in fome uncommon way, are fo many in number, that they cannot be numbered *—Then there is the com-

* Vol. iii. of this work, p. 107.

position of periods, and the division of these into members, more or fewer, and variously connected together, and differing in the sense as well as in the structure of the words —And, *lastly*, in the most perfect language, there is a variety of rhythm and melody, which makes a great part of the beauty of their composition *.

What beauty of composition there is in the barbarous languages, is not easy to say. But, among such nations as are so far advanced in the arts of life, as to hold assemblies, and deliberate about public affairs, it is evident that, in their speeches, there must be more or less of composition. I have heard a story of an Indian orator, who, at a congress or *talk*, as they call it, with the then British governour of Florida, Commodore Johnston, being frequently interrupted by the interpreter, who stopped him, in order to explain to the Governour what he said, at last lost patience; and, says he, ' I can bear this no longer: ' My discourse, cut thus into pieces, can

* Vol. ii. Book iii. Chap. 7.

'have no more effect than the water could
'have upon that great beast of yours,'
pointing to a faw-mill at fome diftance,
' if it were to fall upon it drop by drop.'
Now this orator muft have had as perfect an idea of the *flumen orationis*, and the effects it produces, as a Cicero or Demofthenes.

CHAP. IV.

An account of the Greek language.—This the moſt perfect language the author knows.—Its reſemblance to the Sanſcrit language of India.—From the Greek language the author has formed his notion of what is moſt perfect in language.—Of the ſound of the Greek language.—More ſounds in it than we can pronounce.—Vowels in Homer frequently gaping upon one another.—Alſo rhymes, both of verſes and of hemiſtics.—The words in Greek neither too ſhort nor too long.—The ſhorteſt words are thoſe that occur the moſt frequently, ſuch as Conjunctions and Prepoſitions.—The terminations of the Greek words moſt various and moſt pleaſant to the ear.—None of their words terminate in mute conſonants.—Difference of ſpirits *in Greek.—This ſhould not be confounded with* loud *and* low.*—No ſuch diſtinction* betwixt *the syllables of the same word in Greek or Latin*.

THESE are my observations upon languages in general, as well those of art as the barbarous. I proceed now to apply these observations to particular languages of art, or which are reputed such. And I will begin with the Greek, the language the most perfect that I know, or, I believe, that is known; though, from what we hear of the Indian Sanscrit language, we have reason to think that it is likewise a language of wonderful art, and we are sure that, in some respects, it resembles very much the Greek, particularly in the verbs, of which the Sanscrit has a class that are conjugated in the same manner as the verbs in —μι in Greek *.

---

* This curious fact is averred by a gentleman from India, whom I know, Mr Brassey, who has written a grammar of the Bengallese language, which he says is a dialect of the Sanscrit, as well as the other languages spoken in India. See what I have said of this language, in Vol. ii. p. 530.

When I come to apply my general observations to the Greek, the reader will no doubt perceive that I have formed my idea of a perfect language upon the Greek. Other men, of greater genius and more learned in philosophy, may, from theory and speculation merely, form the idea of what is most perfect in language, and then apply that idea to any particular language they may think proper to study : But, for my part, I begin where those gentlemen end, and not only in language, but in every thing belonging to art or nature, I form my system from facts and observations ; and, as to language in particular, I am sure that, without diligently studying the Greek, I should never have had any notion of what is most perfect in this greatest and most useful art among men.

To begin with the sound of the Greek, it will be found to have all those things I have required to make a language perfect in that respect. For, in the *first* place, it has all the sounds that the human mouth can utter, or ear hear, with any pleasure. And I am persuaded it has a greater variety than we can pronounce; for, besides the vowels which it aspirates, and the consonants θ and φ, it has an aspirated κ or χ, which, when prefixed to a vowel, we cannot distinguish from the vowel aspirated. Thus we cannot distinguish in our pronunciation betwixt the first syllables of the two words 'αμα and χαμαι. Then there is the Æolic *digamma*, which I am persuaded was used by Homer, tho' not marked, I believe, in any manuscript of him, any more than in the printed editions. It had a sound distinct either from the Greek φ, or the Latin *f*; and therefore Claudius invented a new character to mark it *. What is called the proper diphthongs, which raise and swell the sound of the language so much, we can pronounce; but the improper diphthongs, such as α, η, ω, though we are sure

* It was one of the three new letters invented by this Emperor. See Suetonius, in his Life, Cap. 41. and the *notae variorum* on the passage. It is still to be seen in antient inscriptions, and is used, in some words, in place of the V consonant, which shows that it must have had a sound different from that consonant, as well as from the consonant F. See what I have further said of the *Digamma*, Vol. ii. p. 240.

they were not simple sounds but some way compounded, we cannot pronounce.

In so great a variety of sounds, there must be some very harsh, such as the aspirated consonants χ and θ; but they are so mixed with others more sweet and pleasant, that the sound is neither too soft and effeminate, nor too rough and austere, but an admirable composition of both. In some words, they join the two rough sounds, I mentioned, together, as in the word αχθομαι and χμμφθεις: In which last the φ and θ are joined together, and the consonant μ prefixed; which I think does very well by way of variety. And, for the same reason, they sometimes do as the barbarous languages do very frequently, join vowels together, not as diphthongs, but in different syllables, and not only different vowels, but the same vowel, as in that famous line of Homer, which, it is said, deterred Plato from writing verses,

Ηως ριτατο εγιγομεης αλος εξο.

And there is nothing more common in Homer, and nothing more beautiful in point of found than the —Οω. And, in general, in Homer, and in all the Ionic writers, there is a great deal of gaping of vowels upon one another, both in the same and in different words. This, I think, if there be not too much of it, swells the sound of the language, and, I must own, pleases me, though it offended the delicate ears of later times: And, particularly Isocrates has, with what I would call a sophistical nicety, most carefully avoided it. In Homer, too, there are like endings, both of verses and of hemistics, which I think a beauty also, (and so they are reckoned by the antient critics), if they be not too frequent, which they are not in Homer; for he only uses them when he has a mind to adorn his diction, as in his similies, which are the most ornamented part of his poem; nor do I remember that he ever uses them in his narrative or speeches *.

* Homer has followed Aristotle's rules, as in other things, so in stile, which he says ought only to be laboured, and much ornamented, *ις τοις αργοις μερεσι*, that is, in such parts of the poem where there is neither reasoning, character, or sentiments, to be expressed; and he might have added, where there is no nar-

The words in Greek are neither too long, like the words in the barbarous languages, nor too ſhort, like the words of ſome modern languages, by which the flow of the language is much interrupted, (there being neceſſarily, as I have obſerved, a ſtop more or leſs betwixt the words, ſo that the ſpeech muſt be full of breaks), but of a moderate length, with the variety of ſome longer and ſome ſhorter. And it is to be obſerved, that the monoſyllables, or very ſhort words, are almoſt all words that occur very frequently, ſuch as prepoſitions, conjunctions, and the article; theſe, if they were long words, occurring ſo often, would make the diſcourſe cumberſome and tedious.

The terminations of the words in Greek are as various as poſſible conſiſtently with the pleaſure of the ear, being very different, not only in different words, but in the ſame word, by the variation of genders,

rative; for, as by narrative the buſineſs of the poem is carried on, it cannot be ſaid to be ἀργὸς, that is, a part where the action ſtands ſtill, as it does in the ſimilies. See Ariſt. *Poetic.* Cap. 24. *in fine.*

numbers, cafes, and tenfes *. Many words they conclude with a diphthong, fuch as αι, οι, α ου; which makes the pronunciation of fuch words go off with a found that both pleafes and fills the ear, the termination being, as I have obferved, the moft ftriking part of the found of a word. But they end no words with a mute confonant, fuch as β, π, δ, which make a harfh and abrupt conclufion †: Much lefs do they conclude with an afpirated confonant, fuch as θ, with which fo many words in Englifh conclude, but which we fhould think infufferably harfh, and fhould fay with the French, that it *fleaed our ears*, if we were not fo much accuftomed to it ‡.

* Antient Metaph. Vol. iii. p. 220. where I have fhown, that, from the fame Greek verb, there may be formed tenfes and participles of different terminations to the number of two thoufand.

† This is obferved by Ariftotle, in his *Poetics*, Cap. 21. where he obferves alfo that they terminated no noun with a fhort vowel; the reafon of which feems to have been, that the voice could not reft upon a fhort vowel, as on a proper bafis, and therefore the word could not be concluded in fuch a way as to pleafe and fill the ear.

‡ The Greeks have but one little word ending in the mute ς, viz. ις; but, when a vowel follows, they

That the Greeks might have all the variety possible in the sound of their language, they observed that certain syllables were enunciated with a breath much thicker, and more condensed, as it were, than others; and hence the distinction of the two spirits*, which, as I have observed, we must not confound with the distinction of loud and low, in the syllables of our words; a distinction which I am persuaded was unknown both to the Greeks and Latins, who pronounced all the syllables of the words upon a level, as the French pronounce their corrupt dialect of the Latin. And my reason for thinking so is, that, if there had been accents, such as are in our language and some other modern

make it end in *ς*, using *ξ* instead of *ικ*: And, as the word is so used in Latin, I am persuaded it was originally only used in Greek in that way. But, afterwards, where a consonant followed, they threw out the *ς*, for the sake of the better sound, as they frequently did on other occasions.

* See what I have said upon the subject of *Spirits*, Vol. ii. p. 34. where I have shown that the nice Greek ear perceived a third or middle sound betwixt the *tenuis* and the *aspirated*.

languages, making so great a variety in the pronunciation of words, it is impossible to suppose that the antient grammarians would not have taken notice of it.

I will say no more here upon the articulation of the Greek language, but will refer the reader, who may desire to know more of this subject, to a dissertation which I have written upon the sound of the Greek language, and annexed to the Second Volume of this Work; where he will observe how the Greeks have contrived to sweeten and vary the sound of their language, by adding, taking away, changing, or transposing of letters.

CHAP. V.

Of the music of the Greek language.—It consists, like other music, of melody and rhythm.—*It has melody in succession, and may be considered as having music in parts.—Of the difference betwixt the melody of music and that of speech.—Of the* rhythm *of the Greek language, and the beauty it must have given to their pronunciations—The music of language known even among some barbarous nations.—The northern nations of Europe probably got their language from nations who spoke a musical language; but not having a genius for music, they lost that part of the language.—The Greeks a most musical nation—got the elements of music from Egypt, but improved it very much. —Of the music of the Indians of North America—how they came to have music in their language accounted for.—Conclu-*

Chap. V. Progress of Language. 35

sion of what is said upon the sound of the Greek language.—Necessity of analysing it, as has been done, in order to form a right judgment of it.

I come now to speak of the music of the Greek language, for hitherto I have only considered its articulate sounds. This music, like every other music, is a composition of melody and rhythm.

Melody consists of acute and grave sounds, either in succession, or joined together. The melody of the Greek language is the melody of succession; for, when the acute accent is put upon any syllable of a word, and the rest are sounded grave, then is there that melody. But, besides this, the acute and grave are often both put upon the same syllable, which is what is called the circumflex accent. Then the melody of the Greek language may be considered of the other kind, that is, a combination of the acute and grave joined together, which makes what is commonly called *harmony*, or music in parts. For, tho' both sounds are not heard precisely in the same time, as is the cafe of mufic in parts, properly fo called, the acute and grave, being both on the fame fyllable, are fo clofely connected, that they may be confidered as one found; and they certainly have the effect of fwelling and raifing the found, which is one of the chief effects of harmony.

Rhythm is fo neceffary to mufic, that there can be no good mufic without it, nor, indeed, any thing deferving the name of mufic. The rhythm of antient mufic was divided into feet, as well as the rhythm of their verfe; and I am perfuaded it was chiefly by rhythm that their mufic performed the wonderful things afcribed to it. This is likewife a part of the mufic of the Greek language; and it is produced by what we call the quantity of the fyllables, that is, their length compared with one another, the long being to the fhort in the ratio of *two* to *one*. Thefe, mixed together in the language, muft have made a moft pleafant variety to the learned ears of the Greeks. And, though our ears be not formed to that kind of rhythm, yet it muſt be allowed to be very natural; for the vocal ſounds in every language, whether by themſelves or joined with conſonants, may be made ſome long and ſome ſhort, which is much better than if they were all founded of the ſame length, as is the caſe in moſt modern languages, and particularly in the French *.

There are ſome, I know, who think this notion of mine, of the muſic of the Greek language, is a mere fancy. But, is it poſſible that there can be a mixture of grave and acute ſounds, diſtinguiſhed by certain intervals, without a muſic of ſome kind or another? That the ſounds of the Greek language were ſo diſtinguiſhed, we are aſſured by Dionyſius the Halicarnaſſian †. But the muſic of it was different from the common muſic in more than one reſpect. In the *firſt* place, it did not riſe ſo high, not

* See upon this ſubject of *Quantity*, Vol. ii. Book 2. Chap. 5. and 6.

† See a tranſlation of the paſſage, Vol. ii. of this work, p. 284.

above a fifth, as the Halicarnaffian tells us. 2*do*, It had not the variety of the common mufic. And, 3*tio*, what is obferved by the antient critics to have made the chief difference, was, that the common mufic was *diaftematic*, that is, had its tones divided, and feparated from one another by perceptible intervals, and not run together; whereas the mufic of fpeech was ἐν ρυσει, as they expreffed it, that is, going on by flides, the tones infenfibly running into one another. In this way they rofe from the grave to the acute, and defcended again from the acute to the grave. And in this way the Greek language continued ftill to be fpeech, and was neither fong nor recitative, though very different from any fpeech we ever heard *.

And here it may be wondered, that the barbarous languages, particularly fome of

---

* Of the difference betwixt the melody of fpeech and the melody of mufic, fee Vol. ii. p. 286. The whole Chapter, I think, is worth the reading, by thofe who have curiofity enough to know a thing of which we have no practice, and hardly an idea; I mean the mufic of the antient languages.

Chap. V. Progress of Language. 39

North America *, should have tones and rhythms, and yet the modern languages of Europe have none. But the northern nations of Europe, of whom the present inhabitants are descended, appear to have been very little favoured by the Muses and Graces; for, though in the accounts we have of the Scandinavian nations a great deal is said of their poetry, we hear little or nothing of their music; and the most northern of all those nations, I mean the Laplanders, as we are well informed by a Danish missionary, one Lemmius, who was ten years among them, have so little genius for music, as not to be able to learn, without the greatest difficulty, the common church-tunes †: And, as to inventing an art of music, or any other liberal art, I believe them absolutely incapable. Their language, I am persuaded, they learned from some other nation, and perhaps got it with the musical tones and rhythms, but these they have lost; and I think it is not unlikely that they introduced, in place of

---

* See page 11. of this Volume.
† See an account of this country, written by this missionary in very good Latin.

them, what we call *accents*, such as the modern Greeks use in place of their antient accents, and which, I believe, take place in all the dialects of the Gothic and Saxon, as well as in our dialect. These, instead of the music of the human voice, the finest of all music, resemble the beating of a drum, having no other variation but that of loud and soft, quick and slow *. On the other hand, the Greeks were a most musical people ; and, though they may have brought the elements of that as well as of other arts from Egypt, I am persuaded they improved it very much ; and, as to poetry, I believe they invented it, since we do not read of the Egyptians having any poetry, though we know they had music in the most antient times.†. Such being the genius of the Greeks, I think it was almost of necessity that their language should be musical; for a very musical people will speak and move, and do almost every thing, to music.

* See upon the subject of *modern accents*, Vol. ii. Book 2. Chap. 4. and Book 3. Chap. 8.
† Vol. ii. of this work, p. 228.

Chap. V. PROGRESS OF LANGUAGE. 41

As to the Indians of North America, they have not yet got poetry, but they have had mufic as early, I believe, as any art of life, without excepting even language; and their mufic is always accompanied with words*, reciting their own exploits, or thofe of their anceflors, which they fing at their war feafts; nor is there any thing of greater antiquity among them. Now, it was very natural that their words, even when not fung, fhould have fomething of a mufical cadence, efpecially if we fuppofe that mufic and language grew up together.

And here I finifh my obfervations upon the found of the Greek language, where the reader may perhaps think that I have dwelt too long upon trifling and minute things. But it is impoffible to give a

* L'Affiteau, in his work entitled, *Mœurs des Sauvages Ameriquains*, Vol. i. p. 521. obferves, that they fhorten their words in order to adapt them to the rhythm of the mufic. Here we may obferve the beginning of Poetry; for poetry is nothing more than meafured rhythm.

VOL. IV. F

scientific account of the sound of any language, without analysing it, as I have done, into words, syllables, and letters, and likewise into tones and rhythms, observing what each of these has peculiar. Without such a resolution of a language into its elements, we can form no rational judgment, even of the sound of it, nor compare it, in that respect, with other languages.

CHAP. VI.

Of the words of the Greek language, considered as significant.—The art of the Greek language most wonderful in this respect.—Of the noun, and the various things denoted by its declension.—Of the verb, and the still greater variety of expression by it.—Of the words in Greek formed from the Verb.—The Greek verb, though expressing so many different things, not incumbered or overloaded.

I Come now to speak of the words of the Greek language as significant. And here the art of the Greek language appears still more wonderful. For as much as the meaning is of greater excellence than the sound of the words, so much greater skill have the artificers of this language shown by the invention of an analogy, as it is called, whereby all the different circumstances of things, and their relations to one another, are expressed, without making new words, and only by changes made upon the same word: So that the Greek language, at the same time that it is most copious and rich of words, is as frugal of them as possible. I will begin with single words.

Single words are by grammarians divided into what is called parts of speech; and these they make to be eight. But, as I have shown elsewhere *, if we are to speak philosophically, there are but two, corresponding to the grand division of things into substance and accident, viz. the *noun*, by which substances are expressed, and the *verb*, expressing accidents. Now, all the several qualities and relations of substances or nouns to one another, are expressed by what is called the declension of nouns, that is, by their cases, numbers, and genders; which, at the same time that they vary the

* Vol. ii. of this Work, p. 28. and following.

Chap. VI. PROGRESS OF LANGUAGE. 45

termination, and so add much to the pleasure of the ear, express the thing most accurately, particularly with respect to number, distinguishing not only betwixt *one* and *many*, but betwixt *two* and *many* *.

The other part of speech, according to this philosophical division, comprehends the other seven, according to the common division; but I shall speak only of one of them, viz. the verb, which is the glory of the Greek analogy; for, by the several changes made upon it, it expresses, 1*mo*, Whether the action be done, or suffered; 2*do*, Whether the action be perfect or imperfect; 3*tio*, Whether the person who speaks is the actor or sufferer, or whether it be the person spoken to, or some third person or thing; 4*to*, what the number of actors or sufferers is, whether one, two, or more; 5*to*, The time of the action or suffering. And here there is a wonderful va-

* See what I have said of the philosophy of this part of speech, Vol. ii. of this Work, Book. i. Chap. 4. also Chap. 9. where I have given a philosophical account of the cases of nouns, such as hitherto has not been given.

riety; for, not only the three great divisions of time, the *paſt*, *preſent*, and *future*, are expreſſed, but the compoſitions of theſe, the *paſt* with the *preſent*, with the *future*, and with the *paſt*: And, laſtly, there is a form of the word, which expreſſes that the action is ſimply paſt, without determining whether it be likewiſe preſent or not; in ſhort, it denotes the paſt indefinitely. 6*to*, The verb expreſſes alſo the diſpoſition of the mind of the ſpeaker, whether he affirms, commands, wiſhes, or prays. This is expreſſed by three forms of the verb, which we call *moods*, viz. the *indicative*, the *imperative*, the *optative*. 7*mo*, There is a fourth *mood*, which expreſſes ſimply the action of the verb, with the addition only of *time*. This is what is called the *infinitive* mood *. 8*vo*, There is

* This mood, with the article prefixed, is to be conſidered in Greek as an abſtract noun. τὸ τρέττειν, for example, is a noun, as much as πρᾶξις, with the addition only of the ſignification of *time*.——— alſo this explained in Vol. ii. p. 40 The Latins likewiſe uſe the infinitive this way; but, as they have not an article, it often makes the expreſſion obſcure, becauſe it is doubtful whether the infinitive is to be underſtood as a noun, or in the ordinary way as a

a fifth mood, called the *subjunctive* or *conjunctive*, by which it is expressed whether the verb be principal in the sentence, or dependent upon another verb. 9*no*, The object, too, of the action is expressed, as far as that is possible; for, by the nature of things, it is impossible, by any flection, or change of any kind made upon the word, to express all the several things or persons that may be the object of the action. But, if that object is either the person who speaks, or the person spoken to, or the person or thing which is the subject of the discourse, it is expressed by that form of the verb we call the middle voice. *Lastly*, There is a form of the verb which has the signification of an adjective; but, besides *quality*, it expresses *time*. This kind of adjective is what is called a *participle*. And likewise from the verb are formed many substantive nouns; and so rich is the analogy of the Greek in this particular, that, not only from different tenses are nouns derived,

---

mood, and so to be construed with another verb in the sentence.

but from different persons of the same tense, of which there is a remarkable example in the preterperfect tense passive of the verb ποιῶ, viz. πεποιημαι, from every person of the singular number of which are derived as many nouns ; 1*mo*, ποιημα, from the first person, signifying the thing made ; 2*do*, ποιησις, from the second person, signifying the action of making ; and, *lastly*, ποιητης, from the third person, denoting the maker.

What I have said here concerning the Greek verb, I have said shortly, referring to what I have said, at great length, upon the subject, in the Second Volume of this Work *, where those who are not satisfied with having learned at school the common rules of the Greek grammar, and to understand the words and phrases of the language, may, if they please, study the science of the most wonderful art among men, and learn to know that the principles of no art, not even of grammar,

---

* Book i. Chap. 10. and following.

the firſt art we are taught, can be underſtood without philoſophy.

What appears as wonderful, I think, as any thing I have mentioned concerning the Greek verb, is that, with all theſe various expreſſions of different things, with which one ſhould think it would be quite incumbered and overloaded, yet it is not at all difficult to be underſtood, and by the uſe of reading only, without either ſpeaking or hearing, it becomes familiar to us.

Such being the nature of this part of Speech in Greek, I do not wonder that a learned and pious Profeſſor of Divinity, whom I knew, could not be convinced but that it came down from heaven ready made, ſo much he thought it above the invention of men. But, though I think that man, by his natural faculties, having once got ſome uſe of language, might have perfected the verb, as well as every other part of ſpeech; yet, as the beginning of all things is moſt difficult, I think there is reaſon to doubt whether man could of himself have begun to articulate, or whether he muſt not have been at firſt taught by ſome ſuperior intelligence, ſuch as the Egyptians ſay they were by their God *Teuth*. So far, therefore, I agree with the learned Profeſſor.

All the various concomitant ſignifications, ſuperadded to the principal ſignification of the Greek noun and verb, are produced by flexion, which is no doubt one of the greateſt, perhaps the greateſt, artifice of the Greek language; but there are two other likewiſe of ſingular uſe for preventing the too great multiplication of words, and which, therefore, deſerve to be taken notice of, I mean compoſition and derivation.

CHAP. VII.

Of the composition *in Greek.—The use of it in saving words, and making the system of the language more perfect.—Of the variety of its composition with verbs and prepositions.—Of derivation in the Greek language.—The account, given by the author, of the Greek derivation, makes the language a wonderful system of art.—The same was the system of Hempsterhusius.—Not probable that both Hempsterhusius and the Author should have fallen into the same error, without communication with one another.—Other arguments in favour of this system of etymology.—The Greek, according to this system, resembles very much the Sanscrit language.—The language of Homer particularly has a wonderful resemblance to that language.*

BY compoſition, two or more words
of different ſignifications are joined
together, in order to produce another word
that has a connection in its ſignification
with the component words. That this
will often happen in the variety of things
expreſſed by language, is evident ; and
the hearer or reader, knowing the meaning of the words in the compoſition, will
readily know the meaning of the compounded word ; whereas, if it had been
expreſſed by a word quite new, it would
have burthened his memory, and diſtracted
his attention. Beſides, the compounding
words, as well as deriving them, (of which
I ſhall ſpeak anon), makes more uniformity in the language, and more a ſyſtem
of it, than it could be otherwiſe.

Of all the compoſitions in the Greek
language, none is more common, or produces greater effects, than the compoſition of verbs with prepoſitions. It is to it
chiefly that is owing that wonderful accuracy of expreſſion ſo remarkable in Greek,
by which every the leaſt circumſtance of
an action is expreſſed in the ſhorteſt way

possible, and at the same time very clearly; and, if we do not know the force of the prepositions, both single and in composition, we must lose a great part of the beauty, and even of the sense of the Greek language. It is, I believe, singular in the Greek, that they compound often with two, and sometimes even with three, in order to express every circumstance of the thing. Thus Homer, describing water coming out of a rock, uses the word υπεκπρορεειν; where it expresses not only that the water came out of the rock, but that it came from under the rock, and, further, that it did not stagnate at the foot of it, but ran forward*. A language of this kind not only describes but paints, particularly in the use that Homer has made of it; and, accordingly, I believe it is generally agreed by the painters, that Homer has furnished the best subjects for historical painting, of any author, antient or modern.

* See what I have further said upon the subject of the Greek prepositions, and their composition with verbs, Vol. ii. p. 175. 176.

I come now to speak of the derivation in the Greek language. Of this I have given an account in the Second Volume of this Work *; and, if it be a juſt one, the Greek language is certainly a moſt wonderful fyſtem of art, derived from as few principles as I think is poſſible, only five duads of vowels. That I am in the right, I think it is a ſtrong preſumption, that Hempſterhuſius, the greateſt Greek ſcholar of his time, and likewiſe learned in the Oriental languages, formed the fame fyſtem, which he never publiſhed; but a ſcholar of his, one Lennep, has publiſhed it, about five years after my work was publiſhed †. Now, I muſt ſay, that I think that it is much more probable that we are both in the right, than that we have both erred the fame error. But, ſhould the reader think otherwiſe, he muſt allow it to be a moſt curious literary anecdote, that two perſons, entirely unknown

* Page 188.—193. and the diſſertation there referred to.

† He is Profeſſor of Eloquence and Greek in the Univerſity of Groningen; and his book is entitled, *Analogia Linguæ Græcæ*, printed at Utrecht, in 1779.

Chap. VII. PROGRESS OF LANGUAGE. 55

to one another, should have coincided so perfectly, not in one particular thing, but in a whole system of science.

Further, it may be observed, that, as the vowels are essential parts of all language, without which there can be no articulation; and, as they are more pliable by their nature than consonants, and therefore admitting of greater changes and variations, it was most natural to derive the whole language from them; much more natural than to derive the Hebrew from triads of consonants. That the flexions of verbs are chiefly by vowels, must be admitted. If so, is it not natural to suppose that the verb itself has been originally formed in the same way; and, as all the nouns in Greek are derived from verbs [*], it follows that the whole words of the language, except some prepositions and connecting particles, which are to be considered, not as words, but rather as pegs and nails that fasten words together [†], are derived from combinations of vowels.

[*] Vol. ii. p. 169.
[†] Ibid.

Laſtly, The learned language of India, I mean the Sanſcrit, is, as we are well informed, derived from a few words, or rather ſounds, having no determinate ſignification. And, by later diſcoveries, we learn that there is a wonderful reſemblance betwixt the Sanſcrit and the Greek, in that capital part of ſpeech, the verb; for the Sanſcrit has exactly the ſame form of a verb, as that of the verbs in —μι in Greek *. And there is another reſemblance betwixt the Sanſcrit and the oldeſt language in Greek, and I think the beſt, I mean Homer's language, that all the other languages of India are. dialects of the Sanſcrit, as I am perſuaded that all the ſeveral languages, ſpoken in Greece in later times, are dialects of Homer's language. And this perſuades me that the ſyſtem, both of the Sanſcrit and the Greek, has come originally from the parent country of all arts and ſciences, Egypt, though no doubt the words and phraſes would be greatly altered; for there is nothing to hinder the ſame art to be practiſed in different countries, but with very different materials.

* See page 25. of this Volume.

Chap. VII. PROGRESS OF LANGUAGE. 57

There is one advantage which the Sanfcrit language enjoys, I think, in common with the language of Homer; and it is this, that, if you are mafter of the language of the Sanfcrit, you may make as many words in it as you pleafe, and they will be readily underftood by the hearer, if he be alfo mafter of the rules of that analogy *. Now, I think it is evident that we may form numbers of new words according to Homer's analogy, and they will be readily underftood by a fcholar who has ftudied that analogy.

There is another refemblance, as appears to me, betwixt the Sanfcrit and the language of Homer. We are informed that this Indian language never was at any time the language of the vulgar, but of philofophers only. Now, I am perfuaded that Homer's language never was fpoken entire by any one tribe of Greeks, being a language much too various and artificial to have ever been the language of the vul-

* See p. 25. of this Vol. and p. 530. of Vol. ii.

gar in any country. It was therefore the language only of the Poets or Bards, who were at that time the philosophers or wife men of the country.

CHAP. VIII.

Of Composition *in Greek—the greatest beauty of all—requires variety as much as any thing else belonging to language.—The arrangement in Greek wonderfully various.—By a proper arrangement the sense conveyed more forcibly than it could be otherwise.—This composition, though difficult to be understood at first, becomes easy.—It appeared so beautiful to the scholars that flourished after the restoration of letters, that they disdained to write in their vernacular tongue.—Of the many particles used in Greek.—The use of these particles, both with respect to the sense and sound.—Of the wonderful beauty of the composition of Demosthenes, when pronounced by himself.*

I Come now to speak of Composition in Greek, the most material thing in every language, and for the sake of which all the rest of the grammatical art is intended. It is almost needless to observe that by composition here I mean not that composition by which single words are formed, of which I have already treated *, but that composition by which words are put together in sentences; as to which, I have already observed †, that the chief beauty of it is variety; for, if it were always the same, though ever so beautiful, it would soon become disgusting. Now, the Greek language, expressing all the various connections of words by flexion, particularly by genders, numbers, and cases, admits of a wonderful variety of arrangement, in so much, that it is only indeclineable words that require to be connected by juxta-position. In this way, not only the ear must be greatly pleased, but I think I have shown, that, by the position of emphatical words in certain parts of the sentence, the sense is conveyed more forcibly than it could be otherwise ‡; and, as the meaning, where the composition is in periods or long sentences, cannot be divided and taken sepa-

* In the preceding Chapter.
† Chap. 3. of this Volume.
‡ Vol. ii. p. 569. and following,—p. 572. and following.

rately, but muſt be apprehended altogether or not at all, it is evident that the ſenſe in that way comes upon the mind more cloſe and embodied, as it were, and conſequently more forcibly than when broken down, and frittered into ſmall pieces.

This compoſition, ſo various, and ſo different from our uniform compoſition, and which, therefore, appears to us unnatural, is no doubt at firſt difficult to the young beginner, both in Greek and Latin. But it is ſurpriſing how ſoon it becomes eaſy to us, and even familiar; and, at laſt we deſpiſe every other kind of compoſition; which is the reaſon why the learned, after the reſtoration of learning, and for more than one hundred years after that, ſcorned to write in their *vernacular* language, which they conſidered to be fit only for *ſervants* or *ſlaves*, as the word denotes; but they wrote in Latin, (ſometimes in Greek), and converſed in Latin with one another. In Germany, they ſtill write in Latin upon any learned ſubject, though the Latin be not ſo good as might be wifhed. For my own part, if I could write in Latin as well as fome of the fcholars in England, and particularly my friend Sir George Baker phyfician in London, writing, as I do, not for the vulgar, I would never write in Englifh, or in any modern language. When I was at a foreign Univerfity many years ago, I was in the habit of both fpeaking and writing Latin, and could do it tolerably well; but this faculty I have now loft, and I am too old, much too old, to recover it.—But to return to the fubject.

Thefe long periods in Greek or Latin, fo artificially arranged, and confifting of feveral members, various not only in the ftructure of the words but in the matter, (which fhould be the cafe of every long period well compofed,) if they be not well read, with a proper variation of tone fuitable to the difference of matter, will not be intelligible even to the moft learned ears. But this very change of tone, at the fame time that it makes the fenfe quite clear and diftinct, gives a beautiful variety to the pronunciation, as we muft be fen-

Ch. VIII. PROGRESS OF LANGUAGE. 63

fible from hearing well read the periods of Demosthenes or Milton.

There is one thing remaining to be spoken to, which, in my apprehension, gave as great a flow to the Greek composition as any thing I have hitherto mentioned, and made them speak *ore rotundo*, more than any other people in the world. What I mean, is the use of so many particles, or little words, more by far than are to be found, I believe, in any other language in the world. By the flexion of nouns, adjectives, and verbs, words are connected together; but by these particles the sense is connected, so that we know what is to follow by what goes before, and there is no gap or interval in the *flumen orationis*, any more than in a natural stream. Thus, when a μεν goes before, we are sure that something is to follow that has the relation of opposition to the thing preceding, and which is marked by the correspondent particle δε; and, when a τε goes before, we are sure another conjunction is to follow, joining the subsequent thing to the preceding. The particle ϝη gives an emphasis to what follows, which we can hardly express in English even by a circumlocution.

The particle τοι serves a like purpose of raising the attention, though I think not so emphatically as δη. It is the Dorick of σοι, and answers to the Latin *tibi*, which is used by Lucretius in the same sense, where he says,

> His *tibi* me rebus quaedam divina voluptas
> Percipit atque horror [*].——

Ουν I understand to be a particle which connects in the way of reasoning what follows with what goes before, importing that the one is a consequence of the other.

Γε appears to me to be a limiting particle, restricting the generality of the word or proposition to which it is applied. Thus, the meaning of that common expression, εμοι γε δοκει, is, *I at least think so, whatever others may think;* and it may generally be rendered by *at least* in English.

[*] Lib. 3. V. 28.

As the Greeks compound other words, so they compound those particles, and they say, μεντοι τοιγαρουν, &c. all which, I am perſuaded, have a meaning, but which it is very difficult to expreſs in Engliſh or in any other language. And this has inclined many to believe that the greater part of them had no meaning at all, but were employed merely to give a greater flow to the compoſition. But, tho' they certainly have that effect, I cannot believe that a people of ſo correct a taſte as the Greeks would employ words, and ſo many of them too, merely for the ſake of the ſound, without any meaning, eſpecially in their proſe compoſitions, and in their orations, where they were ſpeaking to the people upon buſineſs of the greateſt importance. The learned world, therefore, I think, are much obliged to the German Profeſſor Hoegenville, who has endeavoured, and I think for the greater part ſuccesſfully, to give a meaning to every one of them.

Being obliged, for the reaſon I have mentioned, to write in Engliſh, it often grieves me that I cannot give, both to my words and matter, the connection which the Greeks give by the means of thefe particles, fo that my fentences, do what I can, are often as much unconnected, as if there were no connection in the matter.

If what I have faid of the Greek compofition be true, how wonderful muft the orations of Demofthenes have been, fpoken by himfelf, with all the graces of action and pronunciation? For, befides his action, in which he is allowed to have excelled, what pleafure to the ear muft have given the melody and rhythm of his language, both much ftudied by him *—the variety alfo of his artificial ar-

* Vol. ii. p. 382. Of the melody of the Greek language we have hardly, as I have faid, an idea; and, as to the rhythm, though we know well enough what it was, yet our ears are not formed to perceive the beauty of it, even in their verfe, and much lefs in their profe.—See what I have faid upon this fubject, Vol. ii. p 401. and following, and 409. and following; where I have fhown how effential a part rhythm was, even of their profe compofition.

rangement *, his periods divided into members of different lengths, and containing matter of different kinds, and which, therefore, muſt have been ſpoken, as I have obſerved, with changes of tones †— his ſtile too, adorned with figures very different from the figures now uſed, which ſtick out of the work and alter quite the colour of the ſtile, ſuch as *exclamation*, much uſed even by Cicero, and ſuch as *epithets* which are the diſtinguiſhing characteriſtic of the poetic ſtile, but of which the ſtile of Demoſthenes is almoſt entirely free, (for I have read whole orations of his, where there is not a ſingle epithet); the figures he uſes being ſuch as eſcape the attention of the unlearned, and, though the learned perceive that they give an unuſual caſt to the ſtile, yet they do not know what name to give them?—When I conſider all theſe things, I ſay again that the orations of Demoſthenes, pronounced

* Ibid. p. 363. and following. See alſo the Diſſertation annexed to Vol. ii. on the Compoſition of the antients.

† See an example of a period of Demoſthenes, Vol. iii. p. 60.

by himself, not read even by Eschines *, who, as he was a very good pleader, I suppose, was also a good reader, must have been a most wonderful thing, and of beauty so transcendent, that we cannot have any idea of it †; or, if we could form an idea of it, we should not be able to imitate it, even in writing, much less in speaking, not having the materials upon which he wrought. In other arts, such as statuary, though we have the materials, yet all connoisseurs acknowledge that no modern artist has equalled the beauty of the antient Greek statues; but, when a modern language is the materials upon which the writing ar-

* This alludes to a well known story of Æschines, who having retired to Rhodes, after his banishment, read to some people there Demosthenes's famous oration against him, entitled, περι στιφανου; and, when they admired it very much, ' What would you have thought of it,' said he, ' if you had heard him pronounce it?'—See Vol. ii. p. 417.

† See the account given by the Halicarnassian of the beauty of rhetorical composition, consisting of *melody, rhythm, variety,* or *change,* and, lastly, what is *proper* or *becoming.* I have quoted the passage in Vol. ii. of this Work, p. 381.

tift muft work, it is by nature impoffible to equal the beauty of the Greek compofition, as impoffible as it would be to build a fine palace of rough unhewn pebbles.

Though Demofthenes exceeded, I believe, all the men of his age in the art of pronunciation, yet an oration muft firft be well compofed, before any pronunciation can make it pleafe a man of fenfe and tafte. Now, we know that Demofthenes applied as much to compofition as to pronunciation; and, as a model of compofition, he ftudied the authors before him, particularly Thucydides, whom it is faid he tranfcribed eight times with his own hand; but he has fhown wonderful judgment in the imitation of him, for he has avoided his perplexed and involved periods, fo much crouded with matter, that he was reckoned an obfcure writer in the time of Dionyfius the Halicarnaffian, and, I believe, even when he wrote himfelf; nor do I think that Demofthenes could have been underftood, even by the people of Athens, fenfible and acute as they were, if he had fpoken to them in the ftile of Thu-

cydides; but he has imitated him with so
much difcretion, that, though he have diverfified his ftile by figures without name
or number, yet he has not crouded them
together fo much as Thucydides has done;
(for a ftile may be too much varied as well
as too much the fame); neverthelefs his
ftile, fuch as it is, is fo much varied, and
fo artificial, that he was not well received
at firft by the people, I fuppofe becaufe they
did not perfectly underftand him, till he
had learned the art of pronouncing his
own periods *.

---

* See Vol. ii. p. 363. and following.

CHAP. IX.

Of the Latin *language.—That language the oldest dialect of the Greek—liker therefore to the Oriental Languages.—It has tones, but not so accurately marked as in Greek. —But the quantity of syllables accurately observed in it.—As to* spirits, *much fewer aspirates than in Greek.—The Latin language defective in the elemental sounds, particularly in diphthongs.— These the Latins commonly resolve.—Examples of this.—The greatest difference of all betwixt the sound of the two languages is, that the Latins terminate so many words in mute consonants, the Greeks none at all.—The terminations of* -orum *and* -arum, *in the Latin language, not pleasant.*

THE next language to which I shall apply my general observations is the Latin. This language is the most antient dialect of the Greek known, brought into Italy by a colony of Arcadians, under Oenotrus, about seventeen generations before the Trojan war, resembling more the Doric and Eolic than any other dialect of Greek now known. But, as it came off from the original stock, much earlier than either of these dialects, it has more of the roughness of the Hebrew, or some other Egyptian or Oriental language, from which I am persuaded the Greek is derived. It has, however, accents or tones, which I am persuaded all languages had originally, though they may have lost them in process of time, through ignorance and barbarity; for music being, as I imagine, coëval with language, it was most natural that it should be joined, and, as it were, incorporated with it. Now, the Latins being a musical people, as well as the Greeks, of whom they were descended, preserved the original music of the language, and began the pronunciation of it in the wind-pipe, the greater or less dilation of which gives a language

Chap. IX. PROGRESS OF LANGUAGE. 73

its mufical tones, which the modern languages want entirely, having nothing but articulation produced by the various pofition and action of the organs of the mouth, where our pronunciation begins. But, tho' the Latins had accents, I have a great doubt whether they were fo accurately meafured, or fo exactly obferved in the pronunciation, as thofe of the Greeks were. Their grammarians, who treat of accentuation, though they fpeak of the *acute*, the *grave*, and the *circumflex* *, do not define or meafure them, as the Halicarnaffian has done in regard to the Greek accents: And I do not obferve that any of their authors who have treated of *ftile*, fpeak much of the melody of it as one of its beauties †, or commend it, as the Halicarnaffian does the ftile of Demofthenes, for being 'ευμελης ‡.

* See Prifcian and Diomedes, in the Collection of Latin Grammarians, publifhed by Putchius, p. 1286. et feq. and p. 426. et feq.

† That thefe authors, however, had an idea of fuch a beauty, and the practice of it at leaft in fome degree, is evident from what Cicero fays, Lib. ii. Cap. 8. *De Oratore*, Lib. iii. Cap. 50. *ibid.* And in his *Orator*, Cap. 17. and 18.

‡ See what I have faid upon this ornament of ftile in Greek compofition, Vol. ii. Book iii. Chap. 7.

VOL. IV. K

But, whatever defect there may have been in the melody of the Latin language, the rhythm of it, that is, the quantity of the syllables, appears to have been very accurately observed. But, as to the distinction of spirits, they do not appear to have used it near so much as the Greeks; for they did not aspirate consonants at all *, so that they had not the sound of the Greek letters φ, χ, and θ. And they used very little aspiration even of vowels: Thus, they said *œdi* for *hœdi*, *irci* for *hirci* †. And the reason of this appears to me very plain, namely, that the Latin language came off from the Greek before it was completed either in the sound or in the grammatical part. And from thence arises this defect, and all the others that I shall take occasion to observe, in the Latin language. In later times, when they began to reform their language upon the model of the Greek, they improved the sound of it, by the use of aspirated consonants, as well as vowels. Thus, in place of *pulcer*, which they said

* Cicero, *Orator*, Cap. 48.
† Quintilian, *Institutiones*, Lib. i. Cap. 5.

before, they said *pulcher*; in place of *Gracci* they said *Gracchi*; in place of *triumpi* they said *triumphi*, &c. *; and the use of aspirated vowels became common among them. But, as to consonants, even in the days of Cicero, there were very few of them aspirated, except in words taken from the Greek, such as *philosophia*, which was not Latin till the days of Cicero, though the thing before that was known among them, but it was called *sapientia*; and *sapere* was used for *philosophari*, as late as the days of Horace, who says,

Scribendi recte *sapere* est principium et fons.
Rem tibi Socraticae poterunt ostendere chartae.

And not only did the Latins want those aspirated consonants, which I think give a beautiful variety to the Greek language; but they did not found all the six proper

* Quintilian, *dicto loco*; where he tells us that the Greek fashion of aspirating consonants was carried so far, that some people pronounced *praechones* instead of *praecones*, *chenturiones* instead of *centuriones*, &c.

diphthongs, at leaſt not in later times; for in the days of Cicero they uſed neither the ει nor the ου. The *ai* they appear always to have uſed, particularly in the genitive ſingular of the firſt declenſion; and they ſometimes divided it, as in the words *pa-triaï* and *auraï*. The *au* too, and the *eu*, they appear always to have uſed, as in the words *audio*, and *heu*, and *ſeu*. The *oi* too appears always to have been in uſe among them, as in *Iæna* and *pæna*, and many others, which I am perſuaded they ſounded as the Greeks did the οι; for we cannot doubt that *poena*, for example, is the Greek word ποινη. But in many of their words they leave out one of the vowels of this high ſounding diphthong, and pronounce it as the ſingle vowel. Thus, of the word οικος, they make *focus*, with the Eolic digamma prefixed, and leaving out the vowel *i*; and of *aves*, by leaving out the other vowel, viz. the *o*, they made *viſum*. And, in general, it may be obſerved, that the genius of the language, at leaſt in later times, appears to have been, to reſolve the diphthong, and to ſound only one of t h vowels.——Thus, in the declenſion of

Ch. IX. Progress of Language. 77

animus, in place of the termination οι in the nominative plural, and οις and ους in the dative and accusative, the Latins have *i*, and *is*, and *os*; and in the genitive singular they throw out both vowels, and, in place of ανεμου say *animi* *; and, in the third declension, in the word *omnis*, for example, in place of *omneis* in the nominative plural, they say *omnes* commonly, and some of the old writers *omnis*, always leaving out one or other of the vowels. And it is the same in the verb; as, in *lego*, in place of saying, in the second and third person, *legeis* and *legeit*, they say *legis* and *legit*.—As to the improper diphthongs, of which the Greek Grammarians make also six, it does not appear that the Latins ever founded one of them, (nor does any Latin grammarian, as far as I know, so much as mention them), which must have made the sound of their language of much less variety than that of the Greek †.

* The ancient Greek genitive was ανεμοιο, as it is still used in the Ionic dialect: and from thence I imagine is formed the Latin genitive *animi*, by throwing away first the final *o*, and then the *o* in the diphthong.

† That the improper diphthongs were truly diphthongs, as they are called, and differed in their

Thus it appears that, for want of afpirated confonants, and having fo much few-

found from the fimple vowels, cannot be doubted. At the fame time, we cannot fuppofe that they were founded in the fame manner as the proper diphthongs. Thus, for example, ῳ had certainly a found different from the proper diphthong ω. It had, however, I am perfuaded, a found approaching to it, which I think is evident from the manner of writing it. What, then, was the difference betwixt the two founds? And I apprehend it was this, that, in the proper diphthongs, the founds of the two vowels were fo perfectly mixed, that the ear could not diftinguifh the one from the other; whereas, in the improper diphthongs, the voice dwelt more upon one of the vowels than upon the other, and which, therefore, was better heard in the pronunciation; and, accordingly, in writing, the ι in the improper diphthong ῳ is marked either by a dot under the ω, or by a fmall ι fubjoined to it, which I think plainly indicates, that, in the compofition making this improper diphthong, the ω was predominant, and more ftrongly founded than the ι. Another example may be given of an improper diphthong, where the ω is alfo predominant, but the other vowel, inftead of being *pofiponed*, is *praeponed*; as in the word Παλαιῳ, where, in the fyllable λῳ, the found of ι is heard, if it be rightly pronounced, but faintly. It is faid by the grammarians, and particularly by Euftathius, that thefe two letters are pronounced together by a figure which they call συναφρησις, or συνιξησις. But the vowels cannot be run together, without being pronounced as a diphthong proper or improper.—Thefe

er compounded vocal founds, the Latin language could neither have that variety, nor that fwell in the found, which the Greek language has. And, further, it is evident that the pronunciation of the Latin muft have been very much harfher than the Greek, particularly in their terminations, which, as I have obferved, are a diftinguifhing part of the found of words*. Now, the termination of a great many Latin words is in mute confonants, fuch as *b, c, d,* and particularly *s* †. Such terminations, I am perfuaded, were as common in Greek, in its original ftate, as they are now in Latin; and it is one proof among many others, that it was little better than

---

obfervations I owe to a friend of mine, a learned Profeffor in the Univerfity of St Andrews, Mr John Hunter.

* P. 5.—31.

† In antient times, there were many more words terminating in *d,* as may be feen in antient monuments of the Latin yet preferved. Thus, they faid, *popnlod* for *populo, fentensiad* for *fententia.*—Of the diftinction betwixt the *liquid* and *mute* confonants, Vol. ii. p. 233.

a rude and barbarous language when the Latin came off from it. Several veſtiges of this are to be ſeen in the moſt antient dialect of it, next to the Latin, I mean the Doric, where they ſay λεγοντι in place of λεγουσι. Now, I can have no doubt but that in an earlier period they ſaid λεγοντ, or *legunt* as the Latins now ſay. And they uſed much more the canine letter *r* than they do now,—I believe, as much as the Latins uſe it ; as is evident from a piece of very antient Doric Greek preſerved to us, viz. a decree of the ſenate of Sparta, againſt Timotheus, a muſician, who had corrupted, as they ſaid, the ſimplicity of the antient muſic, by adding a ſtring to the lyre.

This termination in mute conſonants, ſo harſh and abrupt, makes the language flow not ſo pleaſantly. And that common termination in Latin with the *lowing* letter, as it is called, *m*, abſolutely ſhuts the mouth more than any of the letters that are called mute ; and it interrupts the flow of the language ſo much, that it is very frequently elided in their verſe. It is, however, much ufed by them, both in their declenfions and conjugations; particularly in their genitives plural, inftead of the Greek ων, they ufe *orum*, which gives occafion fometimes to rhymes not agreeable, as that of Horace,

<blockquote>Atque alii, *quorum comoedia prifca virorum* eft:</blockquote>

And their *arums* are of the fame kind; as *teftis mearum fententiarum.* Thefe are Monkifh rhymes which I am perfuaded Horace would not have ufed, if he could eafily have avoided it. Now, the ων of the Greek in place of *orum,* and the Æolic αων in place of *arum,* make pleafant enough rhymes at times, as Homer has fhown.

CHAP. X.

The words of the Latin language confidered as fignificant.—In that refpect inferior to the Greek more ftill than in found—particularly in the verb.—Examples of the defect of the Latin language in that part of fpeech—inferior even to the Englifh.—Defective alfo in participles.—The Latins want alfo the variety of two aorifts and three futures.—Defective alfo in moods—wanting alfo a voice which the Greeks have in their verbs, and a dual number both in their verbs and their nouns.—The Latin wants one part of fpeech wholly, viz. the article.—The confequence of this defect is to make the expreffion of the language obfcure and ambiguous.—Examples of this.

Ch. X. PROGRESS OF LANGUAGE. 83

I come now to confider the words in Latin as fignificant. And here it will appear that the Latin is as inferior to the Greek in fenfe and expreffion as in found. The moft important part of fpeech, as well as the moft artificial, is the verb; and in it the Latin is moft deficient. For, in the *firft* place, it has but one paft perfect time in the active voice, fuch as *amavi*, but which cannot exprefs whether that perfect action be now prefent or not; fo that it does not make the diftinction which the Greeks do by their praeterperfect and by their praeterite indefinite, or aorift, for both which *amavi* ftands *. And hence undoubtedly muft arife an ambiguity, which cannot be refolved by the words, but only by the fenfe, or by repeating the verb in another tenfe, and faying, *amavi* et *amo*. And I obferve

* Of the diftinction betwixt the aorift and praeterperfect, fee what I have faid Vol. ii. p. 132. *et feq.* The whole chapter is worth reading by thofe who are not contented with having learned what is called *accidence* in the Englifh fchools, but defire to underftand the fcience of the language, of which the knowledge of the doctrine of the tenfes is, I think, one of the moft difficult parts.

that Horace, in one paſſage, has been obliged to uſe both tenſes, where he ſays,

Manſerunt hodieque *manent* veſtigia ruris [*].

Now this plainly ſhows an imperfection in the language. And accordingly, in the more perfect Greek language, *amavi* is expreſſed as clearly by one word, πεφιληκα, and even in Engliſh, by the words *I have loved*, expreſſing, without any ambiguity, not only that I loved in the time paſt, but that I continue to love, and do now love. In the ſame manner, inſtead of the *manent* and *manſcrunt* of Horace, the Greeks would have uſed a ſingle word, μεμενηκασι.

Again, the Latins, in their active verbs, have not a paſt participle active, whereas the Greeks have two, ſuch as φιλησας and πεφιληκως, expreſſing the paſt time either definitely or indefinitely, as above explained ; the conſequence of which is, that the Latins of neceſſity are obliged to uſe that disjointed gaping compoſition, called the ablative abſolute, which

[*] Epiſt. I. Lib. ii. Verſ. 160.

the Greeks use only some times by way of variety.

Further, as the Latins want a past participle active, so they want a present participle passive; for they have no word that expresses φιλουμενος; nor will an ablative absolute do the business here. They are therefore reduced to hard shifts. Virgil, in place of it, uses the past participle passive, and says, *ventosa per aequora vectis* *; and in another place he says, *elisos oculos* †. And Cicero, in place of the present participle passive, borrows a present participle

---

* *Georgic.* I. v. 206. where *vectis* expresses the Greek word φερομενοις.

† *Æneid.* VIII. v. 261. where Virgil, describing Hercules strangling Cacus, says,

———Angit inhaerens
Elisos oculos.———

Here, if the Latins had had a present participle passive, such as the Greeks have, of the verb *elido*, Virgil would have said *elidomenos oculos*, that is, *eyes in the act of being thrust out*.

from the active voice, and says, *marinis invehens belluis* *.

Besides this want of a participle in the passive voice, there is the same confusion in it of the aorist and praeterperfect that there is in the active, though at first sight it would appear that these two tenses are as much distinguished in the passive voice as they are in Greek; and I once believed it was so, though, in the common grammars, *amatus est* and *amatus fuit* are set down as in the same tense. But the Professor above mentioned, Mr Hunter, who, as the Latin tongue is his profession, is exceedingly learned in it, has shown me that they are truly the same, and that, in the best authors, they are used to denote indiscriminately either εφιλnθn or τεφιλnται, that is, either the aorist or the praeterperfect; in the same manner as *amavi* in the active voice signifies either of the two times; so that

* Cicero, *De Natura Deorum*, Lib. i. Cap. 28. where *invehens* would have been *invehemenus*, if the Latins had used such a form of the verb.

amatus eft, as well as *amatus fuit,* may be applied to a paſt event, which in no ſenſe can be ſaid to be now preſent ; and therefore they are both uſed without diſtinction as the hiſtoric tenſe, in the ſame manner as the aoriſt in Greek. Now, one ſhould think that *amatus eft,* being compounded of the paſt participle *amatus,* and the verb *eft* in the preſent tenſe, muſt denote a time compounded of the paſt and the preſent, that is, the *praeterperfect* : And that *amatus fuit,* being compounded of the paſt participle and a verb in the paſt time, muſt denote an action altogether paſt, but not preſent in any ſenſe: And, if the Latin language had been formed like the Greek, by philoſophers, or men of learning in the ſcience of language, I think it is impoſſible that expreſſions ſo different could have denoted the ſame time : And accordingly Mr Hunter thought at firſt, as I did, that they denoted different times. And, indeed, it is impoſſible to think otherwiſe, if you are learned in the grammatical art, and not one of thoſe who have got by heart the declenſions and conjugations, and have read many Greek authors, but know nothing of the science of language, of whom I am afraid there is a great number. In the same manner, I thought that *amatus erat*, and *amatus fuerat*, signified different things; but now I am convinced that they stand for the same tense, though the one be compounded of a past participle with a verb in the imperfect tense, and the other of the same past participle with the plusquamperfect tense.

Moreover, in the tenses the Latins have, they want the variations which the Greeks have of the same tense. Thus, they have but one future, and one aorist, in place of two of each, which the Greeks have: And there is a third future which the Greeks have also, but of which the Latins know nothing, I mean the *paulo post futurum*. It is true, indeed, that the two aorists have the same signification; and I believe the same is the case of the three futures, being all tenses, as well as the aorists, from themes now obsolete [*]; but they give a variety of

---

[*] See what I have said of the two *aorists*, Vol. ii. p. 147. and of the *paulo post futurum*, p. 131. of the same Volume.

flexion and termination, which makes the language much more copious, in sound at least, if not in signification.

Further, the Latin language wants not only so many tenses which the Greek has, but also a mood, I mean the optative. And this I hold to be a capital defect. For, by the nature of things, there are four dispositions of the mind relating to every verb, and which ought to be expressed by some variation of the word. The first is singly affirming, that is the *indicative* mood. The second is commanding, viz. the *imperative*. The third is wishing or praying, that is the *optative*. And the last is that whereby we express that the verb is not principal in the sentence, but dependent upon another verb; this is done by what is called the *subjunctive* mood *. Now, the Latins express both

---

* See what I have said upon the subject of *moods*, Book i. Chap. 13. Vol. ii. p. 162. where I have given my reasons why I do not number the infinitive among the moods.

these two last mentioned by the same mood, viz. the subjunctive: And, therefore, when they have a mind to distinguish the two significations, and to express only the wish, they are obliged to use another word, *utinam*; or, to express it simply by the subjunctive, which may in some cases occasion an ambiguity.

But even these are not all the defects of the Latin language in the simple article of the verb; for, besides wanting so many tenses and a whole mood, they want a whole voice,—viz. the middle voice, by which is expressed the action of a verb, which has for its subject the person himself who speaks, or something that concerns him; a very interesting part of the expression of a verb. To supply this want, the Latins are forced to use prepositions and pronouns, or sometimes they use active or neutral verbs in a middle sense; and particularly I observe they use *verto* in that way, as where Livy says, speaking of stage-plays, *Ludus in artem paulatim verterat* *.

* Lib. vii. Cap. ii.

I will mention, only in paffing, the want
of a dual number both in their verbs and
nouns, though I think it a defect; as that
additional number not only produces an
additional flexion, and fo makes the found
of the language more rich, but it makes a
very proper diftinction betwixt unity and
number, by marking the firft ftep towards
number*. But I come now to mention the
moft capital defect of all in the Latin language, of fuch importance, that it makes
it a language almoft unfit for reafoning, at
leaft for very ftrict philofophical reafoning.
It is not a defect of any particular modifications or variations of any one part of
fpeech, fuch as the verb, but it is the want
of one part of fpeech entirely, viz. the article, which even the barbarous modern languages have. Now this want is fuch, that,
in the Greek and Latin languages, or in
any other which admits the fame variety
of compofition, when you join two words
together in a propofition by the fubftan-
tive verb, if there be no article, it is impoffible to fay which is the fubject of the

* See what I have faid of the dual number, Vol. ii.
p. 87.

proposition, and which is the predicate. Thus, in that famous γνωμη or *Sententious saying*, of Juvenal,

Nobilitas sola est atque unica *virtus,*

it is impossible to say from the words, whether he means, *that Virtue is the only nobility,* or *that Nobility is the only virtue;* and, indeed, according to our way of arranging the words, the latter is the sense of them. Again, when Virgil says,

Saxa vocant Itali, mediis quae in fluctibus, *Aras* *,

it is impossible to know from the words, whether the stones were called *altars,* or the altars *stones.* Again, in a passage of Livy, where he gives an account of the origin of stage plays among the Romans, you cannot understand from the words he uses, whether he means to say that *Hister* was called *Ludio* by the *Etruscans,* or *Ludio Hister* †. In the in-

* Æneid. i. Verf. 112.
† Livy, Book vii. Cap. 2. where, after telling us that the Romans had their first players from Tuscany, but afterwards got players of their own, he adds, *Ver-*

stances I have mentioned, the sense of the passage removes the ambiguity: But there is a passage in Horace where that is not the case; it is where he says,

> Dixeris egregie, *notum* si calida verbum
> Reddideris junctura *novum*——— †

where I really do not know whether a *known* word is to be rendered *new*, or a *new* word *known*, by a cunning junction.

The article, too, gives an emphasis, and a kind of dignity to proper names, by informing us that they are names well known; and it serves also in place of a relative, letting us know that the thing or person was mentioned before *.

naculis artificibus, quia Hister Tusco verbo Ludio vocabatur, nomen histrionibus inditum.

* See what I have said of the application of the *article* in Greek to proper names, Vol. 2. page 55. & seq. where I have shown, that the article, when applied to a proper name (for it is not always so), has a meaning, and is not, as it is supposed by some, a word altogether insignificant, of which kind I believe there is no word in so perfect a language as the Greek.

CHAP. XI.

Of Composition in Latin—not different in variety of arrangement from the Greek. In some of the Latin poets greater variety of arrangement than in the Greek.—But in the prose authors a tedious sameness in the arrangement, by placing the verb last so often in the sentence.—The want of particles, such as the Greeks have, a great defect in the Latin composition.

HAVING confidered fingle words in Latin, both with refpect to their found, and as fignificant, I come now to fpeak of them in compofition, in which, as far as depends upon the arrangement, there cannot be much difference betwixt it and the Greek, or if there be any as to the variety of arrangement, I think there is more of that at least in some of the Latin authors than is to be found in Greek. Of this I shall say more in the next book, where I am to treat of Stile.

But, in their prose compositions, there is a sameness and uniformity, which does not appear to me to arise from the nature of their language, but certainly predominates very much in their histories, and more or less in all their compositions. What I mean is the terminating their sentences so often with a verb, and generally the governing verb in the sentence. But of this likewise I shall say more when I come to treat of Stile.

But, besides this defect in the Latin composition, there are wanting in it those many connective particles, with which, as I have shown, the Greek abounds so much; and which, besides connecting the sense, give a flow to the composition, not to be found in any other language. Several of these I have already mentioned, and will not here repeat.

And so much for the Latin language; and, as I understand no other antient language, except the Greek and Latin, I will now speak of some modern languages, beginning with the modern Greek.

CHAP. XII.

The words of the modern Greek the same for the greater part with those of the antient—different in the pronunciation and grammar.—Of the sound of the modern Greek—little variety in it.—Five letters sounded the same way.—No diphthongs or aspirates—no melody or rhythm, *but only* accents, *such as ours.—They retain something of the grammatical art—form some cases and tenses by flection—have genders and numbers in their nouns, and persons and numbers in their verbs—but their grammar cannot be reduced to any rule.—The English pronunciation of the antient Greek very like to the pronunciation of the modern Greek—has all the faults that pronunciation can have—formerly it was still worse, as they neglected the quantity, and pronounced the accents as they do the accents in their own language.—A reformation may be made of the English pronunciation of the Greek, without much difficulty.—The advantage of the Scotch pronunciation.—The corruption and debasement of the Greek language should be a warning to other nations to preserve their language, by the study of the grammatical art in the antient languages.*

THE words of the modern Greek language are, for the greater part, the same with those of the antient Greek; so that the difference betwixt the two languages is chiefly in the pronunciation, and the analogy. A man, therefore, who understands the antient language, may in a very short time make himself master of the modern. This I know from my own experience; for, many years ago, I studied the modern Greek New Testament, and, with the assistance of the old Greek Testament, in two or three days I made myself master of the little grammatical art that is now to be found in the language. But what I am now to say of it, is not what I then learned, which I have forgot long ago, but it is from the information I have had from a friend of mine in London, Mr Paradise, whose native language the modern Greek may be said to be, as he was born in *Thessalonica*, now *Salonica*, being the son of a gentleman who was then our consul in that place. And I take this opportunity of returning my thanks to him for the instruction I have got from him in this and several other things concerning the modern Greeks.

To begin with the sound of the language: They have lost even the sound of two of their vowels, the η and υ, in place of which they have substituted the *i*. They have lost also the use of the two diphthongs ει and οι; and these they also sound as *i*; which sound, therefore, holds the place of five in the antient Greek language, viz. ι, η, υ, ει, and οι. This makes a constant *iotacism* run through their whole pronunciation. Now, the sound of this letter is weak and slender, an *exilis sonus*, as the Latins call it;

and therefore it was never used by the antient Greeks in the termination of their nouns, excepting only in three, which Ariſtotle has mentioned *.

2*do*, They have loſt the ſound, not only of the two diphthongs above mentioned, ει and οι, which they confound with *Iota*, but of all the diphthongs, proper and improper; ſo that the ſound of their language is not ſwelled or raiſed by any compounded ſound of vowels.

3*tio*, Neither have they any aſpirated conſonants: They do not, therefore, prounce the letters φ, χ, or θ; nay, they do not aſpirate even vowels.

4*to*, They have loſt the melody of the antient language altogether; and do not appear to have any idea of it any more than the unlearned among us.

* Poetic. Cap. 21. *in fine.*

But, 5*to*, What is still worse, they have no longer any rhythm in their language, which makes it more barbarous than many of those languages we call barbarous *. Their syllables, therefore, are all of an equal length, and only distinguished from one another by what we call *accent*. And this distinction they take from the accentuation in the antient Greek books. Thus, for example, the word ἄνθρωπος having an acute accent upon the first syllable, they pronounce as we do many words in English, and make of it *ánthrŏpos*, neglecting entirely the quantity of the middle syllable.

Thus it appears that they have lost all that variety of sound in their language, which, as I have shown, was the greatest beauty of the antient Greek pronunciation; and, having debased so much the sound of it, we cannot suppose that they have preserved its grammar, though they have retained more of that than could well have been expected, considering how

---

* See pag. 18. of this volume.

much they have loſt of their language in other reſpects; for they ſtill form two caſes by flection, viz. the genitive and accuſative; and they have genders and numbers both in their ſubſtantives and adjectives. They form ſeveral of their tenſes alſo by flection, and likewiſe the perſons and numbers of their verbs. But my friend informs me, that, in their declenſions and conjugations, they hardly follow any rule: So that they cannot be ſaid to have a grammatical art, though they practice ſomething belonging to the art of their antient language.

Before I leave this ſubject of the modern Greek, I cannot help obſerving that the Engliſh pronunciation of the antient Greek is much too like to that of the modern, particularly in the pronunciation of the η and the ει diphthong, both which they ſound like the antient *Iota*, and alſo the ε, which they do not diſtinguiſh from the η by the ſound, but only by the quantity; and ſometimes they alſo pronounce the *Iota* in the ſame way; though more commonly they pronounce it as they do it in their own language, that is, like the diphthong *ai*. And I muſt be forgiven if I ſay further, that the Engliſh pronunciation of the Greek has every fault that pronunciation can have; for they pronounce the ſame letter in different ways, as in the inſtance juſt now mentioned of the *Iota*. 2*dly*, They pronounce different letters the ſame way. Thus, as I have obſerved, they pronounce the three letters ε, η, and αι, and ſometimes *Iota* in the ſame way. They alſo confound in the pronunciation the ſimple υ and the ευ diphthong, and likewiſe the ſimple κ, and the aſpirated κ or χ. And, laſtly, there are ſounds in the Greek language, which they do not pronounce at all, ſuch as the diphthong ου, which they do not pronounce, not having ſuch a ſound in their own language, but confound it with another diphthong quite different, viz. αυ. And there is even a ſimple vowel, that they do not pronounce, viz. υ, which, from the deſcription the Halicarnaſſian gives us of its pronunciation *, ought to be ſounded like the French *u*. Nay, the firſt

---

* Περι συνθεσεως cap. 14.

of the vowels A they do not pronounce as the antient Greeks did, but as they generally pronounce their own A, that is, like the Greek H. So that according to the English pronunciation, the Greek wants the best founding of all the vowels, if we can trust the judgment of the Halicarnaffian *.

* Περι συνθεσεως, ibid. The mechanism of its pronunciation he thus describes, λεγεται επιγομενου του στοματος επι πλειστον, και του πνευματος αναφερομενου προς τον ουρανον.——So that by not opening their mouth sufficiently, the English make their pronunciation of the Greek as faulty, as Milton observes the pronunciation of their own language is.—See Milton's *Tractate of Education ;* He says, that the speech of the scholar ' should be fashioned to a distinct clear pronunci-
' ation, as near as may be to the Italian, especially in
' the vowels. For we Englishmen, being northerly,
' do not open our mouths in the cold air wide enough
' to grace a Southern tongue ; but are observed by all
' other nations, to speak exceeding close and inward :
' So that to smatter Latin with an English mouth, Is
' as ill a hearing, as Law French.' I would recommend the whole treatise to the Reader, as the best thing both for matter and stile, that has been written upon the subject of education, in modern times.

Thus, I think I have shown that the English pronunciation of the Greek, has all the three faults I have mentioned, that is, every fault which pronunciation can have; the confequence of this is, that, in their pronunciation, a great part of that variety of found, which, as I have obferved, diftinguifhes fo much the Greek from other languages, is loft; and by making much ufe of that weak flender found *Iota*, they debafe the found of the language very near as much as the modern Greeks do.

Their pronunciation, however, formerly was ftill much worfe than it is at prefent, and ftill more refembling the modern Greek pronunciation; for they pronounced it according to the accents, as marked in the Greek books, by raifing the voice upon the fyllables that were marked with the acute accent, without any regard to the quantity; or, in other words, accenting the Greek juft as they do their own language; by which means they founded the accented fyllable as if it were long, though it may be fhort. This fault, fo great that it deftroys entirely the meafure of the Greek verfe, they have now corrected; and they pronounce according to the *quantity*, neglecting the accents altogether, for a very good reafon—that they cannot pronounce them; and, indeed, I believe very few, even of the fcholars in England, have any idea how they fhould be pronounced. There are ftill remaining, however, fome veftiges in certain words, of the barbarity of this ancient pronunciation, as in the name of the Ifland *St Heléna*, which being accented upon the penult fyllable, they make that fyllable long: And in the word *Idèa*, they lengthen the fame fyllable for the fame reafon, and I have obferved the like in other words, which I do not at prefent recollect.

The Englifh reader will forgive me for thefe obfervations upon the faults and defects of the pronunciation of Greek in England, as I think it is a pity that a nation, which underftands the Greek fo well, fhould pronounce it fo ill; and I hope, that, as they have already corrected one great fault in their pronunciation, they will alſo correct others. The reformation muſt begin at ſchool, where I ſhould not think that it would be difficult to introduce a new method of pronunciation: And, if any of the maſters of thoſe ſchools have any doubt of the truth of my obſervations upon their preſent pronunciation, I refer them to Dionyſius the Halicarnaſſian, in his treatiſe *upon Compoſition*, where he deſcribes, mechanically, the pronunciation of each letter. Our pronunciation in Scotland comes very near, as I have obſerved elſewhere [*], to the deſcription he gives of that of the ancient Greeks: But, though it be not the ſame, it has clearly this advantage over the Engliſh pronunciation, that it diſtinguiſhes every letter from another, and ſounds every one of them: So that, in the Scotch pronunciation, no part of the variety of the ancient ſound of the language is loſt.——The benefit of this diſtinctneſs of our pronunciation, I have myſelf experienced; for there were ſeveral years of my life, when thro' a weakneſs of my eyes, I read no Greek

[*] Vol. II. pag. 237. 238.

at all, but had it read to me. Now, if it had been read to me with the Englifh pronunciation, fuppofe I had been accuftomed to that pronunciation, I could not have underftood it by the found of fo many letters being comfounded, and fome not founded at all.

Before I conclude this chapter, upon the fubject of modern Greek, I cannot help obferving, how much fo noble a people as the Greeks have degenerated, and loft thofe arts in which they excelled all the world, even that art of the greateft ufe and moft conftant practice, the art of fpeech. This art the Greeks have loft, not by getting another language in place of their own, which has happened to fome, (for the words of their language, with the exceptions of very few, are all Greek), but by lofing the grammatical art, and fo far returning to barbarity, as to fpeak a barbarous language, in place of the politeft and moft cultivated language that ever was fpoken. Their example fhould be a warning to other nations, not to neglect the study of the ancient languages, where only the grammatical art is to be learned, and by the imitation of which, they may improve, or at least preserve from becoming worse, their own language.

CHAP. XIII.

Of the found *of the Englijh language.—It confifts chiefly of monofyllables.--The words crouded with confonants, and many terminated with the afpirated* t.—*This fault of the language aggravated by modern ufe.* —*No* melody or rhythm *in the Englijh language.—The words and fyllables, at the fame time pronounced with a great variety of* tones; *but thefe not reduced to any rule.--The wonderful art of the Greek language in this refpect.—Of* accents *in Englijh.—They give a variety to the pronunciation of the language, and make our verfification more various and beautiful than that of other modern nations.--The abufe of our modern accents in our modern ufe of them.—Not to be compared, though ever fo properly ufed, to the rhythm of Greek and Latin.—The words in Englijh confidered as fignificant.—In this refpect, the language is ftill more inferior to the*

Greek and Latin, particularly in the verb. The time of it not expressed, except by one flexion of the word; nor the numbers except in one instance.—Defective also in the expression of persons.—*We had once a mood expressed by the termination; but that is now lost.—Only two participles expressed by termination.—The English more defective still in voices, than in tenses or moods.—No middle voice.—And no tense, mood, or participle in the passive voice, expressed by flexion.—The clumsy circumlocutions that we are obliged to use to supply the defects of the passive voice.—As to* nouns *in English, they have no genders nor cases, and therefore may be reckoned indeclinable words. —The composition also of words very defective in English; and also the etymology, as it is not an original language.*

THE next modern language I shall mention, is our own language, the English; and I will consider it as I have done other languages, beginning with the sound of it.

The words are, for the greater part, monosyllables, except those of Greek or Roman extraction. Then they are crouded with consonants, and the aspirated *t* is much used, even in the end of words. Now, one cannot well conceive a harsher, or more abrupt sound than a monosyllable, such as we have many concluding with a—*th*. It is a sound that could not be endured by a Greek or Roman ear, and cannot be pronounced by a Frenchman or Italian. The most of our words conclude with mute consonants, such as *b*, *d*, *g*, sometimes a little softened by the addition of an *e* at the end; this must make the sound of the language exceeding harsh and rough, compared with the Greek, or even with the Latin, the voice being so often interrupted by so many stops betwixt words, and the mouth so often shut by those final mute consonants, and by the * termination with *m*. This fault of the language, is not at all mended by the mo-

* See what Milton says upon this subject, pag. 104. of this volume.

dern use, but, on the contrary, is aggravated; for we sometimes shorten our words, by throwing out a syllable in the middle, thus of the trisyllable *Every*, we make a disyllable *Ev'ry*, and the only tense we form by flexion, *viz.* the perfect active, we commonly curtail of its last syllable—Thus of *Loved*, as our forefathers pronounced, we make a monosyllable *Lov'd*; and of *Builded*, as the word is used in our Bible, we make *Built*.

Further, the English language is altogether unmusical, unless we are pleased to call a drum a musical instrument—For it has no melody, that is tones, differing in acuteness and gravity upon different syllables, nor has it rhythm; for though it have some long syllables, they bear no proportion in number to the short, nor is the ratio betwixt them and the short fixed, without which there can be no rhythm; all therefore we have for both the melody and rhythm of the Greeks and Latins, is, that we found one syllable of a word louder than the rest, and so make a mixture of loud and soft sounds, such as we observe in a drum.

But tho' we have no fixed or regulated tones upon our syllables of words, we are not for that to imagine that we pronounce them all with the same tone. Even in a drum, there is some variety of tones, according as the stroke is given nearer to, or farther from the centre. And as to speaking, a man must have a very nice ear, and much practice, to be able to speak a single sentence to an end in a perfect monotony. This, indeed, deaf persons who have been taught to speak, do without any art, and necessarily; for not speaking by the ear, as we do, but mechanically, it is impossible that they can have any idea or practice of variety of tones.

And here we may observe, with what wonderful art the pronunciation of the Greek language has been formed; for the Greeks contrived to reduce to rule that infinite variety of tones with which modern languages are pronounced, and at the same time that they have prescribed rules for their accents, they have given them all the variety that is possible; for every syllable in a Greek word is founded either with an acute accent, a grave, or with both; and besides these nothing, to use a phrase of Aristotle*.—Such being the art of the Greek language, I do not much wonder that it is not comprehensible by those who are but ordinary scholars, and so unlearned in the history and philosophy of man, as to judge of ancient men and arts by what they see in modern times.— But to return to our accents.

Such as they are, they give, I think, a beauty and variety to our pronunciation, which our neighbours the French have not in their language; for they have neither accent nor rhythm: And we are thereby enabled to make much better verse than the French, and of greater beauty and variety, than is to be found in any other modern language, that I know, or have heard of, the Italian only excepted.—Of this versification I have given a system in

* Και παρα ταυτα ουδιν.

the second volume of this work, which the reader, if he think it worth his while, may consult; and if he can devise a better, I shall think myself obliged to him if he would communicate it to me or the public.——But as, by our modern pronunciation, we aggravate the defect of length in our words, so, by a faulty pronu......., which is increasing every day, we are taking from the beauty of our accents, by drawing them too far back, even to the third syllable, and so obscuring the pronunciation of the two final syllables.—Thus a great many pronounce *Révenue*, in place of *Revénue*, where it is evident, that the two last syllables of the word are obscured by the first syllable being accented.—Again, people now generally say, *Ádvertisement* in place of *Advertísement*, as they formerly pronounced; by which two long syllables are sunk in the pronunciation.—Again, almost every body now says, *cómmendable* in place of *comméndable*, by which I think, the rhythm of a very fine period in Milton is spoiled *.

* In Vol. iii. p. 51. the reader will find this period quoted.

—Nay, we endeavour to draw back the accent, even beyond the third syllable; thus we say, *Interested.*—But this being impossible by the nature of things, we are obliged to lay some stress upon the last syllable, *ted.*

But suppose our accents more varied and oftener laid upon the penult, or last syllable, we must not imagine that they could ever be made so agreeable to the ear as the long and short syllables of the antients, not to mention their prosody*, that is, the musical tones of their syllables.—For the variety of long and short in a certain ratio to one another, is true rhythm, and much more pleasant to a musical ear, than any other composition of sounds, where there is no difference but of *loud* and *soft*, the ratio of which to one another cannot be appretiated; and accordingly, in music, tho' there be that difference likewise, the length and shortness of the notes compared toge-

* See what I have said of the abuse of this word by our modern grammarians,—Vol. ii. p. 269.—271.

ther is the chief beauty, without which there is no music of any value; and accordingly, in our notation of music, it is as carefully marked as the tones, and is so essential to music, that we cannot conceive music without it.—And hence the common saying among the antients, ' That rhythm was every thing in music*'—And I am persuaded, that it was chiefly by the rhythm that the antient music produced such wonderful effects ascribed to it; for the rhythm of a tune is the motion of it.—Now, it is well known, how much motion perceived either by the eye or ear affects the human mind; and indeed the motions of the body, or of the features of the face, are the index of all our sentiments and passions.

Before I quit this subject of English accent, I must observe, that the poverty of our language is so great, that we often employ the same word to express both a verb, and a substantive or adjective. Now, ac-

---

* Παν παρα της μετρικης ο ρυθμος.

cording to the common use of the language in my younger days, the verb was distinguished from the noun by the accent being put upon the last syllable of the verb, and the first syllable of the noun. But at present this is neglected. Thus, for example, they said formerly, *a súbject*, and *to be súbject*, but they always said *to subjéct*. Now, many people say, *to súbject*; nay I have heard *súbjected* said, though with the greatest violation to the quantity; by which, a syllable naturally long by position, is almost quite obscured in the pronunciation.

I come now to speak of the words in English as significant, and there it will be found still more inferior to the learned languages, by how much the sense is superior to the sound.—I will begin with the verb, the principal part of speech, expressing the actions and energies of things, by which only we know their nature.—The great artifice of the learned languages is, to express several things necessarily belonging to the verb, by changes made upon the word, without creating new words. One

neceſſary concomitant of all action is time.
Now we have ſeen how ingeniouſly the
learned languages, and particularly the
Greek, expreſſes that by the flexion of the
word; in place of which, the Engliſh mark
only one tenſe by the flexion or termination
of the word, (for the *preſent* I do not reckon a *tenſe*, any more than the *nominative* a
caſe*), viz. the indefinite preterite, *I loved*,
a defect very clumſily ſupplied by what is
called auxiliary verbs.—The next thing to
be conſidered is number, a thing alſo eſſential to the action of th͡ ͡rb; for the
actors muſt be one or ⁒ ⁖y —Now, this
is not at all expreſſed in Engliſh by any
change upon the verb, except in the 3d
perſon of the preſent of the indicative; for
they ſay *I love*, *they love*, *I lov'd*, *they*

---

* See what I have ſaid upon the ſubject of *Caſes*,
Vol. ii. p. 93. And as to *Tenſes*, Ariſtotle calls them
the πτωσις ῥηματος, as he does the caſes the πτωσις
ονοματος. Ariſtotle's *poetics*, cap. 20. So that it appears he did not reckon the *preſent*, from which all
the tenſes are derived, a *Tenſe*, any more than the *nominative* a *caſe*.

lov'd; but in the 3d perſon of the preſent, they diſtinguiſh the numbers; for they ſay *he loves*, but *they love*.

The next thing is to expreſs Perſons, whether it be the firſt, ſecond, or third, that acts. Now, here there is ſomething pretty extraordinary in the Engliſh verb; for in the ſingular number of the preſent, each of the three perſons is marked by different terminations of the word: Thus we ſay, *I love, thou loveſt, he loveth*, or *loves*, as we are now pleaſed to contract it into one ſyllable, not having, as it would ſeem, monoſyllables enough in our language. And in the ſingular number of the preterite tenſe we mark one perſon by a change of the termination: Thus we ſay, *thou lovedſt*; but we ſay, *I loved*, and *he loved*. But, in the plural number in both tenſes, we mark all the perſons by the ſame termination. For we ſay, *we love, ye love*, and *they love*; *we loved, ye loved*, and *they loved*. This defect is ſupplied by a conſtant repetition of the pronoun.

As to Moods, we had once in English a subjunctive mood, marked by the termination; but this termination was no other than the termination of the first person of the present of the indicative, without any variation of the other persons. Thus Milton says, *if I love, if thou love, if he love.* But this mood is, since his time, almost quite out of fashion; tho' we have so little variation in our verbs, that I think not the least should be lost. The defect here is also supplied by auxiliary verbs.

As to Participles, we have but two, marked by the termination, the present active, and the past passive. The present ends in *ing,* as *loving*; but, with respect to the past, such is the tedious similarity of our terminations, that it has no other termination but that of the preterite active tense.

We have, however, with the assistance of our auxiliary verb *have,* one participle which the Latins have not,—an active past participle,—such as *having loved,* the want of which, as I have observed *, the Latins

* Page 84.

supply by the disjointed gapeing composition of an ablative absolute *.

* I have often wondered how it comes, that the
translators of our Bible avail themselves so little of this
advantage, which the language affords them, particularly in the translation of the New Testament, where
I cannot find one instance of that participle being used;
—for instead of saying, *Having done this, he went away*,
they use a circumlocution and say, *when he had done
this, he went away*, or *he did this, and went away*. And
sometimes without any circumlocution, they use the
present participle active, in place of the *past*, as in the
10th verse of the xviith chapter of the *Acts of the A-
postles*, they translate the past participle, παραγινομενοι
by the present English participle *coming*, instead of *having come*.

It may be here observed, that, as the Latins supply
the want of a present participle passive, by using the
past participle passive, as I have noticed p. 85. so they
supply the want of a past participle active by the use
of the present participle active. Thus Virgil says,

Ipse, nemus *linquens* patrium, saltusque Licaei,
" Pan ovium custos, tua si tibi Maenala curae,
" Adûs O Tegeae favens———"
        Georg. lib. i. v. 16.

where *linquens* is plainly λιπων in Greek. In the same
way in prose, Suetonius says, " Cicerone in judicio quo-

As to Voices, the poverty of the language is still greater than in any instance I have mentioned. For besides the want of a middle voice, a defect which is common to us with the Latin, there is not one tense, number, person, mood, or participle in the passive voice, formed by any flexion of the word, but all by auxiliary verbs prefixed to the preterite active, which serves the several purposes of marking that tense, all the passive tenses, and also the participle active past, and the participle passive past.

But even with the assistance of these auxiliaries, there are some tenses in this voice that cannot be expressed but by a very aukward circumlocution. Thus *edificatur*, we can express no otherwise but

---

" dam *deplorante* temporum statum, P. Clodium inimicum
" ejus frustra jam pridem a patribus ad plebem transire
" nitentem, eodem die horaque transduxit Caesar,"—.
Vitae C. Jul. Caesaris, cap. 20. where Casaubon very well observes, that *deplorante* is *cum deplorasset*, or in Greek, not ολοφυρομενον, but ολοφυραμενον, that is, *having deplored*.——See the whole note of Casaubon, which is very well worth the reading.

by saying, *it is in building*, or, as we commonly express it, but without any regard to propriety, *a-building*. Again, *edificabatur* we can express no other way but by *was in building*, or *a-building*. And we are deficient, as well as the Latins are, in a present participle passive; for we cannot express the Greek participle, οικοδομουμενος, otherwise than by the clumsy circumlocution of *being in building*.—And so much for the verb in English.

To the Noun belong genders, numbers, and cases, all marked by flexion in the learned languages. But, in English there are no genders, either of substantives or adjectives, no numbers of adjectives, but only of substantives, marked sometimes by a change of the word, as *man*, *men*, but much more commonly by the addition of *s* to the termination of the singular. But of no nouns, either in the singular or plural number, are there cases; so that the noun in English may be reckoned an indeclinable word, except as to the pronouns, *I*, *thou*, and *he*, which admit greater changes than any other words in English; for they are remarkably changed both as to cafe and number.

As to the Article *the*, it admits of no change, tho' I believe the Englifh language is the only one that has an indeclinable article.

And thus much for the Flexion of the Englifh language. As to the other two great artifices of language, Compofition and Derivation, it is equally defective. With regard to compofition, our harfh monofyllables do not fo eafily run together, and coalefce into one word as the Greek or even the Latin words; and therefore the genius of the language admits but very little compofition, except in words of Greek or Latin origin; and there is one compofition which I have fhown * has fo fine an effect in Greek, I mean compofition with prepofitions, one or more, which is almoft totally wanting in Englifh.

As to Derivation or Etymology.—The Englifh language not being an original

* Page 53.

language like the Greek, but a derived language, and even the third in defcent from the Gothic, and both the Gothic and its immediate parent the Saxon being unknown to us, we hardly know the etymology of any word purely Englifh.

CHAP. XIV.

Of English composition of words in sentences.—The defect of it compared with the Greek and Latin composition.—The want of variety of arrangement in it.—Examples of this from Horace's ode to Pyrrha, translated by Milton.—Milton, in his prose stile as well as verse, has all the variety of arrangement that the language will admit.—The present arrangement, like the French, in what is called the natural order.—Our composition cannot be sufficiently diversified, otherwise than by composition in periods.—Milton's Latin stile composed of very fine periods.—In his English prose, the language does not permit him to vary his stile so much; very different, however, from the fashionable stile at present.—An account of that stile.—It is of two different kinds.

THUS much of single words in English, considered both with regard to their sound and their sense.—I am now to consider the composition of them in sentences. In which, how defective a language must be, that wants genders, numbers, and cases, every scholar must know that understands Greek and Latin, and at the same time knows the science of language, which I doubt is not the case of every man who thinks himself a Greek and Latin scholar. Besides the tiresome repetition of those monosyllables, by which we form our cases, and of our auxiliary verbs, by which we form our tenses, such as, *have, shall, will,* and *can*—*had, should, would,* and *could,* occurring so frequently, the want of numbers, genders, and cases formed by flexion, forbids almost all variety of arrangement, the great beauty, as we have seen, of the antient composition, and obliges us to connect our words in syntax by juxta-position only. To be convinced how contemptible a composition this is, compared with the Greek and

Latin, let him read Horace's ode to Pyrrha, and then Milton's translation of it, as near as possible, not only to the words, but to the arrangement of them, nearer indeed, than the stinted genius of our language will admit; and then he will clearly see how much more beautiful and elegant, as well as shorter, the Latin arrangement is. It is so various, that, in the first stanza, hardly two words that are construed together stand together *.

* The first stanza runs thus.

    Quis multa gracilis te puer in rosa
    Perfusus liquidis urget odoribus
    Grato, Pyrrha, sub antro?

where we may observe, that the only words construed together and placed together, are the prepositions *in* and *sub*; which, being indeclinable words, cannot be otherwise connected with the words they govern, except by juxta-position. The translation, Milton has given us of this ode, was, I am persuaded, intended to show how inferior, in point of composition, the English was to the Latin; for, in the translation of the line,

    Qui nunc te fruitur credulus aureâ,

As much, however, of variety of arrangement as the language will admit, so much I think we should use. And accordingly Milton has done so in his prose, as well as verse, which gives his prose a cast and colour very different from what is fashionable at present among us; for we arrange every thing as the French do, in what we call the Natural Order*, but which is cer-

into the English,

Who now enjoys thee, credulous, all gold,

he must have understood that the word *credulous*, must apply to *thee*, as well as the words *all gold*; whereas in the Latin it is clear, from the genders and cases, that *credulus* applies to the lover, and *aurea* to the mistress. And, in the next verse of the translation,

Who always vacant, always amiable,
Hopes thee, of flattering gales unmindful,

it is evident, that according to our method of arrangement by juxta-position, *always vacant, always amiable*, and likewise the words, *of flattering gales unmindful*, must apply to the lover, and not to the mistress.

* See what I have said of this Natural Order of arrangement, as it is called, Vol. II. B. iii. Ch. 2. 3.

tainly moſt tireſomely uniform. And becauſe Milton does not follow that order, we ſay his proſe is harſh and uncouth, tho' we cannot ſay that it is obſcure, nor conſequently, that he has done any violence to the Language.

But this variety of arrangement, in a Language ſo inartificial as ours, can go but ſhort way in diverſifying the compoſition; and, therefore, as we have neither rhythm nor melody, nor that variety of flexion and termination which we find in the learned Languages, there is no other way remaining, by which we can give any diverſity to our ſtile, except by compoſition in periods conſiſting of different members of various lengths and variouſly connected together, with a different ſtructure of the words, and, what I think is neceſſary to make the period perfectly beautiful, a variety of matter in the ſeveral members. This laſt mentioned variety is particularly agreeable in ſpeaking, as it is gives occaſion to a change of the tone of the voice; which, if it be well executed, is moſt pleaſant to the ear, at the same time, that it conveys the sense better than it could be otherwise conveyed. And for the same reason, *Parenthesis* is a most beautiful figure of Composition.

In this way, Milton composes in Latin, particularly, in his *Defensio pro Populo Anglicano*, where there is a variety and beauty of Composition of the kind I have mentioned, not exceeded, hardly equalled, by any Latin author, with the variety, however, of short commatic sentences thrown in here and there; for the finest things must not be too often repeated. In English, the language not permitting, he has been more sparing in this highly varied composition, but enough of it to make his stile pass for very rough and unpleasant to those who are not classical scholars, and are accustomed to the stile now in fashion, of a colour and complexion perfectly different, where there is either that broken disjointed composition, hardly deserving the name of composition, and which is worse still in English than it is in the Latin of Sallust, Seneca, or Tacitus;—or, if it be composed in periods, it is in periods of two, or perhaps three members, of the same ſtructure of words, inartificially tacked together by the copulative; and, in ſome late authors, who affect to diſtinguiſh themſelves by the beauty of their ſtile, the period is tagged with two nouns, and each its attendant epithet. Such compoſition, I think, is worſe than no compoſition; and therefore I prefer the ſtile of the authors I have mentioned, and their modern imitators in French or Engliſh, who cut their ſtile into ſhreds and patches, to thoſe who compoſe in ſo bad a taſte.———I will only add, that, however rough and unpleaſant Milton's ſtile may appear to the faſhionable reader, I would netherthelefs adviſe him to ſtudy his Polemical writings, both Political and Theological, if not for the ſtile, at leaſt for the matter; for he will find there a variety of argument, with which his moſt extenſive learning, antient and modern, ſacred and prophane, furniſhed him, ſuch as, I think, is not to be found in any other modern author.

CHAP. XV.

The French Language inferior to the English in Sound, having neither accent nor quantity.—It is a fault in speaking French to mark any accent.—They have no perceptible difference in the quantity of their syllables.—This makes their verfification very imperfect, compared with the English.—Their long verse particularly, most tiresomely uniform.—The French words not so much crowded with Consonants as the English, but wanting aspirates too much.—The Grammar of the French Language more complete than of ours, having much more flexion,—but 'of this they do not avail themselves in their composition at present; but did so formerly, particularly in their Verse.

I Come now to speak of the French Language, which I think, in point of sound, is much inferior to the English; for it has neither Accent (I mean what we call Accent) nor Quantity. As to accent, it is a rule among the French, that *good speaking must be without accent* [*]; and they do not distinguish a British man, who has not learned to speak the French well, by any thing sooner, than by his accenting one syllable of a word more than another. And this property of their language, I am persuaded, they have derived from their mother language, the Latin; in which there was not any more than in the Greek, as I have already observed [†], and shall further observe, any such thing as what we call Accent. As to quantity, the English have certainly some syllables in their language longer than others, but not in such proportion to the

* *Pour parler bien, il faut parler sans accent.*

† P. 40. of this Volume.

short in point of number, nor with the ratio in point of quantity so fixed that we can make verse of them, tho' I think they give a variety and beauty to the pronunciation both of our prose and verse. But as to the French, I can hardly perceive that they have one syllable longer than another; which has made a Frenchman say, as I have observed elsewhere[*], judging of all the modern Languages by his own, that there is no quantity in any modern language.—Now, the consequence of their wanting both accent and quantity, is, that they can only make verse by the rhyme and the number of syllables; whereas in English there is great variety of verse, greater I believe, than in any modern language, the Italian only excepted.— The French long verse particularly, consisting all of the same number of syllables, with the Caesura always in the middle, and every two of them tagg'd with a rhyme, is to my ear most tiresomely uniform, tho' they attempt to give it some variety, by what they call male and female rhymes.

[*] Vol. ii. of this work, p. 322.

And the only verse they have, which pleases my ear, is their shorter verse, where the rhymes are alternate, and the number of syllables varied in the verses.

All the advantage, therefore, they can claim over the English in point of sound, is that their words are not so much crowded with consonants as ours are, and they have more variety of terminations, arising from a cause, which I am just to mention. And they have no termination so harsh and uncouth, and which indeed only custom could make us endure, as the termination by an aspirated *t*. This aspiration they want altogether, having it neither in the beginning, middle nor end of their words; but which, besides the want of variety, makes the sound of their language not so strong and masculine as that of ours.

As to their words considered as significant, that is, the grammar of their language, they are certainly superior to the English; for they have genders and numbers both for their nouns and adjectives, and they have more tenses formed by flexion than

Ch. XV. Progress of Language. 139

we have, for befides the prefent and indefinite perfect, they have in the active voice the imperfect and the future formed in that way; and even their moods are diftinguifhed from one another by flexion; for the indicative, imperative, and fubjunctive, have different terminations; and in the fubjunctive there are two tenfes in that way diftinguifhed, the imperfect and the indefinite perfect.

From this advantage over us, one fhould think their compofition would be more various than ours, and confequently better. And fo it certainly fhould be; but the fact is, that the modern French compofition is worfe than even the worft of ours; and there is a famenefs in it, that I really think intolerable; for it is all either cut into fhort unconnected fentences, as Montefquieu writes; or, if the fenfe be carried on thro' feveral lines without any full ftop, the members of the fentence confift of a few words of the fame form and ftructure; and, if they be at all connected, it is only by the copulative *and*: Nor is the meaning fufpended till the end of the sentence, when it is brought out altogether compacted, and as it were embodied; which I hold to be essential to what is called a period.—In short, there is not in the modern French writing, that roundness and circumscription, which is the very definition of a period *. As to Parenthesis, by which, as I have observed elsewhere †, the stile is most beautifully variegated, I have read whole French books, in which there is not one Parenthesis from beginning to end.

* See this definition of a period, from Cicero, Vol. iii. of this work p. 57.——See also the following pages, 58. 59. 60. and 61. where the reader will find examples of periods composed as they ought to be.—See also what I have said of the variety of composition in the learned languages, and how far it is capable of being imitated in English, Vol. ii. p. 354. and following.

† See Vol. iii. p. 72. and following; where I have justified the use of parentheses, by the example of the best authors, and have shown, that a proper parenthesis not only gives an opportunity, to the speaker, to vary his tone agreeably, but excites the attention of the hearer, and conveys the sense more forcibly than it could be otherwise conveyed.

However tediously uniform, or *fade*, to use a word of their own, the French compofition muft appear to a fcholar and a man of tafte, I am forry to obferve, that a great part of our late compofitions in Englifh, are of the fame colour and caft; and, particularly with refpect to Parenthefes, I heard it obferved one day, by an Englifh Gentleman, that there was not in all Mr Gibbon's Roman Hiftory one parenthefis. This muft neceffarily be the cafe, if we forfake the antient ftandards of fine writing, and imitate either modern French writers, or antient writers, but of an age, when the tafte of good writing was corrupted.

In the old French writers, there is a much greater variety of compofition, and I obferve, that they avail themfelves of the advantage, which a more perfect analogy than ours gives them in point of compofition, particularly in their verfe; and therefore I prefer the old French Poetry, written in what they call the *Stile de Marot*, to the modern French poetry, except what has been written in imitation of that ſtile, ſuch as the Tales and Fables of Fontaine, which I think are the beſt Poetry in French [*].

The account I have here given of the French language, is I think favourable enough, as I prefer it in ſeveral reſpects to our own. But, if we believe ſome of their own writers, particularly the Abbé Auger, who has publiſhed tranſlations of Demoſthenes and Eſchines, in 5 vols octavo, with preliminary diſſertations, and particularly one upon the Greek, Latin, and French languages, the French language has every beauty that a language can have; and if *words*, *words*, as Shakeſpear ſays, could per-

---

[*] There is a fine eulogium upon Fontaine, by Voltaire, in his *Temple de Gout*, in the following words.

Toi, favori de la Nature,
Toi, la Fontaine auteur aimable
Qui, bravant et rime et meſure,
Si negligé dans ta parure,
N'en etoit que plus charmant.

Ch. XV. Progress of Language. 143

fuade us, he certainly would perfuade us. I have given the encomium below in his own words *.

* The properties he defcribes to it are, ' Clartè, ' nettetè, vivacitè, dans les tours, force, dèlicateffe, ' fimplicitè, nobleffe, douceur, precifion, harmonie, ' et mème harmonie imitative, elle mêt à tout avec ' affez de facilité dans la compofition, et jufques dans ' la traduction, quoi qu'avec plus de peine et de plus ' longs efforts.'—Vol. iii. p. 130.

Thus the French Abbe has inftructed us in the beauties of his language, not in the old way, by dividing, defining, and analyfing, (which, to be fure, he would think much below a man of his genius), but by multiplying words, very fine ones no doubt, as he thinks, but without any precife or determinate meaning. In the fame way, he examines the merit of Demofthenes, Æfchines, and Cicero, as orators.

CHAP. XVI.

Of the Italian Language.—The words of it long and full.—Of Vowels.—Few of their words terminated by Consonants.—Their pronunciation therefore more flowing than either that of English or French. —They have accents such as the English. —Make therefore Poetry of blank verse. —Have long and short syllables, but no diphthongs, except one.—Their accents not so violent as those in English,—do not obscure the pronunciation of the other syllables.—It is a language better for music than any other now known.—The words not lost in their music.—It is more reconcilable to the rhythm of the language, than the music even of the Greek Tragedy. —The grammar of their language more compleat than that of the English, particularly in their verbs ; but no declension of nouns.—This appears to be the

Ch. XVI. Progress of Language.

most artificial part of language,—one part of speech, it has more than the Latin, viz. the Article,—has greater variety in its accents, and therefore in its poetry than the English.—Some observations upon language in general, arising from the Italian language.—The tone of different languages distinct from the pronunciation of the letters or words.—Very difficult to be acquired by a foreigner.

THE last modern language I shall mention is the Italian, a dialect of Latin, as well as the French and Spanish, but, like them, much corrupted by a mixture of barbarous words more than the modern Greek, and by the loss of the grammatical art. The sound of it is extremely vocal, much more than either Greek or Latin, and more than either of its two sister languages, the French or Spanish. The words of it are long, and, being so vocal, sound very sweetly, indeed I think too sweetly: For there is no aspiration in the language, not even of vowels; and none of the words terminate in confonants, as I am informed, except their article in its different cafes, (for their article is not like the Englifh, indeclinable: The cafes are, *il, del, al, dal.*) and except three prepofitions, *in, con, per.* They have therefore this great advantage over the Latin in point of found, that not one of their words terminate with a mute confonant, or with the liquid M, which, as I have obferved, fhuts the mouth as much or more than any of the mutes; nay, they do not terminate any of the words which are of the growth of their language, and not foreign words, with the hiffing letter S. Sometimes indeed, when the vowel E ends the word, they elide it; and this not only in their verfe, but in their profe. But they never do it, unlefs the preceding letter be fome one of the liquids, not M however; with which, as I have faid, they never clofe a word. Now, I think, this makes an agreeable variety in their ftile, being not unlike many of the elifions ufed in Greek. They have very few monofyllables, much fewer than the French, and very much fewer than the Englifh, which is crouded, as I have ob-

Ch. XVI. Progress of Language. 147

ferved, with monofyllables; a thing that muft neceffarily produce a ftop more or lefs in the pronunciation, betwixt the different words. Neither the French language, therefore, nor the Englifh, can have that flow in fpeaking which the Italian has, nor be pronounced in the way that Milton mentions*, or, as Horace fays, the Greek language was pronounced, *ore rotundo*.

But, however fweet or flowing the found of their language may be, they have loft what I call the mufic of language; I mean the antient accents, which the Latins, no doubt, had, as well as the Greeks, tho', perhaps, not fo perfect. And they have adopted, from the northern nations which fettled among them, and whofe race, I am perfuaded, makes at prefent the greateft part of the inhabitants of Italy, fuch accents as we ufe; for that thefe accents were not ufed by the Greeks and Romans, I think is certain; not only from the filence

---

* See the paffage from Milton, quoted on p. 104. of this Volume.

of all their grammarians, but from this
confideration, that if befides their tones
and their quantity, they had had fuch accents as we have, the pronunciation of their
language would have been too complex
and embarraffed, having both their own
accents and ours, and together with thefe,
their rhythm or quantity *. And befides, I am perfuaded, they would have
very much hurt the mufic of their language by fuch an addition. If there could
be any doubt in this matter, it is, I think,
entirely removed by the want of fuch accents in the French language: For the
Franks, tho' they loft the mufical accents
of the Latins, not being a mufical nation,
I think it is impoffible to believe, that if
the Romans had fpoke with fuch accents
as ours, they would have loft thefe accents
too, while they retained the words. By their
accents, however, fuch as they are, the Italians make their poetry as we do, and not
only rhyming poetry, but blank verfe. And

---

* See further upon this fubject, p. 32.—p. 39. and
42.

it is in this way that our poetry and the Italian have so great an advantage over the French, which can vary its verse no otherwise, than by the number of syllables making it either shorter or longer, or by the rhyme. By these accents, the Italians have as great variety of verse as we have, and I think greater; for they have not only Iambic, Trochaic, and Anapestic feet, as we have *, but also Spondees and Dactyles. I have only further to observe of their accents, that they are much less violent than the English accents, and therefore, when they are drawn back to the antepenult, which they sometimes are in Italian, tho' not so frequently as in English, they do not obscure the pronunciation of the other two syllables; which, as I have observed, is always the case more or less in English †. And for this and the other reasons above mentioned the Italian language

* See upon the subject of English Verse, Vol. II. Book iii. Cap. 8.

† P. 116. and 119.

is very much fitter for mufic than the English, or any other language in Europe, being so adapted to the mufic, that the words not only in their *recitative*, but in their *airs*, are diftinctly heard: So that in their operas, if we underftand the language, we enjoy the pleafure both of mufic and poetry. And according to my information, if the opera be well compofed, the mufic is fo fuited to the words, that there is no violence done either to the accent or quantity; for there never is a long note laid upon a fhort or unaccented fyllable. And in this refpect the mufic of the Italian opera appears to be more perfect than the mufic of the Greek tragedy, at leaft in later times; for there, as the Halicarnaffian has obferved, they often did violence to both the melody and rhythm of the language *.

With refpect to quantity, the Italians have fome long fyllables, as well as we, tho' not fo many of them, or fo commen-

---

* Περι Συνθεσεως, cap. 11.

Ch. XVI. PROGRESS OF LANGUAGE. 151

furate to the fhort as to make poetry of them. But there is one kind of long fyllables, and the higheſt founding of them all, which they want almoſt entirely; I mean the diphthongs: For they uſe only one double found, which they mark by the letters I U, and found them like the diphthong EU; as in the word *fiume* for *flumen*, a river, and *fiamma* for *flamma*, a flame.

As to the grammar of the language, they have all the tenſes, with the variety of three perſons and of two numbers, formed by flexion, except the praeter-perfect tenſe, which they form, as we and the French do, by auxiliary verbs. They have a diſtinction too of moods, as well as the French, which they obſerve very accurately: But as to the declenſion of nouns, their language is as imperfect as ours or the French, and I believe I may add every other modern language of Europe; for their cafes are all formed by prepoſitions or particles. And this perſuades me, that the declenſion of nouns is one of the greateſt artifices in language, which has come lateſt in the progreſs of language towards perfection, and has been first lost in the corruption of it. But the Italian has one great advantage over its mother language; for it has one part of speech more, I mean the Article, which I have no doubt that the Italians have borrowed from the barbarous languages, as well as their accents; for all the barbarous languages of Europe, such as the Celtic, the Gothic and all its different dialects, have an Article as well as the Greek.

I have dwelt thus long upon the Italian language, becaufe, I think, it furnishes some observations of importance in the history of language: And, in the first place, it appears surprising that the Italian, tho' a language much less excellent upon the whole than the Latin, should have the use of that part of speech just now mentioned, which the Latin entirely wants; I mean the article. This, I have no doubt, they got from the Lombards, or other barbarians that settled in their country: For the Greek, at the time the Italian language took the form it now has, was entirely lost in Italy; and, besides, the Italian Article has not the least resemblance to the Greek. Now, the question is, how those barbarous languages should have got this important part of speech, when the Latins had it not? That those barbarians invented it, I cannot believe; for it does not appear to me, that they were capable of inventing so wonderful an art as language, or even of making such an addition to it, which we see the Latins could not make. My conjecture therefore is that those barbarous languages came later off the Greek (or rather off some common parent language) after it was completely formed, and had got all the parts of speech, and, among others, the Article. But, tho' I think it is evident that the Italians did not take their Article from the Greeks, it is remarkable that they use it as the Greeks do, prefixing it not only to appellative, but to proper nouns; and with the very same signification, denoting either a person eminent and well known, or a person that had been mentioned before *.

* See what I have said of this use of the article, p.

Another observation is, that the Italian is of much softer and more pleasant articulation, than its parent the Latin, tho' in other respects so much inferior. This appears the more extraordinary, that the barbarous languages with which it is mixed, and from which, as I have observed, it has got its accents, must be presumed to have been of much harsher and rougher pronunciation than even the Latin. This I think can be accounted for no otherwise than from the natural genius of the Italians for music, and their having cultivated it much more than any other nation in Europe. Their Opera music, I am persuaded, is derived from the theatrical music of the antient Greeks and Romans: And their *Recitative*, I believe, is no other than the manner in which the passionate parts of their tragedies or comedies, called in Latin *cantica*, and in Greek μελωδιαι, were spoken: And the *Airs* in their O-

---

55. and following, of Vol. ii. of this work. See also of the same Volume, Book i. Chap. 7. where I speak of the use of the article in French and in English.

pera, are imitations of the songs of the antient chorus. What makes this extremely probable is, that the opera first appeared in splendour in Venice, whither the people flocked in great numbers, to take shelter in its seas and morasses, when the rest of Italy was over-run by barbarians, and carried with them what remained of the antient arts. To confirm this conjecture, we find another thing, and a very remarkable thing, belonging to the antient theatre, which was preserved in Venice, and from thence was, like the opera, carried to other towns of Italy; I mean the use of masks by the actors in comedy*. About the time that the antient theatrical music was revived in Italy, I suppose that the Italian language was formed, such as we have it at present, and if so, it is no wonder that it is so soft in the pronunciation, and as much adapted to music, as I believe any language ever was.

* See what is said upon this subject, by Dr Brown, in his Dissertation upon poetry and music, p. 200. and following.

After having said so much of the Italian language, I think it is proper to let the reader know, that I do not myself understand it; but that I take the account, I have given of it, from one who resided above ten years in Italy, and who, besides understanding the language perfectly, is more learned in the Italian arts of painting, sculpture, music, and poetry, than any man I ever conversed with. His natural good taste he has improved by the study of the monuments of antient art to be seen in Rome and Florence: And as beauty in all the arts is pretty much the same, consisting of grandeur and simplicity, variety, decorum, and a suitableness to the subject, I think he is a good judge of language and of writing, as well as of painting and sculpture. How much Milton improved his genius by his travels in Italy, and by his study of the Italian arts, is well known: And Mr Thomson the poet, did not, in my opinion, write well, till he went to Italy, and studied there the monuments of antient art, and from them formed that taste of noble simplicity, which is the perfection of all art. After this, he wrote his *Castle of Indolence*, the most perfect by far, in my judgment, of all his works, and the best allegorical and descriptive poem, I believe, in any language. The name of the artist I am speaking of is *Brown*. He was bred a painter, but does not now lay on colours, judging that a mean part of the art compared with *drawing*, which undoubtedly is the most essential part of it, being that without which the colouring would signify nothing: And as he has formed his taste in the art, by drawing the antient statues, and *Bas Reliefs*, he tells me, what I am persuaded is true, that nothing but the colours of Titian could add any beauty to good drawings of those wonderful works of art. He therefore only draws, but better than any body I have ever known, as far as my judgment goes: And I know from gentlemen, who were at Rome while he was in it, that he was there reputed one of the best drawers in Italy. He practises at present in Edinburgh, with the approbation of all those who are judges of the art; but he proposes soon to go to London, where I hope he shall be received and encouraged as he deserves.

Before I conclude this comparison of languages, it is proper to observe, that, besides the sound of the words, and their different flexions and terminations, there is a particular tone belonging to each language, and which is different from the articulation, the accent, or the rhythm of the language. By this tone, a man of a good ear will distinguish a Frenchman from an Englishman, an Italian from either, and even an Englishman from a Scotchman, if he only hear the voice, tho' he do not understand a word of what they say.—This national tone, is the thing the most difficult to be acquired by any foreigner.

CHAP. XVII.

From the comparison of languages in the preceeding chapters, it is evident that the Greek and Latin are much superior to the modern.—These are barbarous in the proper sense of the word.—The author, in this inquiry, has followed the antient method of investigating things.—The advantage to be got from the comparison of different languages.—Impossible that a man, who understands only one language, can know either its excellencies or defects. —Not having the same materials as the antients, it is impossible we can compose so well.—All we can do, is to give as much variety as possible to our stile.—This is to be done chiefly by composition in periods. —Numbers in our prose, not to be affected.—This the fault of some modern English writers.—Of the degeneracy of all languages, the originals of which we know.--The degeneracy most remarkable of the Greek language.—*The degeneracy of the English language in modern times, both in sound and signification of the words.*—Example of this last.—*Reason why the author has insisted so much upon the* sound *of the languages he has compared.*—Written language not spoken, *may be called a dead language, whereas what is spoken, is a living language.*—*The degeneracy of language and other necessary arts of life, cannot be accounted for otherwise than by a degeneracy of the people.*—*The want of an ear and voice for music, makes the northern nations incapable of pronouncing as the antient Greeks did.*—*Of the great difficulty of the invention of language, both as to the* matter *and the* form.—*The* matter *of language not furnished, as that of other arts, by Nature, but by man himself.*—*Of the defect of the pronunciation even of vowels, in sundry nations.*—*The* form *of language still more difficult than the* material *part of it.*—*Wonderful inventions for expressing the infinity of things, by a limited number of words.*—*Language of so difficult invention, that it would not have been invent-*

Ch. XVII. Progress of Language.

ed by men, without supernatural assistance; but, being invented, it might be cultivated and improved without such assistance.—Even for this certain things necessary which are not to be found in this age.—The practice of language, after it is invented, different from the practice of other arts.

THUS I have compared two antient languages, and four modern, in point of beauty and excellency, and have shown, that it is not matter of taste and fancy merely, but is evident from principles of the art, which cannot be disputed, that the Greek and Latin are by many degrees superior to any modern language, at least that I know,--that, therefore, they are very justly named the *learned languages*;— and that these other are to be accounted unlearned, and even barbarous, tho' the national vanity of those, who speak such languages, will, I know, be very much shocked with that appellation. But I hold the want of art, and the defects and imperfections confequent of that, to be the very definition of what we call barbarous in language, or in any thing elfe. In order to prove this, I have gone into a detail which may appear fuperfluous to fome of my readers, if they be of thofe fublime geniufes of this age who defpife the art the antients valued fo much, by which they defined, divided, and diftinguifhed things, and who think they can at once, by the fuperiority of their parts, comprehend the thing, without the trouble of minutely diffecting and explaining it, as I have done language. But for men of my capacity, I find the antient method abfolutely neceffary; and as fome of my readers may be in the fame fituation, I have not grudged the trouble of ufing it, both for my own fake, and for the fake of thofe who will deign to be fo inftructed.

To a man of curiofity, and who has fo much of the philofophical fpirit as to defire to underftand thoroughly the nature of this wonderful art of language, the comparifon I have made of different languages, antient and modern, with one another, in order to know in what they excell or are deficient, muft be very agreeable and inftructive. And indeed it appears to me impoffible, that a man who knows but one language, the Englifh fuppofe, and fo can compare it with no other, fhould be able to know either its defects or excellencies. He could not, for example, perceive how harfh and unmufical its found is, compared with the antient languages, fo much more mufical; nor could he find out that it was loaded with fo many fuperfluous as well as ill founding words, by having an analogy fo much more imperfect than the Greek and Latin; and if he did not underftand French, he could not difcover the great advantage we have over that language by our accents, particularly in the article of verfification. In fhort, by this comparifon, we are led to know, and to know fcientifically, what is moft perfect in the moft ufeful as well as moft wonderful art among men, an object, I think, of great curiofity to a philofopher, if it were to be attended with no profit.

Another thing is evident, from what has been faid, that the antient Greeks and Romans, having fo much better materials to work upon, muſt have compofed very much better than we, not in fpeaking only, but in writing. To vie with thefe, therefore, in beauty and elegance of ſtile, is ridiculous; and all we have for it, is to labour the fenfe as much as poſſible, and to give to our compofition as much variety as the genius of our language will permit. This, as I have obferved, is to be done chiefly by compofing in periods of different lengths, confiſting of members alfo of different lengths, varioufly connected together, with a different ſtructure of the words, and a difference too in the matter, fo as to furniſh a proper occafion for a change of the tone of the voice, which is one of the greateſt beauties of fpeaking. But this kind of compofition is only proper for works of the rhetorical kind. In a plain didactic work, it would be improper to affect it; and even the hiftorical period, as I have obferved elfewhere, is different from the oratorial *. But writing in the plainest manner, and upon the most common subjects, we may avoid a dull and tiresome uniformity. But above all, whatever be the subject upon which we write, we should take care to avoid the affectation of giving numbers to our prose, which was one of the greatest beauties of antient composition, but of which our language, and I believe every other modern language, is absolutely incapable, having neither melody nor rhythm. It is this affectation, which, as I have observed elsewhere, has made the stile of Lord Shaftesbury much worse than it would have been otherwise †, but of which, after all, we may say, as an antient painter said of a work of his own, —*It is more easy to find fault with it than to imitate it* ‡. As to some later writers, who, without the beauties and elegance of

---

* Vol. iii. of this work, p. 62.

† See Vol. iii. of this work, p. 284.

‡ Μωμφεται τις μαλλον, 'η μιμησεται.

Lord Shaftesbury, have affected these numbers, their stile is to me altogether nauseous.

There is another thing which, from what is said, will occur to a reader who has comprehension of mind sufficient to take in the history, not of a single nation only, but of mankind;—that there is a wonderful degeneracy of this greatest, and most useful art among men. For not only do we see this degeneracy from the antient Greek and Latin, in the modern Greek, the Italian, and the French; but in the Gothic languages there is the same falling off. For the English is not so good a language as the Saxon, nor the Saxon, or any other dialect of the Teutonick, so compleat a language as the original Gothic. And I am persuaded the same will be found to be the case, where any language can be traced back to its original.

Of all the instances of this degeneracy, I think the modern Greek is the most remarkable; for the corruption of the other languages I have mentioned, may be accounted for, from the mixture of the nations, who fpoke them, with other nations. But the Greek nation has never been fo mixed; and the prefent Greeks are the defcendants of thofe Greeks who fpoke the fineft language in the world, and excelled mankind in every other fine art. Their degeneracy, therefore, in the article of language, can only be afcribed to ignorance and barbarity prevailing fo much among them, as to make them lofe even their language; and they fhould teach us and every other nation of Europe, that if we lofe the grammatical art, and the knowledge of what was moft perfect in that art among the antient Greeks and Romans, our language will neceffarily grow worfe, and become at laft quite barbarous.

How much our ftile is altered in point of compofition fince the days of Milton and Clarendon, and for the worfe, if the antient authors are to be our ftandards, is evident. But, in much later times, fince I was educated among Englifh gentlemen at a foreign univerfity about fifty years ago,

I perceive a great alteration in the language, both as to the pronunciation and the fenfe of the words. Of the pronunciation I have already fpoken*; and I fhall give but one example, among many that might be given, of an abufe that has crept in, with refpect to the fignification of words; and I choofe this example, the rather that it fhews we can only preferve the purity of our language by keeping to the antient ftandard. The word I mean is *ingenuity*, which is now ufed, even by the beft authors, to fignify what is clever or acute in the operations of the mind; a fenfe which has no connection with the fignification of the Latin word, *ingenuitas*, from which it is derived. In Latin, the adjectives *ingeniofus* and *ingenuus*, fignify things quite different; and the adjectives in Englifh, which we derive from them, viz. *ingenious* and *ingenuous*, have the fame difference of fignification; and alfo the adverbs, which we derive from thefe adjectives, namely, *ingenioufly* and *ingenuoufly*,

* Chap. xiii.

are also quite different in their signification. Why then should we not make the same distinction in the substantives derived from these adjectives that we make in the adverbs, and say, *ingeniousness*, from our adjective *ingenious*; and from the other adjective *ingenuous*, derive, according to rule, *ingenuity*, in Latin *ingenuitas*. And such, I am persuaded, will be found to be the use of the word by the authors of the last century. How much Milton and Doctor Middleton have adorned their stile by using English words derived from Latin in their true classical signification, I have elsewhere observed*.

In these observations upon language, many of my readers may perhaps think that I have insisted too much upon the sound of it. But such readers should consider, that language was made to be spoken; and that, for many ages of the world, no other use was made of it: And in several nations at this day, such as the Indians of North America, where they hold

* Vol. iii. of this work, p. 27.—30.

councils, harangue, and deliberate, with great gravity and wisdom upon public affairs, there is no use of letters. And even after the invention of letters, we know, that, among the Greeks and Romans, their national business was carried on chiefly by speaking: And in every free country it must be so. Now, when that is the case, the sound of language becomes a matter of importance; for the pleasure of the ear contributes not a little to persuasion; and setting aside that consideration, language spoken may be said to be *living language*, compared with *written language*, which may be called *the dead letter*, being altogether *inanimate*, and nothing more than marks or signs of language, wanting that chief beauty of elocution, which is given it by pronunciation and action. How studious the Greeks were of the sound of their language I have shown, in a dissertation written upon that subject, annexed to the second volume of this work.

From what has been said in this book, an observation will occur to the philosopher, that the history of language makes not an inconfiderable part in the hiftory of man: And there is not, perhaps, any thing belonging to a people, by which we can better judge of their genius and underftanding. Such being the cafe, I would have thofe confider, who maintain that man has been always the fame in all ages of the world, how they are to reconcile their fyftem with the univerfal degeneracy that we obferve in the languages of all nations, whofe antient language we know. Can that be accounted for otherwife, than by the people, who fpeak the language, becoming barbarous and ignorant? It may be faid, that fome of thofe people, fuch as the Greeks and Romans, have been over-run and conquered by barbarians; and fo have become barbarous like them. But what fhall we fay of the Goths and Saxons, who never were conquered themfelves, but conquered other nations? Yet the Saxon is a much worfe language than its parent the Gothic*, nor is the Englifh

---

* I had an intimate acquaintance, who was very learned in languages, and had made a particular ftudy of the Gothic, of which there is only one book extant, viz. a tranflation of the Four Gofpels, which is

near so perfect a language as the Saxon, from which it is immediately descended. And when we go to the other side of the Globe, I mean to India, we find there the same degeneracy of language. The Sanscrit, which is the most ancient language of that country, all the other dialects of the Hindoo language being derived from it, is, I believe, the language of the greatest art that ever existed: For with respect to the pronunciation, it has all the variety of tone, and of rhythm that the Greek has; and as to the gram-

---

preserved in Upsal in Sweden, together with some fragments of the Epistle to the Romans. In all the Four Gospels, he told me, he could not find one Greek or Latin word, or any word derived from either of these languages, tho' the translators must have had many things to express, for which there were not words in their language. But it would seem they made words for those things, according to the rules of derivation or composition in their own language. In short, he said, it was a language which had all its roots within itself, as well as the Greek. He further said, that it had an *article* of three genders, and he added, that it had likewise a dual number.——See what I have further said of this language, p. 552.—, 555. of Vol. I. of this work, 2d edition.

mar of it, it has all the flexions that can well be imagined, having no lefs than feven declenfions, with a fingular, dual, and plural number *. And in the other two great artifices of language, viz. compofition and derivation, it appears to exceed all the languages we have ever heard of †. Now, the other dialects fpoken in India, derived, as I have faid, from the Sanfcrit, are all corruptions of it more or lefs‡. Such being the cafe, I afk whence comes this degeneracy of the language of fo many nations? And not only of their language, but of other arts that were practifed by them, fuch as building; for the edifices they erected, are not only grander, and more magnificent, but of

* See the tranflation of the code of Gentoo's laws, by Mr Braffey Halhed, with a preface, in which he gives this account of the Sanfcrit Language.

† See what I have faid of the compofition and derivation of the Sanfcrit Language, p. 210.—492.—530. of Vol. II. and p. 56. of this Vol.

‡ See Mr Braffey Halhed's Bengalefe Grammar, and particularly p. 65.—127. and 137.

greater solidity and much more durable than our modern buildings. And there is another very useful art, which was much better practised by them than by us, I mean the writing art; for there are antient charters in Scotland, some of which I have seen, that are above five hundred years old and yet appear as fresh as if they had been written yesterday. And the oldest record, I believe, in Europe, Doomsday book, which is now seven hundred years old, is in such preservation, that a copy of it has been lately made and printed. And I have seen some *fac similes* of it, which show it to be perfectly legible by those who have studied the hand. Whereas, our later writings, that are not above a hundred or a hundred and fifty years old, are hardly legible; and what we write at present, will not be legible in much less time. Now, is it possible, that there can be such a corruption of arts among a people, and some of them the most necessary for human life, without a degeneracy of the people? for I think it cannot be disputed, that the excellency of all the works of art must depend upon the genius, the underſtanding, the application, and the induſtry of thoſe who practiſe them.

There is one bodily faculty, which is found very defective among the northern nations, and which, if we were equal to the Greeks and Romans in every other reſpect, would render us unable to pronounce their language as they did, I mean the want of an ear and voice for muſic. The northern nations do not appear at any time to have been ſo muſical a people as the antient Greeks and even Romans. But at preſent among us there are many who have no ear or voice at all for muſic, a thing which, I am told, is hardly known in Italy, and I believe far leſs among the Greeks, even degenerate as they are at preſent. Now ſuch men, tho' they might articulate the antient Greek, could not give it the proper tones and rhythms which made that language truly muſical, and diſtinguiſhes it from all the modern languages of Europe. It is a thing ſo remote from our practice of ſpeaking, that we can hardly, as I have obſerved, form an idea of it. And tho' we have muſic with words in our ſongs, it is a muſic of a very different kind from the muſic of ſpeech among the Greeks, as I have elſewhere ſhown *. What ſhould make us aſhamed of our incapacity in this reſpect is, that there is a brute animal among us, who comes nearer to the Greek pronunciation than any thing I know; I mean the Cuckow, who articulates his name moſt diſtinctly, and, at the ſame time, pronounces it to muſic, raiſing the tone of the firſt ſyllable, not ſo high as the acute accent among the Greeks, that is a *fifth*, but only a *third*, above the laſt.

The laſt obſervation, with which I ſhall conclude this book, is alſo of the philoſophical kind, ariſing naturally from the obſervations I have made upon the ſeveral languages that I have examined and compared, and it is this, that, of all the arts which have been invented by men, language is not only the moſt uſeful, being that, without which civil ſociety never could have been

---

* P. 37. and 38.

established, but the art of most difficult invention, (if it be the invention of man,) and, after it is invented, of most difficult practice. To be convinced of this, let us consider, first, the materials of which language is composed. These are articulate sounds, which we cannot form by instinct or our natural powers, as some of the brutes do, such as the Cuckow above mentioned, and another bird they call the *Kockatoo*; so called likewise from this articulate sound which he utters, but we must learn it from teaching, as we see deaf men learn it, or from imitation. Nature, therefore, has not furnished us the materials of this art, as she has done of other arts; but we must furnish, from our own stock, both the *matter* and the *form* of language. How difficult this is, appears from the example of deaf men just now mentioned, who are taught to articulate with labour and pains hardly to be credited, except by those who have seen it; and from the example of nations far advanced in other arts of life, but who are very defective in articulation, not to speak of the

grammatical part, which, as articulation is
so familiar to us, we are apt to consider
as the only art of language. The Chinese,
who are by many thought to be a most
ingenious people and do certainly practice some arts very well, have not yet learned to pronounce even all the vowels, which
are by far of easier pronunciation than the
consonants, requiring nothing more than
a certain form and configuration of the
organs of the mouth. Yet the Chinese
cannot pronounce even the first of them,
at least not as we do; and another of them,
viz. the *O* they cannot pronounce at all.
Nor can the Siamese pronounce the *U* *.
And what is more wonderful still, the
English, far avdanced as they are in arts
and civility, cannot pronounce, any more
than the Siamese, this vowel *U*, but make
a diphthong of it, and pronounce it *IU*;
not distinguishing, as the French do, these
two sounds, the one simple, and the other

* These facts I take from Bullet's Memoirs of the
Celtic Language, Vol. i. Chap. 4. who, I suppose, must
mean, that those nations do not pronounce the letters
he mentions as his countrymen the French do.

compounded †. As to the confonants, there is more difficulty in the pronunciation of them; for it requires not only a certain configuration of the mouth, but each of them a different action of the organs of the mouth, and which is taught to the deaf men with much more difficulty than the fimple configuration of thofe organs, as I have been informed by Mr Braidwood, the famous teacher of the dumb to fpeak, who now practifes his art in London, but formerly in Edinburgh; where, having occafion to fee him frequently, and to converfe a good deal with him, I advifed him to begin with teaching his fcholars the pronunciation of the vowels, inftead of teaching them the letters, as they ftand in the order of the alphabet; and which he told me, he did with great fuccefs.— It is not therefore to be wondered, that there are feveral of the confonants which

† That the French pronounce this vowel U rightly and as the Greeks pronounced it, is evident from the mechanical account that Dionyfius the Halicarnaffian gives of its pronunciation in his moft valuable work περι Συνθεσεως, cap. 14.

whole nations do not pronounce *. Even
the labial confonants, fuch as B, P, M,
which appear to us to be of fuch eafy pronunciation, being among the firſt that our
children learn, the nation of the Hurons
cannot articulate; and the Baron Hontan
tells us, that he fpent four days to no purpofe, in endeavouring to teach a Huron
to pronounce them: The reafon of which
is, that there is one organ of pronunciation,
which the Huron does not ufe at all, namely, the lips; for he always fpeaks with o-
pen mouth †. Even a Frenchman cannot

---

* See in Vol. I. of this work, Book iii. Chap. 7.
examples of many barbarous nations, who cannot
pronounce different confonants, particularly the Pe-
ruvians, who cannot pronounce the confonants S, B,
D, F, G, H. Ibid. p. 505.

† See Vol. I. of this work, p. 502. See alfo p.
470. The whole chapter is well worth reading by a-
ny man, who is curious about the origin of this wonderful art, which is beſt difcovered by the ſtudy of
fuch a rude and imperfect a language as the Huron,
very near, as I imagine, to the origin of the art; for it
confiſts of cries, fuch as the brute animals utter with
open mouth, and is only articulated by a few gutteral
confonants, fuch as K, Q, and X, with the afpirated H.

pronounce the aspirated *T*, or *Th*; for he cannot say *Thee*; nor can an Englishman pronounce the aspirated *K*, or *Ch*, for he says *Akilles*, not *Achilles*.

As to melody and rhythm, they are not essential to language; neither do I think the invention of them near so difficult as of articulation; for I am persuaded, that language began in the southern countries, where all the inhabitants were naturally musical, as much as certain birds among us. It was therefore natural, and indeed in some sort necessary, that the men, who first articulated, should join with it both musical tones and rhythms. But when from those people the language was propagated to the barbarous and unmusical northern nations, the musical part of it would soon be lost: But it continued among the nations of the south, particularly the Greeks, where it was formed into an art, as regular as their vocal and instrumental music.

The *form* of language, as it is more excellent than the *matter* *, so it is much more difficult: And indeed the contrivance, to express the infinite variety of things by a number of words, not so great but that they may be retained by the memory and readily used, is to a philosopher by far the most wonderful of all the inventions of men; tho', to a vulgar man, not learned in the science of language, it appears not at all surprising. That the number of things, even of genuses and specieses, is infinite, at least with respect to our capacities, cannot be denied: And yet, if a language be in any degree compleat, all that infinity of things must be expressed accurately and distinctly by words, very much limited in number compared with the things expressed by them. Now, by what wonderful art is this to be done, not by one means as we have seen, but by four, *derivation*, *composition*, *flexion*, and lastly, *the use of words in a figurative sense*. Of all these I have spoken, both in this volume and

---

* Of this great division of language into *matter* and *form*, which I have made the foundation of the science of language, delivered by me in the 3d volume of this work, see p. 53. of that volume.

the second volume of this work. But suppose words invented to express all the conceptions of the human mind, distinguishing accurately each thing from another, the *substance*, for example, from the *accident*, the *action* from the *agent*, or the subject of the action; and all the different circumstances of the action, from the action itself; there remains still as great a difficulty, perhaps greater than any yet mentioned, how to join together so many words in a sentence, so as to mark their connection one with another, without which, there could be no sense or meaning in the sentence. This is done, as we have seen, in the learned languages, chiefly, by the means of *flexion*, which I hold to be the greatest artifice of language, as it serves a double purpose, both to save the multiplication of words, and to shew their relation and connection with one another*. And thus it appears, that whether we consider the *matter* of language, furnished

* See what I have said of the nature of syntax, and the different ways by which words can be connected together, Vol. II. Book iii. Chap. 1.

not by God and nature, but by man himself, the *mechanifm* of it, and the *form*, that is, the words confidered not as founds merely, but as fignificant, it muft appear to be, as I have faid, the moft wonderful of all human arts *.

And here a queftion will naturally occur to every intelligent reader, whether the invention of fuch an art does not exceed the faculties of man. And tho' I have no doubt that men, after the art is invented, may cultivate and improve it, and make of it as perfect a language as I have fhown the Greek to be, I can hardly believe but that, in the firft difcovery of this fo artificial a method of communication, men had fupernatural affiftance; and, therefore, I am much inclined to liften to what the Egyptians tell us, of a God, as they call him, that is, an intelligence fuperior to

* If the reader, after all that I have faid here, fhould doubt of the extreme difficulty of this moft wonderful art, I muft refer him to what I have faid in Chapters 7. 8. and 9. Book iii. Vol. I. of this work, II. edition.

man, having firſt taught them the uſe of language: For that the art of language was firſt practiſed in Egypt, and from thence propagated all over the world, I have endeavoured to prove in the firſt volume of this work; and, the more I conſider the thing, the more I am confirmed in that opinion, for which I will give many additional reaſons in the fourth volume of my Metaphyſics, if I ſhall live to publiſh it. Here I will only ſay further, that if we believe that Providence has ever at any time interpoſed in the affairs of men, and aſſiſted them in their recovery from their fallen ſtate* by enabling them to invent arts and form ſocieties, which only could make them intellectual creatures, it muſt, I think, have been in the invention of this art, without which there could have been no civil ſociety, nor art or ſcience among men.

Vol. IV. A a

* In this 4th Volume of Mataphyſics I propoſe to ſhow, that the fall of Man is a truth of philoſophy as well as of religion; and that he was aſſiſted to recover his former ſtate, ſo far at leaſt as to become an intellectual creature, by extraordinary interpoſitions of Providence not only in Judea, but in other countries.

As Providence does every thing that is neceſſary for accompliſhing its great purpoſes, ſo it does nothing more: And, therefore, after language was diſcovered and once ſet a-going, it was left to the natural faculties of men to cultivate and improve it. But this muſt have been the work of ages, and could not have been performed but in a nation that appears to have laſted ſo long as that of Egypt, and where there was a claſs of men ſet apart for religion and the ſtudy of arts and ſciences*. Nor do I think, that even in ſuch a country it could have been brought to any great degree of perfection, if men had lived as ſhort time as they do now, and died before age and experience had matured their judgment, after living a few years with crazy and infirm bodies. In theſe later times, tho' we may add ſomething to former diſcoveries, (for according to the common ſaying, *facile eſt inventis addere*). I think it is hardly poſſible, that we could invent an art of any great conſequence, much leſs an art

---

* See Vol. II. Book iii. Chap. 13.—See alſo Vol. I. p. 566. of the ſecond edition.

so extremely difficult as that of language. All therefore we should aim at is, to preserve the arts that have been handed down to us from our forefathers, or to restore them when lost; and I think, it is one of the greatest eulogiums that Horace bestows upon Augustus, when he says that, *veteres revocavit artes*.

I will conclude with observing a very singular thing concerning this wonderful art, and which shows, more than any thing else that I know, the power of that faculty of imitation, which distinguishes our species so much from every other. And it is this, that other arts we cannot practice without being artists, that is, without having learned the principles and rules of the art: Whereas, we see women, and even children, speak a language very well, nay, write it well, without knowing one rule of grammar, or understanding any thing of the art or science of language. It is indeed true, that music is practised, in the same way as language, by mere imitation; but I am persuaded, that in music we are more assisted by our natural instinct; and I have little doubt, but that men *sung* before they *spoke*: For we have from nature those tones of which music is composed; whereas, even the matter of language, I mean articulate sounds, are not given by nature to us, as they are to some brutes, but are a work of art, and as I have shown, of the greatest art.

BOOK II.

Of Stile, and its different Kinds.

CHAP. I.

Public speaking *an art—also* private conversation.—Writing *an art likewise.—The best orations could not please, if they were not first well written.—The art of writing different, according to the different subjects.—In writing upon certain sciences, such as mathematics, no art of stile is required.—Of the nature of that study, and how much it engrosses a man.*

IN the preceeding book I have examined and compared the materials for ſtile, which different languages afford. In this book I intend to treat of ſtile itſelf, by way of ſupplement to what I have written upon the ſubject in the preceeding volume of this work.

Altho' language, as I have obſerved, however difficult the invention of it may have been, is, by means of that wonderful faculty of imitation belonging to human nature, ſo eaſy in the practice, that men ſpeak it and even write it without any art at all, yet we are not for that to imagine, that there is no art of ſpeaking. That there is an art of public ſpeaking, I think impoſſible to doubt, tho' many men ſpeak even in public, as if they thought it could be performed without any ſtudy or art. But even in private ſpeaking, if it be of the elegant and polite kind, there is an art, and an art not commonly underſtood, as I ſhall ſhow, when I come to treat of the ſtile of converſation.

Speaking, is no doubt, an art more difficult than writing, requiring, befides the words and their compofition, a proper elocution; for which purpofe certain bodily qualities are neceffary, fuch as an agreeable countenance, and a good voice both clear and fweet, with a diftinct articulation*. But writing is likewife an art, and a very great art too; nor would the orations of Demofthenes have pleafed us near fo much as they do, if they had not been written and compofed with as much art as they were pronounced. Yet there are many who think, there is no art of writing, any more than of fpeaking: And hence it is, that *Scribimus indocti doctique*, as Horace has obferved of the men of his age. But thofe, who have ftudied writing, know not only that there is an art of ftile and fpeaking, but that it is different, according to the different fubjects of which

---

* See upon this fubject, what Cicero fays, in his dialogue *De Oratore*, where he fays, that fome people are by nature fo deficient in voice and articulation, in countenance too and movement, that tho' they excel ever fo much in genius and art, yet they never could be orators, Lib. I. Chap. 25.

it treats; and that there is a poetical ſtile, a dialogue ſtile, an oratorial, an hiſtorical, and a didactic.

As to the laſt ſtile, it may be obſerved, that there is one kind of it, which requires no art at all, and where it would be ridiculous to affect any thing like art or ornament in words or compoſition. What I mean, is the language of mathematics, the ſubject of which are lines and figures, numbers, calculation, and menſuration. And it is well for the mathematicians, that their ſcience requires nothing that deſerves the name of ſtile; for there are few of them that are ſcholars, and fewer ſtill that are men of taſte: And according to my obſervation, there is no ſtudy or application, which engroſſes a man ſo entirely as mathematics, rendering him ſometimes unfit not only for the buſineſs, but even the ordinary commerce of life; and indeed I have known methematicians, that I thought had hardly the common feelings of humanity. Upon ſuch men as theſe Dr Swift has, in the voyage to Laputa, beſtowed a great deal of ridicule, repreſenting them as living in some sort out of the world. This may be thought by many to be very much exaggerated, but we are to confider, that, when the Doctor wrote, mathematics were much more in fashion than they are now; for they had come in place of the antient philosophy, which was then generally cried down all over Europe, and particularly in England, where the *philosophy* of Sir Isaac Newton, as it is called, was put in place of it*. There are, however, exceptions to this rule; and I know one man particularly, whose mind is so enlarged, that, tho' he be one of the greatest mathematicians of this age, and particularly learned in Sir Isaac Newton's astronomy, he is at the same time a scholar and a philosopher, and withal an agreeable companion. By this description, every man who

---

* It was about this time, that Lord Shaftesbury, in his *Advice to an Author*, part iii. sect. 1. says, ' That a ' man, who dedicated himself to the study of *triangles* ' and *circles*, came off well, if by good fortune he kept ' his head sound.'

knows Dr Horsley, will know that I mean him *.

In a stile not unlike the mathematical are written Aristotle's *esoteric* books, or

* By what I have said here, I hope it will not be understood that I mean to discourage the study of mathematics; on the contrary, I maintain, that geometry and arithmetic (by which I mean the science of numbers, not the practice merely), ought to be the first sciences a young man learns: And accordingly they were first taught, as I have elsewhere observed, in the school of Pythagoras, which produced the greatest men in arms and government, as well as science and philosophy, that ever existed—(See what I have said upon this subject, in the preface to the third Volume of Antient Matephysics, p. 7. 23. and following). But this I maintain, that, tho' arithmetic and geometry be the best preparation for philosophy, yet if a man addict himself wholly to these studies, he will not only be unfit for the business of the world, but even for good company: For he will want that taste and sense of what is becoming in conduct and behaviour, which is essential to the character of a gentleman, and an agreeable companion. And indeed I observe, that such men lose almost the idea of mind, to which only beauty and grace belong. Those of them who are so vain of excelling in the science of lines and figures, (for arithmetic among us can hardly be called a science), ought to consider, that it is only what may be called the elements of science, being the first effort of the human mind to abstract itself

books of abstruse philosophy. But in his writings upon popular subjects, such as morals, poetry, and rhetoric, in which he treats of the actions, character, and sentiments of men, his stile is very different: For it is as much ornamented as any didactic stile should be; and there is composition in periods in it, particularly there is one period, with which he begins his *po-*

from matter, in which we are assisted by visible signs. And as the ideas are so simple and so determinate, and the conclusions deduced from propositions self-evident, it is not, one should think, any matter of great glory to excell in it. But, where *mind* is the subject, and not *body* or its dimensions, and where the ideas are so much more complex, and cannot be typified by any thing falling under the senses;—there to excell, is indeed worthy of praise.—And such is the nature of logic, morals and metaphysics. To be vain therefore of excelling in geometry or arithmetic, is as ridiculous, as if a scholar should be vain of having learned his alphabet: For these sciences are truly no more than the A, B, C, of science. They are however, as I have said, an excellent preparation for philosophy, and very proper to give a young mind a taste of demonstration and accurate science. But whoever mistakes them for philosophy, does not know what philosophy is: For philosophy is the science of causes, being the science of mind, which is the cause of every thing.

etics, as well compofed as any in Demofthenes *.

Now, neither geometry nor arithmetic will apply to the inveftigation of the caufes and principles of things; and as often as they have been attempted to be employed in that way, fo often the attempt has failed.

* See what I have further faid of Ariftotle's ftile, Vol. III. of this work, Book IV. Chap. xix. p. 358.

CHAP. II.

*Writing, being an art, muſt be either in-
vented or learned.—Was not invented a-
mong the northern nations, any more than
any other liberal art.—Muſt be learned
from the Greeks, as well as ſtatuary and
painting.—Good writing more difficult
than either of theſe arts.—The compari-
ſon of them with the writing art, both
as to the ſubject and the materials.—The
beſt models of the writing art ſtill extant.*

HAVING ſhewn in the preceding chapter that ſtile in writing, as well as in
ſpeaking, is an art, it follows of neceſſary
conſequence, that every man who writes
muſt either have invented the art or learned it. As to invention, I have a great
doubt whether we of the northern re-
gions, not favoured ſo much by the muſes

and graces as those of the southern, have the capacity, or ever had, of inventing any liberal art; but be that as it will, the fact is certain, that we have invented none. Some mechanical arts, indeed, we have invented, such as printing; and of some accidental discoveries of powers of Nature, such as that of gun-powder, we have made an art, but which we never should have done, had we been as wise as the Indians who discovered it long before us, but forbade the use of it*. But as to the liberal arts, we have contented ourselves with imitating those that have come down to us from the Greeks and Romans.

It appears, therefore, that we must learn the writing art. Now we learn either by teaching or imitation, or both ways, which last is no doubt the most perfect way of learning every thing. But if we are to learn to write by only one of these two ways, I hold that style, as well as language, is better learned by imitation than by teaching.

---

* See the preface to the Code of the Gentoo laws, published by Brassey Halhed.

The queſtion then is, who are to be our maſters, and whom we are to imitate? And I ſay it is the antient Greeks and Romans, from whom we muſt learn the writing art, as well as every other ingenious and liberal art. But of the two, it will be aſked, who ſhould be our principal maſters? and I ſay it ſhould be the Greeks, not the Romans, who were themſelves taught by the Greeks *, a people who appear to me to have been deſtined by God and Nature to excell all others in genius and the fine arts, as much as the Egyptians in ſcience and philoſophy: For, as I have obſerved elſewhere †, there is a difference of character in nations as well as individuals; nor has nature profuſely beſtowed all her gifts upon any one nation, any more than upon any one individual.

There are I know among us *free ſpirits*, as they call themſelves, who ſcorn this ſla-

* See what I have ſaid upon the ſubject of the imitation of the Greek writers, Vol. III. Book iv. Chap. 20.

† In the Preface to Volume iii. of Metaphyſics, p. 6.

vifh fubjection to the antients, and infift to ufe their natural liberty, and be themfelves their own mafters in ftile and compofition. At the fame time they confefs, that in other arts, fuch as ftatuary and painting, we muft fubmit to be taught by the antients; and without ftudying the antient monuments which the Greeks have left us of their fculpture, we cannot excell in either of the two above mentioned arts. But, fay they, the writing art is not fo difficult as either of thefe. Now I fay, that in this they are miftaken, and that good writing is more difficult than any other of the fine arts, oratory alone excepted, which, befides ftile and compofition, includes pronunciation, an art of itfelf very difficult. But I fhall confine what I have to fay upon the fubject of this comparifon to ftatuary and painting.

That poetry, or writing in verfe, is a greater art than painting or fculpture, no man, who has ftudied in Ariftotle's poetics the fcience and philofophy of the fine arts, can have any doubt. But I fhall here only fpeak of what is, no doubt, an art inferior to poetry, writing in profe. That it is preferable to landscape painting, or the representation of the animal life either in sculpture or painting, is evident to every body who knows that the beauty of those arts consists chiefly in the value of the subjects they imitate, not merely in the imitation, which, however perfect, is but little valued by the real connoisseur. It is therefore only the painting or sculpture of human actions that can be compared with writing; and I shall compare them first with respect to the subject, and then with respect to the materials with which they work.

The subject of the painter and sculptor's art is the characters, sentiments, and actions of men. The same is the subject of the writer, if he write of human things, with this difference, that the writer exhibits them in succession, and so gives you the progress of them, which, if well executed, both moves and instructs us more than any single scene of them, which is all that painting or sculpture can represent; for these arts are confined to an instant of time, and to one place. It is true, that Hogarth has enlarged the bounds of his art, by giving us fucceffive fcenes, and making a hiftory and kind of drama of fome of his pieces, fuch as the rake and harlot's progrefs; and in this, I think, he has fhown a genius fuperior to any painter of the age. But no body will compare his pieces, however excellent of the kind, to the hiftories of Herodotus or Livy. And indeed, it is of neceffity, that the works of writing fhould be much grander and more comprehenfive, than thofe of painting or fculpture; and I muft confefs, that even a fingle fcene of fentiment or paffion well written, affects me more than any reprefentation of it in painting or fculpture that I ever faw. But befides paffions, fentiments, and actions, by writing are expreffed the operations of our prime faculty, intellect, in reafoning, which cannot be reprefented by fculpture or painting. Such are works of philofophy: Such are fpeeches in hiftory: Such are the orations of Demofthenes; which, if they had not been written, muft have been loft to us.

The subject therefore of writing is much more extensive, and more noble too, than the subject of the other two arts: And as to the materials with which they work; those, employed by sculpture, are stone or metal; those by painting, colours and canvas; and those by the writing art, words. Now, words are of more ready use, more abundant, of greater variety, and therefore better adapted to express the infinite variety of things, which are the subject of the writing art, than the materials of the other two arts.

Thus, I think, I have proved that writing, even in prose, is a nobler as well as more difficult art than painting or sculpture; and, therefore, if we must have recourse to antient models for these arts, much more is it necessary that we should form our taste in the writing art by the imitation of the best authors Greek or Latin, and particularly the Greek authors: And we have this encouragement to do so, as I have observed elsewhere*, that we are sure the very best models of the writing

* See Vol. III. p. 378. et seq.

art have come down to us; whereas we are by no means sure that the best statues of antient Greece are preserved to us *.—Upon this subject of the imitation of the antients I will say a good deal more in the sequel of this work; I shall only add at present, that I believe no example can be given of any modern having succeeded in writing either prose or verse, who did not form his taste upon the best antient models.

* Winkleman has a doubt, whether any one statue of the best days of Greece is now extant.—Certain it is, that many of them, which were in Constantinople in the twelfth century, are now not to be found,

CHAP. III.

Variety the great beauty of stile, as well as of language.—Of the variety of single words.—There may be too great variety of these.—Examples of authors who exceed in that way, such as Plato, Cicero, and Lord Shaftesbury.—Demosthenes a model in that respect, as well as in others; —also Horace.—The rule to be followed in this matter.

WRITING having been shewn to be an art, in the preceding chapter, what is the chief beauty, as I have elsewhere observed, in language, and indeed in every thing of art, being that, without which there can be no other beauty, the same is necessary in stile; I mean *variety* *. For in the

---

* See the passages upon this subject, that I have

two things of which ſtile confiſts, the words and the compoſition, if there was not a certain variety, tho' the words were ever ſo well choſen, and put together in the beſt manner poſſible, yet the ſtile would be tedious and difguſting.

I will begin with ſingle words.—The abundance and variety of them is what makes what we call a *copious* ſtile, which, no doubt, pleaſes very much; but, as in other things, ſo in it there may be an exceſs as well as a defect; for if the language be too much varied by tropes, or by uſing too many different words to expreſs the ſame thing, every judicious reader or hearer will be offended. This fault is very conſpicuous in many of our modern writings, and indeed is to be found more or leſs in almoſt all our late productions. My Lord Shaftef-

---

quoted from Quintilian and the Halicarnaſſian, Vol. III. p 152.—Here the reader may obſerve, that the two beauties of variety of language and variety of ſtile, muſt in ſome degree go together; for it is only in a language that admits of ſuch variety of arrangement of the words as the Greek and Latin do, that there can be any great variety of ſtile.

bury, as I have elsewhere observed, is, in my judgment, the most copious as well as elegant writer we have in prose: But he commonly exceeds very much in this particular, and may be said to play very often and wanton with the language; as particularly in his *Advice to an author*, how many changes has he rung upon *soliloquy* or *self-converse*, indeed more than I should have thought the language could have furnished. Among the antients, Plato has something of this fault, but Cicero much more, especially in his orations; and indeed he seems every where to labour to convince the reader of the justice of his observation, but of which however he has not convinced me, that the Latin language is more rich in words than the Greek[*].

[*] *O inopem Graeciam*, speaking of the Greek language, is an exclamation of his somewhere: For, as I have observed, he deals much in that figure.— At the same time, I do not deny that the Latin language is a rich language, especially as Cicero has used it; but that it is a richer language than the Greek, I cannot believe. And in other passages Cicero himself acknowledges the poverty of his language; as where he tells us, that the words *Physica* and *Dialectica*

208   THE ORIGIN AND   Book II.

In this, as well as every thing else belonging to stile, Demosthenes excels. For he is copious in words, but not super-abun-

---

were borrowed from the Greek. Even the name of *Philosophy* was taken from that language; and what is more extraordinary, the Romans had no name for his own art, till they naturalised the word *Rhetorica*. (See *Academic*. lib. i. cap. 7.) And in his philosophical works, he very often uses Greek terms for want of Latin: And Lucretius, tho' he does not use the same freedom, complains of the poverty of the language;

> Nec me animus fallit, Graiorum obscura reperta
> Difficile illustrare Latinis versibus esse:
> Multa novis verbis praesertim cum sit agendum,
> Propter aegestatem linguae et rerum novitatem.
>
> Lib. i. in Prooemio.

Neither can I believe, that the Romans in genius exceeded all other nations; which, however, Cicero affirms, without even excepting the Greeks. (Lib. i. *De Oratore*, Cap. 4.) Nor can I approve of his treating the Greeks in the manner he does, calling them *Graeculi* (Ibid. cap. 11.) and *Otiosi et loquaces*, and only *fortasse docti et eruditi* (Ibid. cap. 22.) For tho' it be true, that they had then a great deal of leisure, not being employed, as they were formerly, in arms and government, they were for that very reason much more learned, not only in philosophy, but in every art, and among others in the art of speaking;

dant. And here again, I cannot help differing from Cicero, who says, that even Demosthenes did not fill his ears: For I say, his ears were vitiated by the practice of the schools of declamation, where, in order to draw the applause of boys or any ignorant crowd, the same things were said over and over again, with much exaggeration and amplification. But Demosthenes had formed his taste upon the practice of real business, not upon

which, as Cicero himself tells us, his countrymen learned chiefly from the Greeks: And the fact most certainly is, that the Romans got all their learning from the Greeks, and had nothing they could call their own, except the science of government and arms, as their own poet Virgil has confessed, who in oratory particularly, as well as in other arts, has given the preference to the Greeks in these famous lines.

> Excudent alii spirantia mollius aera;
> (Credo equidem); vivos ducent de marmore voltus;
> Orabunt causas mellus; coelique meatus
> Describent radio, et surgentia sidera dicent:
> Tu regere imperio populos, Romane, memento;
> (Hae tibi erunt artes); pacifque imponere morem;
> Parcere subjectis, et debellare superbos.
> Æneid, Lib. 6. v. 847.

the mimicry of it in fictitious cauſes. The author in Latin, who of all others has varied his expreſſion the moſt agreeably, is in my opinion Horace, who is rich and copious in words and phraſes, particularly in his odes, but without affectation or vain ſhew. And tho' it be evident to every man who knows what fine writing is, that ſuch a variety of choice words and phraſes muſt have coſt him a great deal of pains, yet they appear ſo eaſy and natural, that he well deſerves the eulogium, Petronius beſtows upon him, of *Curioſa felicitas*. The Rule in this matter ſeems to be, that the change ought not to be too frequent, ſo as to appear to be merely for the ſake of variety; and when it is made, the new word, ſhould, if poſſible, expreſs the thing more fully and accurately, or with more force and emphaſis.

CHAP. IV.

Of the composition of words.—Of the variety, which the rhythms *and* accents *of the Greek language gave to their pronunciation.—Those were a beauty of their prose, as well as of their verse composition.—No* melody *or* rhythm *in the pronunciation of English.—We have only what we call* accents.*—These measure our verse but not our prose.—The French have neither* quantity *nor* accent.*—The Italians have* accents.*--The modern Greeks have* accents *such as ours.—We want one of the greatest beauties of antient composition, variety of arrangement of words. —Not easy to set bounds to that variety in the antient languages.—That arrangement not so artificial in their conversation, and in their laws and decrees;—very artificial in their poetry.—Examples of this from Horace's odes.—Not so much of it in*

I Come now to speak of the composition of words in sentences, which being so much more excellent, and of so much greater variety, Stile is in English, from its principal part, not unfitly denominated *Composition*. How much the Greek language must have been varied in its pronunciation, and how beautifully, by long and short syllables, and by grave, acute, and circumflex accents, the one the rhythm the other the melody of the language, I have already observed [*]. What a wonderful variety the accents alone must have produced, the reader may imagine, when he considers that every accent he sees marked in a Greek book, and which are now become quite insignificant, except sometimes to distinguish one word from another, were pronounced. The variety of these accents was a beauty even of their prose composition, as I have else-

* Lib. i. Chap. 5. and 8. of this Volume.

where observed*, and shall say a great deal more of it in the next chapter. And as to their rhythm, that it was perceived in their prose as well as in their verse, which was formed by it, and that it was a thing of importance in their rhetorical composition, we have not only the testimony of Dionysius the Halicarnassian, but the authority of Aristotle, who treats of it in his books of *rhetorick* as a material part of the oratorial stile †. And if the reader be not satisfied with these two authorities, and will still believe that there is no such thing as rhythm in Greek or Latin prose, because it is not in his own or any other modern language, I will add a third, viz. Cicero, who has treated of it at greater length than any of the two authors I have mentioned, in his *Orator, ad*

---

* Lib. 1. Cap. 5.

† See the Halicarnassian upon this subject, *De Compositione Verborum*, cap. 25. where he quotes the authority of Aristotle, and I think he could not have quoted a better, to prove that what he says of the rhythm of the Greek orations was not fanciful. The passage in Aristotle he refers to is Rhetor. Lib. iii. cap.

Marcum Brutum*. Now, if the periods of Demosthenes so well composed, and pronounced with such variety of rhythms and tones, could not fill the ears of Cicero, they must have been indeed, as he says, very proud and fastidious.

As the English do not make their verse by long and short syllables, they cannot be supposed to have any *rhythm* of that kind in their prose. And with respect to *accents* such as the Greeks used, I believe very few men in England have so much as an idea how a language could be pronounced with such a variety of musical tones, and not be mere cant or sing-song. But their learned ears knew how to distinguish betwixt the melody of speech and of music, properly so called, as I have elsewhere explained †. But, tho' we have not rhythm neither in our verse nor prose, we have what we call *accents*, by which we distinguish the syllables from one another, not by musical tones, but by sounding one louder

---

* Cap. 51. et sequens.

† Lib. i. Chap. 5. of this Volume.

than another. In this way we form our verse; and tho' it give an agreeable pronunciation to our prose, it has not yet been formed into an art, nor reduced to feet, measuring our prose composition, as I have shewn, it measures our verse [*]. But if it be drawn too far back, as is the fashion now, instead of being a beauty to our language, it becomes a great fault in our pronunciation.

The French, as I have observed, have neither *quantity*, nor even what we call *accent*, in their language. They cannot therefore have blank verse, and it makes the pronunciation of their prose wonderfully uniform, being varied only by a certain tone, which some of them give to the last words of their sentences, but which I observe is not practised by their best speakers.

The Italians have *accents* such as we have; they therefore have blank verse: And I do not observe that they use their ac-

[*] Vol. II. of this work, p. 383. and following.

cents so improperly as we do, by drawing them too far back; and in general I think their pronunciation is not only sweet and soft, but very diſtinct and articulate *.

As to the modern Greeks, they have converted their antient accents into accents such as ours; and, neglecting quantity altogether, but obſerving the accents as they are marked in the Greek books, they pronounce the Greek juſt as the Engliſh did some years ago.

One of the great beauties of antient compoſition, and such as gives it a variety to which it is not eaſy to set bounds, is the various arrangement of the words. This is a beauty, which the defects of the grammar of our language will not admit, except in a very ſmall degree, even in our poetry; and ſtill leſs in our proſe, where, beſides the ſtinted genius of our language, cuſtom has confined us ſo much, that to depart

---

* See what I have ſaid of that language, p. 144. of this Volume.

from one certain arrangement, is reckoned pedantic and affected. In this respect, I think the French are at present still more stinted than we, tho' their language, by having genders and numbers not only in their nouns but in their adjectives and verbs, admits much more latitude.

I have said, that in Greek and Latin it is not easy to set bounds to the variety of arrangement: But that it had its bounds is certain: For we plainly perceive the arrangement of Cicero to be very different from that of Ammianus Marcellinus, or any other writer of the lower empire; and we say the one is classical, and the other not. Further, we know also, that among the Greeks and Romans, there was an arrangement that was ordinary and familiar, and another that was artificial and not common, being used only in particular stiles. What the ordinary composition was, we may judge from their familiar letters [*],

---

[*] See the collection of Cicero's letters, *ad familiares*, being the 16th book of his Letters, where the arrangement is such, that the words may be translated

which were, no doubt, written in the ſtile of converſation; but in their laws and decrees, in which the greateſt perſpicuity was ſtudied, the compoſition was ſtill ſimpler and plainer, and coming much nearer to the arrangement in modern languages. This is evident from what is preſerved to us of that kind of writing, among the Athenians and Romans *. The other kind of arrangement is to be found in their rhetorical and poetical works, but chiefly in their poetry, and I think I have obſerved that it is more uſed by the Latin than by the Greek poets; nor do I know any thing in Greek compoſed ſo artificially as the beginning of Horace's ode to Pyrrha,

into Engliſh, in an order not very different from that in which they ſtand in the original.

* In Demoſthenes we have ſeveral laws and decrees inſerted in his orations, where the arrangement of the words is very different from the arrangement in the ſpeeches upon theſe laws and decrees. The ſame inartificial order of words we ſee in the Roman Laws, or *Senatus-conſulta*, and in the edicts of their Praetors, preſerved to us in the collection of their laws made by the Emperor Juſtinian.

Quis multa gracilis te puer in rosa
Perfusus liquidis urget odoribus
Grato, Pyrrha, sub antro?

Where, except it be the two prepositions *in* and *sub*, which, being indeclinable words, cannot be connected with the words they govern otherwise than by juxta-position, there are no other words which are construed together, that are joined together by position.

Of this kind of composition there is a great deal in his Odes: And it is certainly very proper for that exalted kind of poetry, which ought to speak a language very different from the common. But in his Satires, where both the subject and language are of the familiar kind, there is very little of it; nor is there much of it in his Epistles, except in one where he seems to have thought, that the subject required a more elevated stile, and a finer flow of verse than ordinary. The epistle I mean, is that to Lollius in praise of Homer, where, in describing the subject of the Iliad, he says,

Ch. IV. Progress of Language. 221

> Fabula, qua Paridis propter narratur amorem
> Graecia Barbariae lento collisa duello,
> Stultorum regum et populorum continet aestus.

Here the two first lines are as artificial, and flow as well as any of Virgil's.

And this leads me to speak of him, who has used this artifice of composition, called by the rhetoricians *hyperbaton*, more I think than any other poet Greek or Latin. This gives his verse that peculiar flow, which distinguishes it from that of every other poet; and it must be confessed, that there is a sweetness in his composition, not to be found in that of any other Latin poet, as we may perceive by comparing his versification with that of Ovid, who uses it very little, or with that of Lucretius, who does not use it at all, except in the introductions to some of his books*. The reason of this I take

---

* In the exordium of his first book he makes Venus supplicate Mars to give peace to the Romans, in these admirable lines; where, joined to the finest composition, there is presented to the reader as beautiful a picture as is to be found in any poem.

to be, that it will often happen, that by putting together, in so artificial a manner, words of different terminations, the sound will be made more agreeable to the ear. 2dly, Such an uncommon arrangement gives a wonderful variety to the stile, which, as I have more than once observed, is one of the chief beauties of writing, and without which, in some degree, there can be no beauty in that or any other art. And, Lastly, I think I have shown, that in the best writers, this artificial arrangement not only gives pleasure to the ear, but conveys the sense with more emphasis than it would otherwise be conveyed*. But be the reason what it will, we are sure that the beauty of the periods of Demosthenes and Cicero, were they to be stripped of the artificial arrangement, and the words put together as they are construed in syntax, would be entirely lost;

  Hunc tu, diva, tuo recubantem corpore sancto
  Circumfusa super, suaveis ex ore loquelas
  Funde, petens placidam Romanis inclyta pacem.

* See the essay upon the composition of the antients, annexed to Volume ii. of this work.

Ch. IV. PROGRESS OF LANGUAGE.   223

and the same would be the case of such artificial verse as that of Virgil, tho' the quantity of the syllables should allow it to be so taken down.

But there may be too much of the best things; and I must own I think Virgil has used this artifice too much, particularly in his narrative poem, I mean the Æneid. Whereas Homer, tho' he has used it sometimes in the ornamented parts of the Iliad and Odyssey, such as the similies *, has very seldom used it in the narrative; and for

* As in the fine comparison of Nausicaa and her maids to Diana and her Virgins ;

Οἵη δ' Ἄρτεμις εἶσι κατ' οὔρεος ἰοχέαιρα,
Ἢ κατα Τηΰγετον περιμήκετον ἢ Ἐρύμανθον,
Τερπομένη κάπροισι καὶ ὠκείῃς ἐλάφοισι·
Τῇ δέ θ' ἅμα Νύμφαι, κοῦραι Διὸς αἰγιόχοιο,
Ἀγρονόμοι παίζουσι· (γέγηθε δέ τε φρένα Λητώ.)
Πασάων δ' ὑπὲρ ἥγε κάρη ἔχει ἠδὲ μέτωπα·
Ῥεῖα δ' ἀριγνώτη πέλεται, καλαὶ δέ τε πᾶσαι.
Ὣς ἥγ' ἀμφιπόλοισι μετέπρεπε παρθένος ἀδμής.

Odyss. vi. V. 102.

This simile Virgil has imitated in the following manner.

this among other reasons, the narrative of Homer is much more simple than that of Virgil, and very much less obscure.

> Qualis in Eurotae ripis aut per juga Cynthi
> Exercet Diana choros, quam mille secutae
> Hinc atque hinc glomerantur Oreades: illa pharetram
> Fert humero, gradiensque Deas supereminet omnes:
> Latonae tacitum pertehtant gaudia pectus.
> Talis erat Dido, talem se laeta ferebat
> Per medios, instans operi regnisque futuris.
> Æn. i. V. 502.

Here we may observe, that Homer has excelled Virgil even in the artifice and variety of his arrangement, which, as I have said, is the chief excellence of Virgil's versification: For he separates Αερμος and its epithet αχταιρα, by the words κατ' οζεας. After that he returns again to *the mountains* and 'throws in the line Η κατα Ταϋγιτον, &c. Then he returns a second time to Diana, in the line Τιςπομιη ναςφιςι, &c. where the reader may observe the figure of *like endings*, or *rhyme*, as we call it: Which, I think, is a beauty, and gives not only a variety, but an agreeable flow to the composition, when sparingly used, as it is by Homer, never as far as I remember, except in his similies, (See what I have said on this subject, in Vol. iii. of this work, p. 84.) where he studies the ornaments of diction more than in the busy active parts of his poems, according to Aristotle's rule, who has said, that the ornaments of stile

Before I have done with the arrangement of words, I cannot help observing,

should be chiefly employed ἐν τοῖς ἀγῶσι μέρεσι that is, where the action of the poem stands. (*Poetic.* Cap. 24. *in fine*—where the philosopher adds, what is certainly true, that whatever there are reasonings or sentiments and characters expressed, that is, τὰ διανοητικὰ καὶ τὰ ἠθικὰ, the ornaments of words ought not to be studied;—ἀποκρύπτει γὰρ ἡ λίαν λαμπρὰ λέξις τὰ τε ἤθη καὶ τὰς διανοίας.)—But to return to Homer: After describing the attendants of Diana, he interjects a kind of parenthesis, where he introduces her mother Latona and describes her joy. Then he comes back again to Diana, who being principal in the simile is never out of sight, and concludes with describing her fine appearance, and eminence above the nymphs of her train. Now this variety of composition, which, at the same time that it pleases so much, does not produce the least confusion, is not to be found in Virgil's lines. Nor is his versification so flowing and high sounding; particularly in one line, viz. *Hinc atque hinc glomerantur Oreades*, which has no Caesura, and therefore sounds disagreeably. Now, tho' this may be admitted by way of variety in other parts of the poem, it ought not to be in a part so much ornamented as the similes should be. With respect to the sense and matter of the simile, Virgil is still more inferior; for, in the first place, he distinguishes Diana from the nymphs in her train by her wearing a quiver, which certainly was no mark of distinction; for they

that, tho' the antient critics speak much of
that figure of composition they call Hyperbaton, none of them has attempted to
define it otherwise than by telling us, that
it is, as the word imports, putting the
words of a sentence out of their natural
order. But what that natural order is they
do not tell us, nor do I believe they could
tell us, otherwise than by reference to common use. Now, I am persuaded, that even
in common use, there was an arrangement

all had quivers. Then he has omitted the circumstance that distinguishes Diana more than any thing
else, which is, that, tho' they were all handsome, yet she
was conspicuous among them all: And, lastly, that
emphatical description in Homer of the joy of Latona
in two words, γηθει φρενα, is very insipidly paraphrased
as I think in a whole line:—See an excellent criticism
of one Valerius Probus, preserved to us by Aulus Gel-
lius upon this imitation of Homer by Virgil, where
he says, what I think is certainly true, *Nihil quicquam
tam improspere Virgilium ex Homero vertisse*. And besides what I have said, he observes that the whole simile is improper, because there was no likeness betwixt Diana hunting with her quivered nymphs, and
Dido in the middle of her town, surrounded by her
Court, and *instans operi regnisque futuris*.

different from what we ufe in our language*, and different from that in which a fchoolboy arranges the words of the learned languages, when he conftrues them. This I think is evident, from the familiar letters and the edicts and decrees I have mentioned. The difference therefore betwixt the common arrangement and the figured, muft only be of more or lefs, which would be readily perceived by the Greeks and Romans, but is not to be defined.

Before I conclude this fubject of the Greek and Latin arrangement of words, I muft obferve, that there is fomething fingular in the Latin arrangement, which diftinguifhes the Latin compofition from the Greek, or that of any other language I know. It is the pofition of the verb, almoft always at the end of the fentence: And if it be a period confifting of feveral members, it very often likewife terminates each of thefe members. Now, as I hold variety to be effential to the beauty of lan-

---

* See of the arrangement in Englifh, Vol. II. of this work, book iii. cap. 2.

guage and ſtile, this arrangement gives an uniformity and fameneſs to the compoſition, which I muſt own, does not pleaſe me: Nor can it, I think, pleaſe any one, whoſe ear is formed to the variety of the Greek compoſition.

This obſervation upon the Latin compoſition, I have made in the diſſertation upon the compoſition of the antients, annexed to the ſecond volume of this work*; but I will beg leave to ſay a little more here upon the ſubject. If every ſentence was to be concluded with the ſame word, it would, no doubt, be very much worſe, and not to be endured; but it is not, I think, good when the concluſion is with a word of the ſame kind, that is, the ſame part of ſpeech. When I read Latin proſe, I expect the verb at the full ſtop, as much as I do a rhyme at the end of Mr. Pope's Diſticks: And, beſides, the terminations of the Latin verbs in *it* and *unt*, in *erit* and *erunt*, *abant*, *ebant*, and *ibant*, are founds, which, by themſelves, were very unpleaſant, I am perſuaded, to a Greek ear, even when in-

* Page 587.

terfperfed with the reft of the compofition, but much more fo, when they made a gingle at the end of fentences, or members of fentences. It is true that the verb is a principal part of fpeech, and the glory, as I have faid, of the grammatical art, being more artificial, and admitting of greater variety than any other part of fpeech. It is true alfo, as I have obferved elfewhere*, that the laft place of the fentence is a place of honour, and gives a particular emphafis to the word that is put there. But, however diftinguifhed the verb may be by the grammatical art, in the nature of things the noun expreffing the *fubftance* is prior in dignity to any word denoting an *accident* †. And tho' the concluding verb go-

---

* Differtation on the Compofition of the antients, Vol. ii. p. 572.

† This the Halicarnaffian has obferved before me; for he has faid, τα μεν γαρ (τα σωματα) των ουσιων δηλουν, τα δε (τα ῥηματα) τι συμβεβηκος· πρoτιζoν δε ἡ φυσις ειναι των ουσιων των συμβεβηκοτων. *De Compofitione* cap. 5. This whole chapter and the next are well worth the reading, as they fhow that it is neither precedence in the nature of things, nor the grammatical conftruction of the words, that regulates their order and rank in the fentence.

vern nouns, and perhaps other verbs in the sentence, yet it may not be the word to which the speaker or writer desires to draw the chief attention of the hearer or reader, and for that reason it may not be worthy of the last place, or in that order it may not give an agreeable cadence to the period.

In the composition of the best Greek writers, I think I have shown*, that not only the pleasure of the ear was studied, but also the sense: And if so, it was necessary that the sentence or period, and its different members, should be terminated with different parts of speech, sometimes, no doubt, with the verb; but oftener, according to my observation, with substantives, adjectives (under which I include participles, these being as I have said, no other than words denoting *qualities* with the addition of *time* †,) and sometimes pronouns, and even adverbs, nay

---

* Ibidem, page 570. and following.

† Page 47. of this Volume.

particles*, which gives a wonderful variety to the Greek compofition, with refpect both to the found and the fenfe.

To be convinced that there is not the

---

* Of this many examples may be given; but I will only mention two, which happen to occur to me in reading the third *Olynthiad* of Demofthenes; there he fays, Οτι γαρ εις τουτο περιεστηται τα πραγματα, και τα παροντα περιοριδα, σχεδον ισμεν απαντες ἐν τοι, p. 22. Editionis Morelli.—Here the conclufion is with two particles of affirmation. In the fame way he concludes another fentence in the fame oration; Ουκ γαρ ει τοις των πολεμων αυθεσιν, των φευγοντες ουδεις ιαστιε κατηγορει· αλλα και των στρατηγων και των πλησιοι και παντων μαλλον. Ηττωνται δ᾽ ομως δια παντας τους φευγοντας ἐν τοι. Then follows immediately a very fingular conclufion, with the potential Particle, αν. Μισον γαρ εξει το κατηγορουντι των αλλων· ει δε τουτο εποιει ‘ιαυτοι, ιτιαοι αν, Ibid. p. 23. And the fentence immediately before thofe that I have quoted concludes with the pronoun of the firft perfon, in this manner, παρων ουδε τουτ᾽ εγω. Thus we have, in the fame paffage, the fentences terminated with almoft all the feveral parts of fpeech, excepting only the participle, which, tho' it happen not to conclude any of the fentences in this paffage, is a very frequent conclufion in Greek, for the Greeks, as the antient grammarians obferve, were φιλομετοχοι.— It may be obferved, that even when the Greeks terminate with a verb, it is not the governing verb in the fentence, but an infinitive governed by that verb.

fame variety in the Latin compofition, neither in their hiftorical nor rhetorical ftile, we need only compare in this view the Greek hiftories with the Latin, or the Greek orations with the Latin. There is I think no better hiftorical ftile in Latin than that of Julius Caefar, fo much, and fo juftly recommended by Cicero. Now, let any man read but the firft page of his commentaries *de Bello Gallico*, and there he will find every fentence terminated with a verb, and generally the feveral members of the fentence, as where fpeaking of the feveral nations that inhabited Gaul, he fays, ' *Horum omnium fortiffimi*
' *funt Belgae, propterea quod a cultu atque*
' *humanitate provinciae longiffime abfunt;*
' *minimeque ad eos mercatores faepe comeant*
' *atque ea, quae ad effeminandos animos perti-*
' *nent, important.*' And immediately following this, is another fentence confifting of feveral more members, all terminated in the fame way: It is in thefe words, where, fpeaking of the Helvetii, he fays, ' *Prox-*
' *imi funt Germanis qui trans Rhenum inco-*
' *lunt, quibufcum continenter bellum gerunt:*
' *qua de caufa Helvetii quoque reliquos Gal-*
' *los virtute praecedunt, quod fere quotidi-*

Ch. IV. PROGRESS OF LANGUAGE. 233

'*anis praeliis cum Germanis contendunt,*
'*quum aut suis finibus eos prohibent, aut*
'*ipsi in eorum finibus bellum gerunt.*' Where
we may obferve, that in the laſt ſentence,
there is a quadruple rhyme of *unts*; for
there is *gerunt, praecedunt, contendunt,* and
gerunt again. Now, compare with this,
the narrative of Xenophon (whoſe ſtile,
of all the Greek writers, is the likeſt to
that of Julius,) in the beginning of the narrative of his *Cyropaedia*; and we ſhall
find his clauſules moſt agreeably varied
with other words as well as verbs: And
one of his ſentences, it may be obſerved,
concludes with the adverb 'ετεκα; for he
ſays, παντα δε κινδυνον 'υπουσιναι του επαι-
ρεισθαι 'ετεκα. And Thucydides, in the beginning of his narrative, where he deſcribes the town of *Epidamnis,* goes on for
five ſentences, all terminated with nouns
or participles: And it is not till the ſixth
ſentence that he concludes with a verb.

In the Latin oratorial ſtile, there is ſtill
more of the ſameneſs of compoſition, of
which any man may convince himſelf, by

comparing the orations of Cicero with those of Demosthenes. In the beginning of his oration for Milo, which, I am persuaded, was more studied in the composition than any he ever wrote, tho' as it is said, he failed much in the speaking of it, I have counted above ten periods all concluding with verbs, and even the members of these periods ending for the greater part in the same way. I will give an instance only of one of them: 'Quam-
'obrem illa arma, centuriones, cohortes,
'non periculum nobis sed praesidium *denun-*
'*tiunt*: neque solum ut quieto, sed etiam
'ut magno animo simus *hortantur:* neque
'auxilium modo defensioni meae verum
'etiam silentium *pollicentur.*' And it is well known, that there was one clausule with a verb, which was observed, in his own time, to recur too often in his orations; I mean the *esse videatur*: And there is a remarkable passage from his *Orator ad M. Brutum*, which I have quoted, in Volume iii.* from which it appears, that in the days of Cicero no composition was esteemed, unless the sentences terminated in a verb.

* Page 54.

What made the Romans so fond of such endings, was, I believe, that they thought the verb furnished a firm basis upon which the period might rest *, and gave it a density and a compactness, by bringing the sense of it altogether and as it were in a body upon the hearer; so that, without such a basis, the composition was loose and diffluent, as he expresses it in the passage above quoted. And it is, no doubt, for the same reason, that the Greeks use it more in their rhetorical stile than in any other. But as I have observed more than once, there can be no beauty of stile without variety. And besides, it will often happen, that the verb is not the most important word in the sentence, and therefore not entitled either to the first or last place, as I think I have shown, in my Treatise above quoted, ' *upon the compofi-* ' *tion of the antients.*' And accordingly Demosthenes, as appears from the exam-

---

* 'The Halicarnassian commending a period of Plato, says, that βασις πλαγι ασφαλης.—(Περι της διυοτητος των Δημοσθινος, cap. 24). Yet it does not end with a verb; for it runs thus, Εγγυς μεν ειμι δἰ ιχνων τα πραγματα ὁρινι αντοις, ὁι τυχοντες, περιοντες τηι ἱμερμινη ποιησι.

ples I have given, very often chooses to conclude his periods with some other part of speech. And, if the reader be not satisfied with these examples, he may find many more of the same kind in the same Olynthiac, particularly in that famous passage, so much admired by the Halicarnassian *, where he compares the Athenians of his time with their ancestors. This comparison begins with these words, Καιτοι σκεψασθε, Ο ἀνδρες Αθηναιοι, 'α τις ἂν κεφαλαια ειπειν εχοι των τ'επι των προγονων 'εργων και των εφ' 'υμων. Then he goes on for two folio pages of the edition I use, where, I say, that there are more periods and members of periods terminated by other parts of speech, than by verbs. The whole oration is well worth the reader's perusal; for I think it the finest thing of the kind, both for matter and stile, I ever read: And particularly Demosthenes has shewn in it, that he well deserves the praise, which even his enemy Eschines bestowed upon him, and which the Halicarnassian † tells us,

---

* Περι της δεινοτητος του Δημοσθενους, cap. 22.

† Περι της δεινοτητος του Δημοσθενους cap. 35. and 36.

was so clear, that it could not be disputed, of excelling all other orators in composition.

The Latins, I observe, in their epistolary stile, have not near so much of it; which persuades me, that, in their conversation, of which the epistolary stile is an imitation, it was not so common. And accordingly Cicero in his dialogues does not use it so much. But in all their grave compositions, such as their histories and orations, it is very much used. And even in their didactic stile they use it more than the Greeks; as we may judge by comparing Cicero's *books de officiis*, with Aristotle's didactic works, and particularly his *Treatise on poetry*, where you may read whole pages without the conclusion of one sentence by a verb.—And so much with respect to the arrangement of words in the antient languages.

In the modern, such as the French and English, the verb not being so artificial a part of speech, nor of such importance in the sentence, there is no such uniformity

in their compofition; nor indeed do I
obferve, that there is one kind of word
in them that concludes the fentence oftner than another.

From what I have here faid, and in other
parts of this work, it is, I think, evident,
1*mo*, That we cannot vary our compofition
by the arrangement of words, as the antients did. 2*do*, Neither can we do it by long
and fhort fyllables; for befides the defect
of the modern languages in that particular,
our ears are fo little formed to that kind
of rhythm, that even in reading the antient verfe we do not mark it as we fhould
do*: And, *laftly*, as to the accents or melody of their language, as they called it,
we have hardly an idea of it.—It remains
therefore, that the only variety we can
give to our ftile, is by compofition in periods, fitly divided into members of different lengths and ftructures, and varioufly
connected together. Whoever, therefore,
compofes in fhort fentences, where the fubject makes periods proper, appears to me to

---

* Vol. II. Book ii. Chap. 6.

be entirely ignorant of the beauty of compoſition, nor indeed to know that there cannot be any beauty in any art without variety, and that variety cannot be, except where there is a whole of ſome extent or ſize. And accordingly we obſerve, that this ſhort cut of a ſtile, as I call it, which has been introduced among us from France, but is not at preſent ſo faſhionable as it was ſome years ago, is tediouſly uniform and diſguſting to the ear, which in matter of compoſition muſt be the judge, ſince, as I have elſewhere obſerved, reading is the teſt of good writing *. The ear is alſo offended by the frequent breaks or ſtops, which make a kind of bounding hopping ſtile, without any thing like that flow, that *flumen orationis*, of which the antients ſpeak ſo much. And beſides all this, I maintain that the ſenſe, collected in a well compoſed period, comes upon you more fully and forcibly, than when it is cut into ſhreds, and frittered down into ſhort and unconnected ſentences. I will add, that the compoſing in this way has a bad effect upon the readers or hearers; for it weakens their com-

---

* Introduction to Volume iii. p. 4.

prehenfion, by accuftoming them to take in the fenfe only in fmall parcels, and broken down as it were into pap to feed children. Now, the moft valuable faculty of the human mind, is *comprehenfion*, by which we are enabled to fee a whole at once. In acquiring this faculty, as in acquiring other habits, the mind muft proceed by degrees, and before it can take in a whole oration, an epick poem, a tragedy, or a fyftem of fcience, it muft have learned to comprehend a period. Further, by not being accuftomed to fuch compofitions, one becomes unable to read or pronounce what is compofed in the antient way, or even to underftand it, tho' it be ever fo well read to him; and he is in the cafe of a young beginner to learn Latin, who will not underftand the moft fimple and ordinary compofition in that language, till the words are put in the order of conftruction to which he has been accuftomed in his own language. It is alfo to be confidered, that to pronounce fuch compofition, a good deal of breath is required, and one muft be well-winded, according to the common expreffion. Now, that is to be acquired by practice: And accordingly we are told, that Demosthenes, by exercises of different kinds lengthened his wind, which was naturally short, so as to be able to pronounce his long periods *una continuatione verborum*, as Cicero says *, that is *in one breath*. Mr Garrick, the famous player, not having practised the speaking of such kind of composition, very different from that of Shakespeare, which he had been accustomed to speak, could not, as I have been well assured, pronounce the periods of Milton †; and therefore he avoided acting

---

* Cicero, *de Oratore*, Lib. I. cap. 61.

† There is a period in Satan's speech to Beelzebub, in the first book of Paradise lost, consisting of no less than seventeen lines running into one another; in which, tho' it be so well composed that I think the sense is perfectly clear, those, who are not accustomed to such composition, are, as I have observed, very apt to lose their way. But the scholar knows, that nothing can be truly beautiful, which has not a certain extent and greatness. See Aristotle's *Poetics*, cap. 7. The running the lines into one another, as Milton does, not only makes the versification more beautiful by making the pauses more various, but gives to verse

in any play compofed in that way *: And perhaps that was the reafon which made him refufe the beft play, as it is now generally acknowledged to be, in the Englifh language; I mean the Douglas, a great part of which is compofed in periods †. The ftudy of the antient authors will form our tafte to that kind of compofition; and if we join to the ftudy of them, the practice of tranflating and reciting them, we fhall acquire the habit of writing and fpeaking in

the beauty of profe compofition in periods, as the Halicarnaffian has obferved. See the paffage from him quoted, Vol. ii. p. 396. But Shakefpear, not being a fcholar, and having no idea of this beauty, commonly terminates the fenfe with the verfe, fo that the ftop muft always be at the end of the verfe; which makes his verfification almoft as uniformly tedious as our rhyming verfe, compofed all of fentences confifting each of ten fyllables, with a gingle at the end of every fecond verfe.

* This anecdote I had from the late Mr Glover, who was very well acquainted with Mr Garrick, and, being himfelf a play-writer, attended the theatre very much.

† I doubt there are very few players now in Britain, that can fpeak, as they ought to be fpoken, the

periods, so as to do it as it were naturally. For such is the force of custom, as the Halicarnassian has observed, that by it we can bring ourselves to do with ease the most difficult things; even to compose and pronounce such periods as those of Demosthenes; and for proof of this he gives an example, which to me is most convincing, of our learning the grammatical art, by which we are taught to know all the differences of words, and to read and write readily and easily,—a most wonderful art, he says*. He might have added a more wonderful art still, which we acquire by mere imitation and practice, without being taught, or indeed without being capable of learning the grammatical art, or any other; I

---

first eight lines of this play, where the verses are run together, and the sense suspended to the end, in a way never used in rhyme, and very seldom in blank verse as it is now composed. This composition should be spoken in such a way, that the verse should be marked not only by the accents, but by some little stop at the end of the verse, but much shorter, and of a different kind from the pauses which the sense requires. This is a matter of pretty nice discrimination.

* Περι της συνθεσεως των ὀνοματων, cap. 52.

mean *speaking*. The practice of reciting the orations of antient authors I would recommend particularly to those who would form themselves to be public speakers. I have heard that the Marquis of Wharton formed his son, the Duke, to be one of the greatest, and at the same time one of the readiest speakers that ever was in England, by making him get by heart whole orations of Demosthenes, and repeat them with all the graces of action and pronunciation.

How much stile may be varied by tropes and figures, I have explained at length in the preceding volume. And I shall only add here, that in this, and every thing else which varies and embellishes the stile, a measure must be observed, and there must not be too much any more than too little. For, in that consists the το πρεπον or what is decent and becoming, which is required in every art, and without which there can be nothing truly beautiful in any art [*]. Yet it is not comprehended in a-

[*] See what the Halicarnassian says upon the subject of the το πρεπον, in his admirable treatise περι της δει-

ny art or science, nor can it, by the nature of the thing, be so comprehended, according to the opinion of the Halicarnaffian, tho' Gorgias, as he tells us, endeavoured to reduce it to an art *. Before I come to speak of it, I will bestow a chapter more upon some things relating to the Greek composition, which were reduced to an art among them.

περι των Αμαρτιων, cap. 48, where he says, that if what is becoming and suitable to the subject is not studied, no other beauty in the diction will be of any value. And in this, he says, as well as in other virtues of an orator, Demosthenes was most eminent.

* Περι ρητορικης επιματος, cap. 12.

CHAP. V.

*The beauty of the Greek composition perceived even by the people —Of the difference betwixt a learned and an unlearned judge, in the matter of oratory and of popular writing.—The art of composition best learned from Dionysius the Halicarnassian;—he divides the art into two branches, the choice of the words, and the joining them properly together.—This last, the most difficult of the two.—Two things required to make fine composition, that it should be pleasant, and that it should be beautiful.—These must depend upon the elements of speech properly joined together.—Of the letters, the syllables, and the words in Greek.—Of the changes which their orators made upon their words.—The composition of words into periods, of great variety and beauty.— Four things required to make fine compo-*sition, melody, rhythm, variety, and

Ch. V. Progress of Language. 247

*what is suitable or proper to the subject.
—Of the melody of the Greek language.
—Different tones upon different words
in other languages as well as the Greek,
but not regulated by art.—Of the* rhythm
in Greek.—*Shown that there is a rhythm
in the prose as well as the verse.—A
difference of rhythms suited to different stiles in prose.—Of the difference betwixt the rhythm of verse and of prose.—
The mind much affected by rhythm as
well as by other kinds of motion.—The
greatest excellence of prose is to resemble
verse, and of verse to resemble prose.—
This explained.—Prose resembles verse
by rhythm,—but it must not be the rhythm
of verse —Examples given in the Greek
Lyric poetry, of rhythms that do not appear to be regular or measured.—Examples of such rhythms in Demosthenes.—
That there are such rhythms in prose, attested by Aristotle as well as by the Halicarnassian.--Of poetry in English in which
the verse is concealed.—Of prose in English resembling verse.—How verse is
made to resemble prose.—Examples of
this from Homer and from Milton.—Of*

variety in the prose stile.—That absolutely necessary to make it pleasant.—There must be a variety not only in the words, but of the rhythms and the melody.— Little variety at present in our English prose.—Milton imitates the antients in this as in other things.—Opinions of certain critics in the days of the Halicarnassian, that Demosthenes did not labour his words so much as the Halicarnassian supposes.—Answer to this objection.— The writing of numerous prose, tho' difficult at first, becomes easy by practice.— Examples of this from other arts.—The art of fine speaking and writing more difficult than the other arts;—requires greater labour to excell in it.—A great memory necessarily required in an antient orator.—An art of memory among them, unknown in modern times.—The nature of this art.—If the moderns excell or equal the antients in oratory, it must be by superiority of genius.—Commendation of the Halicarnassian's writings.

THAT there is a wonderful beauty in the Greek compofition, not only in verfe but in profe, and particularly in their orations, every man, who underftands their language, and has any natural tafte or fenfe of what is beautiful, muft acknowledge; for not only can the people judge of an oration whom it is fpoken, and can determine very juftly upon the merit of different orators whom they hear, but they can judge alfo of an oration when they read it. And I am of the opinion of Cicero, that, in the matter of oratory, there is no difference between the judgment of the learned and of the unlearned; for oratory, and fpeaking or writing upon any fubject belonging to common life, is a popular art, which being addreffed to the people, muft pleafe them, otherwife it would not be good of the kind. And tho', as the fame author obferves, the people may approve of a very forry orator, not having heard a better, yet when they have an opportunity of hearing a better, and fo making the comparifon, they will give the preference to the beft *.

Is there then no difference, it will be faid, betwixt the judgment of the learned and the unlearned in this matter? My anfwer is, that there is a very great; for the people, tho' they be pleafed, and rightly pleafed, cannot give any rational account why they are fo: Whereas, the learned judge can inform them by what fkill, and what arts, the orator is able to pleafe them fo much †. In fhort, he underftands the art, while they only perceive the effects of it.

In what this art confifts, no author that I know, has explained fo well as the author I have fo often quoted, the Halicarnaffian, in two treatifes that have come down to us, the one of them upon the fubject *Of the compofition of words*, and which we have entire; the other upon the ftile

* Cicero *De Claris Oratoribus*, cap. 52. and 53.

† Cicero, ibidem, cap. 54.

of Demosthenes; but this is a good deal mutilated and imperfect in many places. In the treatise on composition, he begins, after the manner of the antients when they treat of any art or science, with the first principles of the art, and examines the nature of the first elements of speech, I mean the letters; then he proceeds to syllables, from syllables to words, and from words to sentences and periods. And indeed it is evident, that the pleasure of the ear, about which he only inquires in this treatise, must depend upon all these.

The speaking or writing art consists, he says, of two things, the choice of the words, and the composition; of these, the composition is by far the most difficult; and tho' it be last in practice, he says, it is first in dignity and excellence: This he proves, by comparing it with other arts, such as architecture, where the preparing and polishing the stones is not near so great an art as the putting them together in the building, and also by examples from authors, and particularly from Homer, who of the moſt common words, has, by the art of compoſition, made moſt beautiful poetry *.

To make compoſition fine, he requires two things, *firſt*, That it ſhould be pleaſant or ſweet: And, *ſecondly*, That it ſhould be beautiful†, under which he includes the grave and the dignified. That both theſe things muſt depend upon the five things I have mentioned, viz. the letters, the ſyllables, the words, the ſentences, and the periods, is evident.

As to the Greek letters, I have already obſerved, that the Greek language has in it all the elemental ſounds, which the human mouth, as far as I know, is able to utter. And, in this reſpect, it is different from many other languages I have taken occaſion to mention. I have alſo obſerved, that it compounds ſome of theſe elemental ſounds, making diphthongs both proper and improper: And the Halicarnaſſian, in

---

* Ibid. cap. 2. and 3.

† The τε ἡδυ and the το καλον, as he expreſſes it, Ibid. cap. 10.

Ch. V. Progress of Language. 253

what he writes upon the subject of the letters, observes, that they compound also consonants, making what they call *double* consonants, of which they have three marked by the characters ψ, ζ, ξ, all compounded of the σ for one of the sounds, the first of π and ς; the second of κ and ς; and the third of ς and δ; the σ being first in the last of them, according to the account the Halicarnassian gives of its composition*, if there be no error in the MSS. or printed editions: So that we ought to say, not Νομιδσω, as it is usually pronounced, but Νομισδω†.

As to syllables, I have likewise observed, that the Greek syllables are almost all composed of letters that join easily together, to make one sound; and that they have no syllables compounded of many consonants, some of them mute, some of them liquid, some of them aspirated, and some

* Ibid. cap. 14.

† That this is the true pronunciation, and that there is no error in the MSS. or printed editions, I think Lambert Bos, in his Greek Grammar, p. 36. has very clearly proved.

of them not afpirated; fuch as the word *ftrength* in Englifh, in which there are no lefs than fix confonants, and the laft of them afpirated, of which termination there is no example in Greek.

Of fyllables are compofed words, which by flexion undergo wonderful changes, as I have fhown, in the feveral genders, cafes, tenfes, numbers, and perfons.

The next compofition is of words into fhort fentences, or Κωλα, as they are called by the Halicarnaffian: And here he obferves an art of compofition which is peculiar to the Greek language; for, fays he, in order to make the compofition in thefe fentences pleafant, we muft not only chufe words that fitly join together, and give thofe words fuch a form by flexion, as fuits beft the place they are in; but if even with that, they do not make a pleafant found, we muft alter them by what he calls μετασκευη, that is by adding, taking away, or altering letters. Examples of this will readily occur to every one that is learned in the Greek language; and the

Ch. V. PROGRESS OF LANGUAGE. 255

Halicarnaffian furnifhes two from Demofthenes*.

The next and laſt compoſition, and which crowns the whole work, is of the ſentences into periods, which, as it is the greateſt compoſition of all, there is in it the greateſt variety, and conſequently the greateſt beauty.

All theſe things being attended to, one ſhould think the compoſition would be complete. Antient art, however, did not ſtop here, but required four things more, to make the compoſition pleaſant or beautiful, or both; the firſt is melody, the ſecond rhythm, the third variety, and the

---

* One of them is where Demoſthenes inſtead of ſaying εις τουτον τον αγωνα ſays, εις τουτοις τον αγωνα, In the beginning of the famous oration *pro Corona*; again, he ſays, in the beginning of the oration againſt Ariſtocrates, Μητ' ιδιαν ιχθρας μαθωσας 'ινα' ακιν, where we obſerve an apocope of the vowels ι and α. And he obſerves alſo, the leaving cut or adding the letter ν in the firſt aoriſts, ſuch as ηγαγον; and he mentions alſo their uſing αφαιρισυκαι in place of αφαιριτηριμαι, ibid. cap. 6.

fourth, which he says ought to accompany these three, is, what is becoming and suitable to the subject, or the το πρεπον in one word [*].

What the melody of the Greek language is, I have explained at pretty great length in the second volume of this work, and have mentioned it in several passages of this volume. I shall only add here, that, but for the Halicarnassian, we should have known no more of the science of it, than we do of the practice, and should have believed, that there was no more art in the Greek accents, than in the Chinese, or those of some barbarous nations, or even our own, which we know are various, as I have observed, and different upon different words and syllables, but we cannot reduce them to any rule. There are however, several, who will not believe, even upon the credit of the Halicarnassian, that ever any language was spoken as he says the Greek was spoken. But, in the first place, I think, no man who has learned

[*] Ibid. cap. 11.

but the elements of mufic, can deny, that it is poffible to flide up and down a fifth upon the fame word, or even upon the fame fyllable of a word, if it be a long fyllable. The Chinefe, who pronounce the fame monofyllables with fo many different tones, fpeak with as much eafe as other men, tho' their tones are not regulated with any art, as far as I know. And, 2*dly*, I think it can as little be denied, that a variety of tones, conducted by art and rule, would make an agreeable melody. And, *laftly*, I think it is probable in the higheft degree, fetting afide the authority of the antient authors, that a people fo mufical as the Greeks would join mufic to their language, and make an art of it as much as of mufic, vocal or inftrumental; from which, as the Halicarnaffian tells us, the melody of this language differed only in degree, not in kind or quality *. But fuch arguments, I know, will be loft upon thofe who only learn the antient languages, but who do not make

* Τῃ ποιῃ ᾳ τῳ ποιᾳ, Ibid. cap. 11.

what I think the proper ufe of them, which is to live in the antient world, and there to ftudy the men and the manners, the arts and the fciences. Unlefs we do fo, it is very natural to believe that men are and always have been the fame, in all ages and nations; and that the antient languages, tho' different from the modern, as we fee one modern language is from another, are no better in any refpect.

This notion, of men and their arts having been always the fame in all ages and nations, would difpofe fuch critics to believe, that all that we read in the Halicarnaffian, in Ariftotle, and in Cicero, of the rhythm of the antient profe, was mere imagination: But they have at leaft the idea of the rhythm of long and fhort fyllables; tho' we have not the practice of it, even in reading the antient verfe*. None of thefe gentlemen, however, will be fo bold as to deny that the antient verfe was formed by this rhythm, and not by accent, fuch as that with which we read it. And, as their

* Vol. II. book ii. cap. 6.

prose was composed in the same language as their verse, it is impossible to deny, that their ears must have perceived the quantity of the syllables, in the one as well as the other: And if so, I think it is also impossible to deny, but that they must have judged the rhythms in one prose composition, to be more agreeable than in another.

The only question therefore is, whether this rhythm of prose can be reduced to an art, as well as the rhythm of verse? Now, this is done both by Aristotle and the Halicarnassian, and particularly by the Halicarnassian, who has told us the feet that are proper for the grave and dignified composition, or for such as is rather pleasant and sweet than grave*. And he has illustrated his doctrine by examples from the best prose writers, whose compositions he has scanned, and measured by feet, as carefully as we do Greek or Latin verse; and shown that the feet they use are very well suited to that colour of stile in which they write; and, to illustrate this matter

* Ibid. cap. 17. and 22. 23.

further, he has contrasted the rhythms of those good writers, with the rhythms of a very bad writer, of his own time as it appears, one *Hegesius* *; for, as he tells us in another place, the art of that numerous composition began to be lost about his time. And he shows us, that proper rhythms not only give a beautiful colour to the stile, but are imitative and expressive, particularly of motion, of which he gives a fine example, from the description of Sysiphus and his stone in Homer †. If any body be not convinced of the effect of rhythm in prose, by what Aristotle and the Halicarnassian have said, I refer him to Cicero in his book entitled *Orator*, where, in the passage I have quoted from him above, he speaks of all composition without numbers as loose and dissolute, and no better than the language of vulgar men. He there examines the matter most accurately, and inquires, *first*, Whether there be such a thing as rhythm in prose, which he determines

---

* Ibid. cap. 18.

† Cap. 20.

very clearly in the affirmative: And, 2*dly*, Whether the feet, which conftitute that rhythm, are not the fame with the feet that make verfe. And he fays they are, and fhows what poetical feet are proper for the rhythm of profe*. And, in the fame place, he gives us the hiftory of this art of numerous profe, which, being the completion of the oratorial ftile, was not difcovered till later times †.

But how are we to diftinguifh the rhythm of verfe from that of profe? And the Halicarnaffian tells us, that it is by the rhythm of verfe being exactly meafured, and the fame rhythms returning again at certain intervals: Whereas the rhythm of profe is not reftricted to any certain meafure; nor does it return at certain intervals, but is diffufed thro' the whole compofition, and ufed by the writer or fpeaker in fuch a manner, as, he thinks, moft agreeable to the fubject he treats. And he compares the mixture

* Cap. 56. and 57.
† Ibid. cap. 52.

of the different rhythms in the same composition, to the mixture of colours in a picture, which is very different, according to the genius and taste of the painter, or the subject of the picture *.

That those rhythms of the antient prose, as well as of the antient verse, must have had a wonderful effect upon the minds of the hearers, I cannot doubt. And I believe what the Halicarnaſſian says, that there is nothing of such power to please the ears, or affect the mind †: For, as I have observed elsewhere, it is by motion, more than by any thing else, that paſſions and sentiments are expreſſed; and accordingly, it is in that way the *pantomime art* moves us more perhaps than any other art. Now, rhythm is nothing but various modifications of the motion of the voice. In short, it is just what Time in muſic is; and what the effect of that is, every muſician knows.

* Cap. 21.

† Περι της διοτητος του Δημοσθενος, cap. 39.

I think it is a fine obfervation of the Halicarnaffian, that, with refpect to the compofition, (for he fpeaks only of that part of ftile, not of the choice of words), the greateft beauty of profe is to be like verfe, and of verfe to be like profe *. This re-
*quires fome explanation, and accordingly he gives it †. As to profe refembling verfe, he tells us, that verfe has a certain regular meafure returning at certain intervals, at the diftance of one verfe, as in the heroic poetry, or of feveral, as in ftrophes and antiftrophes in the lyrick poetry; and it confifts of certain feet arranged in a certain order: Whereas profe has no regular return of the fame rhythms, nor is it con-. fined to certain feet in a certain order, but mixes them together as the writer thinks proper; the confequence of which is, that good profe is ευρυθμος, or ευμετρος, not ερρυθμος, or εμμετρος, as verfe is; and again, with refpect to the accents and tones, it is ευμελης, not εμμελης, as mufic is. Thefe

* Ibid. cap. 20. in finn.

† Cap. 25.

terms I cannot render in Englifh, becaufe as we have not the thing, we have not the words for it; but after what I have faid, I am fure the Greek fcholar will underftand them; or if I have not fufficiently explained the matter, let him have recourfe to the Halicarnaffian himfelf, who has explained them much more copioufly and elegantly than I am capable of doing; and he has taken the more pains to do it, that, as it appears from what he fays, it was a myftery to the critics of his time; therefore he invites thofe only, to hear 'οις θεμις εστι, θυρας ετέσεθε βεβηλοις, the form of words they ufed in the myfteries.

What makes the matter very clear to my apprehenfion, is the example he gives of certain fpeciefes of the Greek lyrick poetry whereof the periods or ftrophes as they were called, were fo long, and fo much varied in the compofition, that the regular return of the meafure was forgot*; and in the dithyrambic poetry, he tells us, they mixed the different melodies of the diatonick, the

---

* Cap. 26.

chromatic, and the en-harmonic*, and the Dorian, Phrygian, and Lydian modes †. So that the mufic was as much varied as the poetry; and the rhythms of the poetry were fuch, that it might be faid to be, like the orations of Demofthenes, ευρυθμος not ερρυθμος.

The examples of fuch numerous compofition in profe he takes chiefly from Demofthenes; and particularly from two orations of his, the one the famous oration for *Ctefiphon*, and the other againft Ariftocrates ‡, where he is at pains to fhow, that the rhythms in thofe orations were not accidental, but ftudied: And he compares them to fundry pieces of poetry, where there are the fame rhythms, only Demofthenes has added perhaps or taken away a foot, that it might ftill continue profe.

Vol IV.   L l

* Cap. 19.

† Ibid.

‡ Ibid. cap. 25.

I muſt confeſs, that my ear is not ſo learned, nor I believe is any modern ear, as to perceive thoſe rhythms. But that is no reaſon, why we ſhould diſbelieve what ſo great a critic as the Halicarnaſſian, and himſelf too ſo fine a writer, ſays of them. Or if we ſhould not give credit to the Halicarnaſſian, I think it is impoſſible we can reject the authority of Ariſtotle, who tells us, as the Halicarnaſſian does, that the ſtile of oratory muſt have rhythms, tho' at the ſame time, it muſt not be metre or meaſured rhythm: And he mentions the metrical feet that he thinks proper for oratory *.

But tho' we cannot perceive the rhythms of Demoſthenes, there is certainly a great deal of art in his ſtile, but more concealed than that of any other writer I know, ſo much as not to be diſcovered, except by a learned reader, who has formed his taſte upon the ſtudy of the beſt antient authors, and knows the art, by which, of common words, ſuch as thoſe of Demoſthenes, an uncommon

* *Rhetorica*, lib. 3. cap. 8.

Ch. V. Progress of Language. 267

ſtile may be formed. But of the ſtile of Demoſthenes, which the Halicarnaſſian, I think, with great juſtice, conſiders as the moſt perfect ſtile of oratory, I ſhall ſay a great deal more in the ſequel.

What the Halicarnaſſian ſays, of numbers being concealed even in poetry, may be illuſtrated from ſome Engliſh poetry we have, ſuch as the beginning of the *L' Allegro* and *Il Penſeroſo* of Milton, and particularly from Dryden's ode to St Cecilia, where the rhymes are ſometimes at ſuch a diſtance from one another, that the ear hardly perceives them, nor diſcovers that ſome of the lines do not rhyme at all with any other; and when, beſides that, the verſes are of ſuch unequal length, and differing alſo ſo much in meaſure, ſome of them being *iambics*, others *trochaics*, others *anapeſts*, I think they may be accounted rather meaſured proſe than poetry, but, at the ſame time, more pleaſant to my ear than any regular verſification we have.

What in our proſe comes the neareſt to the looſe numbers, which the Halicarnaſsian requires in fine profe, is the rhapfodies of Theocles in Lord Shaftefbury's dialogue, entitled *the Moralifts*; only the numbers are not concealed as the Halicarnaffian would have them to be, but are too apparent, and therefore make the compofition to be like poetry. There is fome meafured profe of the fame kind, written by his kinfman the late Mr Harris, and fubjoined to his dialogue upon art. The numbers in it are better concealed, but the words are not fo fplendid; nor is there fo much of good compofition in periods, but the fenfe and matter are very good.—And fo much the refemblance of profe to verfe.

As to the making verfe like profe, this is done by compofing poetry, as we do profe, in periods, and making the periods and their feveral members cut the verfe, and run into different verfes. Of this he gives fome beautiful examples from Homer [*], the greateft author, according to his judgment, that ever wrote, and the moft perfect mo-

---

[*] Chap. 16.

del of every beauty of ſtile, either in the words or compoſition *. Of this Milton's blank verſe in the *Paradiſe Loſt* is as good an example as we could have; for we have there periods often of ten or twelve lines, and one I have obſerved in Satan's firſt ſpeech to Beelzebub, in the firſt book, of no leſs than twenty-one lines, divided among the ſeveral verſes; which has a fine effect, giving to verſe all the beauty and variety of proſe compoſition †. How different, in this reſpect, the blank verſe of Shakeſpeare is from Milton's, every reader of taſte and judgment muſt obſerve.

The third thing required to make a fine ſtile is variety, without which, as I have more than once ſaid, there is no beauty in language any more than in ſtile, nor indeed in any work of art. For, as the Halicarnaſſian has obſerved, variety is by na-

* Chap. 24.

† See what I have further ſaid on this ſubject, Vol. II. p. 396.

ture so agreeable to us, that nothing pleases us without it; so that even the finest and most pleasant things do not please us if long continued without variation*; and he requires, that there should not only be a change of words of different kinds, some long and some short, and with different flections; and sometimes composed into periods of different members of various lengths, and sometimes in short sentences without periods, with a variety too of rhythms; but even the tones, he requires, should be varied, so that words of the same tone should not be put together †.

How much variety is wanted both in our verse and prose at present, we may judge by comparing them with those of Milton, who in this, as well as every

---

* Cap. 19. and cap. 12. where he says, Μεταβολη παντος γγου γραμα 'ηδυ. Homer has said long before him,

Παντων μεν κορος εστι, και 'υπνου και φιλοτητος.

† Chap. 12. and 19.

Ch. V. Progress of Language. 171

thing elfe, has imitated the antient compofition as far as the ftinted genius of his language would permit him. How agreeably he has varied his verfe by compofition in periods of different lengths, confifting too of members different both in length and number, I have juft now obferved; and as to his profe, I have given, in the third Volume of this work *, an example of his fkill in compofing rhetorical periods. As to his plain ftile, didactic or narrative, he periodifes it alfo, but in a manner very different. Of this plain ftile you have a very good example in his preface to the *Paradife Loft*, which, tho' it be not fo much varied in the compofition as his rhetorical ftile, (nor indeed ought it to be fo), has nothing of that tedious uniformity, which is to be obferved in our prefent writings.

I will only add upon this fubject, that, as I have elfewhere obferved, to make a fine period, there muft not only be variety in the compofition but in the matter;

* Vol. iii. p. 51.

because it gives occasion to vary properly the tone of the voice, which is the greatest beauty of pronunciation, either in speaking or reading. The players often do this affectedly, and merely to avoid a monotony. This, I think, is more disagreeable, than even a monotony, if the sense require it should be so spoken. But where that is the case, it is a fault in the composition, which is not to be found in the preface that I have mentioned, where there is variety enough in the matter, as well as in the structure of the words, to make a variation of voice, both proper and necessary for making the sense well understood. Let the reader compare the composition of this preface, with the present English and French compositions, (I name them together, because I am afraid they are too like one another), and if he has any taste or judgment, he will perceive the difference more clearly than any words can explain it. As to Milton's Latin, there is as much variety in it as in any Roman writer. In this beauty of stile, more if possible than in any other, Demosthenes excels; and is in that way peculiarly diſtinguiſhed from Iſocrates in Greek, and Cicero in Latin.

I ſhould now ſpeak of the fourth thing, which the Halicarnaſſian requires to make a fine ſtile, I mean *decorum* and *ſuitableneſs to the ſubject*: But of this I am to treat in the next chapter; and I will conclude this with ſome obſervations, which naturally ariſe from what I have ſaid.

And, in the firſt place, tho' it be evident from what I have ſaid, that we cannot have tones and rhythms, ſuch as adorned the antient languages, yet I do not think it impoſſible to vary our proſe compoſition agreeably by our accents. Of this I have given a hint in my third volume * of this work. Our poetry is undoubtedly made by accents, and by accents only and a certain number of ſyllables in our blank verſe. Of theſe we compoſe feet of different kinds, as I have ſhown elſewhere †.

Vol. IV.   M m

* Page 49. and 50.

† Vol. II. p. 383. and following.

such as iambic, trochaic, and anapestic. Now, I know nothing to hinder us to give to our prose certain numbers by a proper mixture of these feet, not returning regularly in a certain order, as in our poetry, but so diffused thro' the stile, as to affect the ear agreeably. The great fault I find with the prose of that kind, which has been attempted in English, is that only one of these feet is used, namely the iambic, and sometimes so used as to make an entire heroic verse, such as we find in Lord Shaftesbury's rhapsody. Now, I would have the other two feet likewise used: In this way Milton has diversified his verse, very finely I think, in the *Comus*; and I am not sure but our prose stile might be agreeably varied in the same way, without being run into poetry. Cicero has made the same observation with respect to the rhythms of antient prose, and finds fault with Aristotle for confining that rhythm to one foot, viz. the *paean*; whereas he thinks, that other feet, such as the *dactyle* and *anapest*, may be admitted, and in short all feet, but so varied and blended together, that the composition may appear not loose or diffolute, yet not altogether numerous or poetical *. These obfervations upon the numbers of our Englifh profe, I only throw out as conjectures, of which perhaps fomething may be made by thofe who have more leifure than I to fpeculate upon fuch fubjects. One certain way of varying not only our ftile in profe, but likewife in verfe, I have already fuggefted; I mean by compofition in periods of various lengths, and confifting of members differing both in length and number. And in thefe periods, there may be ufed thofe ornaments of which I have treated at fome length elfewhere †, by which like is referred to like, contraries oppofed to contraries, with a like ftructure or compofition of words, and claufules or cadencies of the fame kind. Such ornaments our language admits; and thefe, fays Cicero ‡, do of themfelves give numbers to the ftile. But they muft not be intem-

* Orator, cap. 57.

† Vol. III. p. 85. and following.

‡ Orator, cap. 65.

perately or immoderately ufed, otherwife they become difgufting, and in hiftory or narrative of any kind, they deftroy the appearance of truth and reality.

In the next place, the Halicarnaffian tells us, that there were thofe in his time, who could not be perfuaded that Demofthenes was at fo much pains, and beftowed fo much time in meafuring fyllables, and joining words fo artificially together in periods, or members of periods, and in fhort, ringing all the changes upon them poffible. This they thought a drudgery, that no man of fpirit could fubmit to [*]. And, indeed, I do not wonder that the art of compofition being, as he tells us, for the greater part loft in his time, there fhould be critics that did not think that it ever was practifed, to the degree of perfection mentioned by the Halicarnaffian. Neither am I much furprifed, that modern critics, who have not made an accurate ftudy of the pronunciation of the Greek language,

[*] *De Compofitione*, cap. 25.

Ch. V. Progress of Language. 277

and of all the powers of the human voice, should doubt whether it was possible, that any language could be spoken with such a variety of rhythms and accents as he describes: Whereas, the critics of his time, when the Greek was still a living language, and spoken with all that variety, could not but believe that it was possible to compose such prose as he has described, though they might not believe that ever it was practised, or if practised, could have such effects as he ascribes to it.

The answer, which the Halicarnassian makes to this objection, I think, is a good one. He says, that at the time Demosthenes composed those orations, the art of writing was so much studied at Athens, and particularly by Plato and Isocrates, that their compositions appeared to be polished and turned, as it were in a turning loom. Isocrates, he says, bestowed ten years at least, some say more, upon a single oration, viz. his *Panagyric*. And Plato did not give over labouring in the arrangement and trimming of words, when he was eighty years of age, as appeared from his pocket book when he died, in which the firſt ſentence of his work upon Polity was found variouſly arranged. As therefore Demoſthenes laboured ſo much, as is well known he did, to excell every body in the oratorial art, he thought it was neceſſary for him to labour the words as well as the matter, and to make his orations pleaſe the ear as much as the underſtanding. If, ſays the Halicarnaſſian, ſculptors and painters beſtow ſo much time and pains in executing every the leaſt thing belonging to their art in the higheſt degree of perfection, how can we ſuppoſe that Demoſthenes would be at leſs pains, working, not upon corruptible materials ſuch as they wrought upon, but upon ſuch as were to laſt for ever, and to acquire him much greater glory than they could aſpire to. This example, from theſe other arts he mentions, appears to me to be very convincing: For we know, from what remains of the antient ſtatues, that beſides the noble ideas expreſſed by them, and the grace and elegance of the figures, there is an exactneſs, and what we would call a minuteneſs in the execution, that is really wonderful; for the marble is poliſhed in the higheſt degree; and all the ſinews and muſcles ſo finiſhed, that nothing can exceed it.

The Halicarnaſſian then proceeds to tell us, that however operoſe and difficult ſuch elaborate compoſitions as thoſe of Demoſthenes might be at firſt, yet by aſſiduous practice, they would be performed at laſt with tolerable eaſe; and he gives an example to prove this from another art, which I think very appoſite. A man, ſays he, who has learned and practiſed muſic very much, will upon the firſt hearing of a new piece, be able with very little trouble to perform it: And accordingly now-a-days, we ſee that a girl, who has practiſed the harpſicord much, will be able almoſt at ſight to perform a new piece, and will play you at once three or four parts of a tune, after ſhe has ſtudied it a little, with ſo much eaſe, that ſhe will be talking to you all the while.

At the fame time I am perfuaded it is true, what the Halicarnaffian fays, that fuch orations as thofe of Demoſthenes, could not have been compofed without great labour, greater I believe, than any work of painting, fculpture, or mufic. But after the compofition was finiſhed, the labour was not at an end; for the moſt difficult part of the orator's art remained to be performed; I mean the fpeaking, or what they called the *action*: Under which they included not only the gefture of the body, which was very confiderable, (for befides the action of their arms, they walked backward and forward, or to either fide, as I am told the pleaders in Italy do at this day), but the look and action of the face in fpeaking, and alfo the management of the voice, or what we call the pronunciation*. Now action, as Demoſthenes tells us, was the firſt, the fecond, and the third quality

---

* Cicero, *de Oratore*, Lib. i. cap. 5. Quid ego de actione ipfa plura dicam, quae motu corporis, quae geſtu, quae vultu, quae vocis conformatione ac varietate moderanda eſt ? Quae fola per fe ipfa quanta fit, hiſtrionum levis ars et fcena declarant.

of an orator: And the more I attend to public speaking, the more I am convinced of the truth of the observation; for it is by it chiefly that the character of the speaker is indicated, one of the three great sources of persuasion mentioned by Aristotle, and more by it than by what he says are the passions of the hearers excited, which are the second source of persuasion according to Aristotle: And even the arguments from the nature of the thing, the third and last source of persuasion, have a very much greater effect when well spoken, than they have otherwise.

But there is still more in the art of the antient orator: For, before the speech is pronounced, it must be got by heart; as it does not appear that those antient orators used any notes while they were speaking; and yet, among the many defects of orators, which Cicero mentions, I do not remember that any where he speaks of want of memory, except once, where he tells us, that the orator's memory having failed him,

he said he was bewitched *. It is therefore
not without reason that Cicero says, that
without memory, every thing else in an
orator, however great and excellent, is of
no signification †. Now, there was among
them a thing utterly unknown in modern
times, I mean an art of memory; for e-
very thing among them appears to have
been reduced to art and rule: And indeed
I think it is impossible, that without some
such art they could have pronounced o-
rations so very long, and so very well composed, that they could not have been spoken extempore. But we are not left to
argument or conjecture upon this subject;
for that they had an art of memory, is a
fact so well attested, that we cannot doubt
of it. Cicero has spoken of it at some

---

* *Orator*, cap. 37.

† Cicero *de Oratore*, lib. 1. cap. 5. The words are.
'Quid dicam de thesauro rerum omnium memoria,
'quae, nisi custos inventis cogitatifque rebus et verbis
'adhibeatur, intelligimus omnia, etiamsi praeclarissima
'fuerint in oratore, peritura.'

length in his second book *de oratore*, as a thing of common use at that time; for he says, that it is *res nota et pervulgata*. And he tells us, that not only things were preserved in the memory by this art, but even words *. The author of the books, *ad Herennium*, by some critics ascribed to one Cornificius, but undoubtedly the work of an antient rhetorician, treats more fully of it, and is at a great deal of pains to make us understand wherein the art consists †. Both Cicero and he agree in this, that it was by a reference to sensible objects that the memory both of things and of words was preserved. They therefore imagined to themselves certain places or *loci* as they called them, such as houses or porticos; and in these they conceived certain images of things and of words, which places and images suggested to them whatever they were to say. The author, *ad Herennium*, compares the *places* to the

* Lib. 2. *de Oratore*, cap. 87. and 88.

† Lib. 3. *ad Herennium*, cap. 16. and 21.

wax or paper on which they wrote, the *images* to the letters and words composed of those letters, the difposition and placing of those images to the writing, and the pronunciation to reading *. As to the images for the words, Cicero obferves, that that there were fome words, of which there could be no natural image or reprefentation, fuch as the words that connect the feveral parts of difcourfe, commonly called conjunctions: But of thefe, fays he, we muft, from our own imagination, form images which we are conftantly to ufe †. By this art, he tells us, in the fame place, that the natural memory was not oppreffed or impaired, as fome people imagined, but greatly improved. And it was not only practiced in Rome, but in Greece; for Antonius, who there fpeaks, fays, that he himfelf knew two famous men in that country, *Carneades* and *Sceptius Metrodorus*, who both faid that they could in thofe *places*, in their memory, fix the images of things and words, as they could fix letters in wax.

* Ibid. cap. 17.
† *De Oratore*, lib. 2. cap. 88.

Whether this art, from the account given of it by those two authors, could be revived and practiced now a days, I will not take upon me to say. But we are assured by both of them, that the use of it could not be learned without the greatest diligence and most assiduous practice. Yet it was but a small part of the orator's art among the antients, and is now thought so little necessary, that it is not at all studied. But, when we join to it all the other parts of the art practiced among the antients, and all that variety of things which an orator must know to be perfect of his kind *;—And when to all this we further add certain qualities of the body, not required in any other of the fine arts, such as a fine person, a commanding aspect, and a clear and strong voice,

* Crassus, in Cicero *de Oratore*, requires that he should be learned in all arts and sciences; and indeed, if he is to speak eloquently upon any of them, he must understand it; and, even in speaking upon any common subject, he may use illustrations from arts and sciences, which will both adorn his stile, and serve to make his subject better understood.

————*populares*
Vincentem strepitus, et natam rebus agendis [*],

I think we must conclude, as Cicero does, that it is a most wonderful art, and that no other reason can be given why so few have excelled in it, even in countries such as Greece and Italy, where such rewards were proposed to excellence in it, " *nisi rei quandam incredibilem magnitudinem ac difficultatem* [†].' One part of the art only, I mean the composition, tho' not the greatest in the opinion of Demosthenes, required, as I have described it, a diligence and attention, such as there is no example of in our time: So that, if we equal or excel, as some imagine, the antients in the writing art, it must be by a wonderful superiority of genius, which enables us with very much worse materials, and much less industry, to make finer or even as fine compositions.

To those who are not of that opinion but who think as I do, that we never could

---

[*] *Horatii Epistola ad Pisones*; see the quotation from Cicero upon this subject, p. 191.

[†] *De Oratore*, lib. 1. cap. 5.

have invented nor cannot excel in any of
the fine arts, except by the imitation of the
antients, I would earnestly recommend the
reading and the studying diligently of the
Halicarnassian's critical works, without
which, I think it is hardly possible to be a
great performer, or even a good judge in
the writing art. In Aristotle's poetics and
his books upon rhetoric, we have the general and philosophical principles of criticism and good taste very accurately laid
down. But Dionysius is more particular
and instructs you as accurately and minutely, as I believe he did his pupils he taught
at Rome, to one of whom he dedicates his
work *upon composition*, which I have so often quoted. I read him with the greatest
pleasure, not only for the *matter* but for
the *stile*, which, as far as I am able to
judge, is truly Attic, and the most copious
as well as most elegant stile of criticism
that is extant. I do not think that he deserves at all the censure of Photius upon
some Attic writers, that they are too Attic;
by which he means, that their stile is so
artificial as to be obscure, which I think is
true of one great Attic writer, namely Thu-

cydides. This fault the Halicarnaffian has noted in him, but I think has himfelf avoided altogether; for, unlefs where his text is corrupted, I think he is a very clear author, fo clear that, in many places, a good Greek fcholar can, at the firft reading, correct the error of the manufcript. Hudfon's edition from the Oxford prefs is an excellent one; only I think he fhould have taken into the text all the corrections from MSS. which he mentions at the bottom of his page, particularly from the Vattican MS. And there are fome emendations fuggefted by fuch critics as Sylbrugius and Harry Stephen, which are fo evident, that I think he ought to have admitted them into the text, and degraded the common reading to the bottom of the page: And I fhould be very glad if the learned in Oxford would take the trouble to publifh an edition of him in that form, and without a tranflation, fo that it might be carried about in two or three pocket volumes. For it is a book that a fcholar ought

Nocturna verfare manu, verfare diurna.

CHAP. VI.

In judging of what is proper in writing, the subject only to be considered.—Stile, divided according to the subject, is of six kinds,—1. Epistolary stile,—*should be concise, and without any thing like composition in periods.*—*The ancients excelled in that kind of writing as well as in every other.*—2. Dialogue writing,—*That nothing else but conversation written.*—*Of the stile of conversation,—few excel in it.*—*Bodily qualities necessary for that excellence.*—*Some so deficient in these, that it is impossible they can converse agreeably.*—Speaking *and* moving *distinguish a gentleman and lady more than any thing else.*—*Both studied more in France than in Britain.*—*Defects of pronunciation in private conversation may be corrected.*—*Of the fault of too fast speaking.*--*Of the con-*

trary extreme.—Of speaking too slow and with an affected gravity.—Of too strong emphasis in speaking.—Too much study to speak well must not be shown in private conversation.—Provincial and professional dialects to be avoided.—Verses well repeated, an ornament of conversation.—Of politeness in conversation;—four things required in order to be polite.

WHAT is *decent*, *proper*, and *becoming* is principal in all the arts, being that, without which no performance in any art can please; yet it is not nor cannot be comprehended in any art, as Cicero informs us [*] : Nor can it be otherwise perceived, but by a natural sense of the *pulchrum and decorum*, which is the foundation of excellence in all the arts, but which no art or teaching can bestow, if nature has denied it.

[*] (Cicero *De Oratore*, lib. i. cap. 29.) And for this he quotes a great artist in his time, I mean Roscius, so great, that a man, who excelled in any art, was said to be ' a *Roscius* in that art.'

Ch. VI. Progress of Language.

What is fit, decent, or proper in the practice of the writing art, depends upon three things: The nature of the subject; the character of the writer; and, *lastly*, the character and disposition of the persons to whom he writes. The two last considerations belong to public speaking or oratory, rather than to writing; for the author may be altogether unknown, or, if known, his character has commonly nothing to do with his work; and as to those to whom it is addressed, it is the world in general for whom most authors write. It is therefore the subject of the writing which I shall only consider, as that which must determine what is fit, proper, and becoming in the stile and manner of treating it.

According to this way of considering stile, there will be six different kinds of stile to be examined: The epistolary stile; The dialogue stile; The narrative or historical; The didactic; The rhetorical; And, lastly, the poetical. I will begin with the epistolary.

As the subject of a letter is commonly the ordinary affairs of life, such as are talked of in converfation, the ftile of it, as well as of converfation, fhould be plain and fimple, confifting of words of common ufe, and without periods or any thing that can be called compofition. It fhould be lefs diffufe than the ftile of converfation, but it muft have nothing of the affected and obfcure brevity of Tacitus. It may be compared with the philofophical ftile in this refpect, that it ought to be both accurate and concife, and without any afcititious ornaments: And therefore it is not to be wondered that Ariftotle, whofe philofophical ftile is fo admirable, fhould excell fo much in letter writing, as we are told he did *. There are no letters of his preferved; but there are many of other antients, more than fufficient to fhew their excellence in that kind of writing, as well as in every other †.

---

* Vol. iii. of this work, p. 353.

† In p. 206. of the fame Volume, I have given the words of a letter of Lentulus, preferved to us by Salluft. I will give here the words of a letter of Julius Caefar, to his friends Appius and Cornelius, which Cicero has preferved to us, lib. ix. *epift. ad Atticum* epift. 16.

Ch. VI. Progress of Language. 293

I am now to speak of the stile of dialogue, which, being no other than a writ-

' *A. D. vii. Id. Mart. Brundusium veni: ad murum
' castra posui. Pompeius est Brundusii; misit ad me Cn. Ma-
' gium de pace. Quae visa sunt respondi. Hoc vos statim
' scire volui. Quum in spem venero de compositione aliquid
' me conficere, statim vos certiores faciam. Valete.*'

If his Commentaries had been written in the same stile, it would, no doubt, have been approved of by the late French writers, particularly by Montesquieu, who writes great works much in the same stile. But the stile of Caesar's Commentaries is quite different; and is, I think, the best memoir-stile that ever was written, though it has not that elaborate composition, which a formal history requires. I will mention another letter of Julius, which has more of composition in it, very suitable, I think, to the noble sentiment expressed in it. It is also preserved to us by Cicero, in the 10. book of his letters to Atticus, epist. 9.; and appears to be an answer to a letter of Cicero, in which he told Caesar, that several of the Pompeian faction, who had fallen into his hands and whom he had dismissed, had taken up arms against him. The words are, ' *Neque illud me movet, quod ii, qui a me di-
' missi sunt, discessisse dicuntur, ut mihi rursus bellum infer-
' rent; nihil enim malo, quam et me mei similem esse, et illos
' sui.*' See what I have further said upon the epistolary stile of the ancients, p. 218. of this volume; where I have shown, that in their epistolary stile

ten converfation, muft of neceffity imitate
the ftile of real converfation. This leads
me naturally to fay fomething of that ftile,
for which I do not find any precepts given
in any antient author: And Cicero feems
to doubt, whether it could be reduced to
an art. But he adds, that tho' there
were very many mafters of rhetoric, there
were none of the ftile of converfation, as
there were none who defired to learn it [*].
But whether it be reducible to art or not,
it is certain that it is better and worfe
performed; and though it be of more
common ufe than any art, it is furprifing
how few excel in it. The reafon of this
is, that, befides tafte and judgment, converfation, as well as public fpeaking, re-

they made much lefs ufe of that artificial arrangement
of words, which their language permitted, than in o-
ther ftiles. And in general it may be obferved, that
by compofition the antients diverfified their ftile much
more, than by the choice of words; for it is by the
arrangement of the words, and by compofition in periods, that Demofthenes has made, of common words,
the fineft profe ftile that ever was written.

[*] *De Officiis*, lib i. cap. 37.

quires some bodily talents not commonly met with. And first, there must be a good voice, sweet and clear, if not strong and commanding like that of a public speaker. I have known some, who were blessed by nature with so sweet a tone of voice, that almost every word they spoke went to the heart of the hearer. Then there must be a distinct articulation, a pleasant look, and an agreeable action of the face in speaking. In all those natural endowments, I have known many so deficient, that it was impossible, by any teaching or practice, to make them agreeable in private conversation, any more than good public speakers.

There are two things which distinguish a gentleman and lady in company, more than any other thing I know. These are moving and speaking, both of which we have occasion to practice as often as we are in company, but neither of which is sufficiently cultivated in Britain. In France, the grace of motion is very much studied, and the people of that country have so high a taste of beauty, that they prefer the beauty of that kind to the beauty of either face or shape; and it is undoubtedly by nature preferable, as it is more expressive of mind, the source of all beauty, than either of the other two. They are therefore at pains to form every motion a gentleman or lady has occasion to make in company, and particularly their motion when they first enter a room. And the effect of this culture is very visible in their behaviour; for I have frequently seen a Frenchman, without any advantages of face or person, enter a room, and present himself, as they call it, with an air and presence that surprised me*. Nor is the other accomplishment, of speaking agreeably, neglected among them: And accordingly I have known many French gentlemen and ladies, who excelled also in that qualification.

Of these two so essential parts of education, one is almost entirely neglected in

* The highest eulogium the French can make upon a man's person, is to say Il a l'air noble; on the other hand, the worst thing they can say of a man's appearance, is Il a l'air ignoble.

Ch. VI. Progress of Language.

Britain; I mean the grace of motion, which is but too vifible in the appearance and behaviour of many of our people of the firft rank. The other is cultivated in the fchools of England, but only in the way of public fpeaking, the tone and manner of which is, and ought to be, quite different from private converfation, but upon which there is no attention at all beftowed; and the boys are allowed to prate in private as they think fit. Neither is it minded by their tutors and preceptors when they grow up and come into the world; the confequence of which is that, as I have faid, fo few fpeak well in converfation. Now, it is evident that defects of voice, articulation, and action, may in fome degree be remedied, and any natural advantages improved by art and teaching. And particularly there is one very great fault in fpeaking, and which prevails more and more every day, efpecially among the young people, that might be entirely cured, if parents and mafters would give a proper attention to it. The fault I mean is speaking too fast. In my younger days, the people of fashion in England spoke with a certain gravity and dignity becoming their rank; and there was a remarkable difference in that respect betwixt the city and the court end of the town. Now, a young gentleman of the first rank talks or rather prates like a waiter in a city tavern, in such a glib, pert, flippant manner, as to me is very offensive, and indeed, sometimes not intelligible. At the same time the contrary extreme is to be avoided; for we should not speak too slow, nor affect a gravity and dignity which only belong to public speaking, and this too upon great and important occasions. Nor should we lay too many or too strong emphases: For that is a fault even in public speaking, because it destroys the smoothness and flow of the speech, making it proceed by hops and bounds; and besides, if there be too many emphases, there is truly none at all. There are many who speak too low, more than speak too loud, at least in good company. But we should suit the pitch of our voice to the number of the company. There are many too,

Ch. VI. Progress of Language.

who speak while they are laughing: But this is not right. To speak with a smile is agreeable, especially if the action of the face in smiling is beautiful. But to speak and laugh at the same time, is not graceful; and besides, it makes the pronunciation inarticulate, and very often not intelligible. As to the words, they should be of common use, and not affectedly learned, or *Johnsonian*, as I have heard them called *. And there should be nothing like composition in periods in private conversation, any more than in letter writing; and in general, we ought not to seem to labour to speak well. This persons are apt to do when they speak any language other than their native; and I have particularly observed it in Scotsmen

* There is a definition of *Network* in Johnson's dictionary, which has been shown me, and, I think, is a curiosity of the kind. ' *Nettwork*,' says he, ' is Any thing reticulated or decussated at equal distances, with interstices between the interfections.' This may not be a good definition of Network, but it is a very good description of the author; for nothing characterises a pedant more than the use of hard words, not intelligible except to a few, in describing a common thing.

who have learned to speak English after they were become men, and who, though they speak it well, may be discovered by a nice ear to speak a language that is not native to them. It was in this way, that the herb woman in Athens discovered Theophrastus, when he was cheapening some of her herbs, to be a foreigner; for he spoke, as she said, *Nimis Attice*, though he had been then twenty years, as I remember, in Athens: But it seems, the habit he had formed, when he first began to speak the Attic, still remained with him.

There is an Attic in every country, as well as there was in Greece. The Attic in England is the language of the court and of the universities. But there are many provincial dialects: And besides these, there is what may be called a professional dialect, belonging to men of certain professions; for I have observed several gentlemen of the law, and more of the clergy, who had not been much in good company, speak in a tone and manner very different from people of fashion, and which I thought not at all beautiful. Such peculiarities ought to be avoided. And, lastly, I would advise the student of this art of conversation, to learn to repeat *with good accent and good discretion*, verses in English or any other language, which he and the company may understand, and to acquire that *suavitas oris*, which, Cornelius Nepos tells us*, recommended Pomponius Atticus so much to the great men of Rome. And indeed, good verses, properly introduced and well repeated, are in modern times, as they were in antient, one of the greatest ornaments of conversation.

A good deal more might be said upon the subject of conversation: And it is a subject worthy to be treated of at much greater length ; for it is in conversation that politeness is chiefly shewn. Now, I don't know that, in the state of society in which we live, there is any greater enjoyment than polite conversation, which may be considered as productive of the greatest blessing of human life, friendship. But my subject confines me to speak only of

---

* *In vita Attici,* cap. 1. 4. et 20.

the stile of conversation; however, as I have mentioned politeness, I will add that four things appear to me to be necessary ingredients of politeness. In the *first* place, a general benevolence or love of mankind, which makes what the French call the *politesse naturelle*, and without which politeness is mere form and etiquette. Now, there are many men of this age, that have not in their nature the philanthropy of a Newfoundland dog, who will not bark or growl at a stranger who comes to his master's house at a proper time, but, on the contrary, will fawn upon him, bidding him as it were welcome to the house. Nay, I know men, who are not only wanting in general benevolence, but have not that attachment to any one of their own species, which every dog has to his master. 2*do*, A polite man must know the company in which he converses, and what measure of respect is due to each of them. For an undistinguishing civility, without regard to rank, worth, sense, or knowledge, is not politeness. 3*tio*, He must be so much of a philosopher, as to know himself, and not to assume more, in regard of any of the particulars above mentioned, than belongs to him. In one word, he muſt not be vain; for vanity, tho' it may be concealed for ſome time, will break out upon certain occaſions, and give great offence to thoſe you converſe with. And, *laſtly*, a man, in order to be polite, muſt have the ſenſe of the *pulchrum* and *decorum*, and of what is graceful and becoming in ſentiments and behaviour, without which there is nothing amiable or praiſe-worthy among men. And, as this ſenſe is the foundation of all virtue, it was not, I think, without reaſon that the Stoics reckoned politeneſs, or *urbanity* as they called it, among the virtues.

CHAP. VII.

Dialogue writing is conversation upon the subject of some art or science.—Not a mere catechism, but of the poetic kind, having a fable with characters and manners;—not therefore real conversation, such as the Socratic conversations recorded by Xenophon.—Plato the great dialogist of antiquity.—His dialogues fictious even as to the matter.—Some of them admirable pieces of poetry;—but he does not succeed when he delivers whole systems of science in that way.—Aristotle's manner in such works much better.—The stile of dialogue should be simple.—Plato's stile not so in some of his dialogues.—A poetical arrangement of the words affected by him.—Cicero the next great dialogist of antiquity;—his manner quite different from Plato's:—Wherein that difference consists.—His stile also very different from Plato's;—great variety of matter in his phi-

Ch. VII. PROGRESS OF LANGUAGE. 305

lofophical dialogues.—*The fect of philofophy, to which he was addicted, furnished arguments upon both fides of a queftion.*—*They are full alfo of examples from both Greek and Roman hiftory.*—*The rhetoric of them better than of his orations,*—*his dialogues on the fubject of eloquence, and in general his writings upon eloquence, the beft part of his works.*—*Eloquence the delight and ftudy of his life;*—*philofophy he only applied to when he could do nothing better.*—*Nothing therefore new or excellent in his philofophical works;*—*but his rhetorical, admirable of the kind.*—*Only two rhetorical dialogues;*—*of thefe the one* De Oratore, *the beft thing that ever Cicero wrote;*—*it is perfect of the kind, having both fable and characters:*—*The perfonages in this dialogue;*—*not all the fame the fecond day that they were the firft:*—*The difference accounted for:*—*The time and place of the dialogue marked:*—*The endurance of it alfo:*—*That more confiftent with probability, than the length of fome of Plato's difputations:*—*It is divided into*

VOL IV. Q q

two days.—*The disputation of the first contained in Cicero's first book.—The subject of that disputation.—The second day's disputation divided into two conversations; the one in the forenoon, the other in the afternoon.—The forenoon's conversation contained in the second book.*—Antonius *the speaker there, who goes thro' all the subject matter:—The narration is agreeably diversified by one of the personages explaining that part of eloquence, which consists in pleasantry and facetiousness.—The* third *conversation in the afternoon of the second day.—This contained in Cicero's third book.—The scene of it changed.*—Crassus *the chief speaker there, who explains all the ornaments of speech.—The exordium of this third book very fine, and very pathetical, giving an account of the calamities, which after that befel the commonwealth, and in which most of the speakers in that dialogue perished.—Of the grand idea of an orator which Crassus had.—It comprehends, according to him, the knowledge of arts and sciences.—In antient times, the knowledge of things and words was* not divided.—This division first made in the schools of philosophers.—Answer to the objection that it is impossible to learn so many things.—A pause after this in the conversation, which is interrupted by Cotta putting Crassus in mind of the province he had undertaken, which was to explain the manner of an oration, as Antonius had done the matter;—Crassus accordingly explains the ornaments of single words;—of words in composition;—of rhythms;—of what is decent and proper; and lastly, of pronunciation and accent.—Cicero concludes the dialogue, with a compliment to his friend Hortensius from the mouth of Crassus.—Of the decorum observed in this last day's conversation with respect to those who speak.—The speech of Crassus the most laboured part of the dialogue.—Cicero there gives his own idea of the perfect orator.—That idea a true idea;—without that universal knowledge, an orator cannot be rich in the ornaments of speech, nor have that elevation of mind necessary for a great speaker.—He cannot be such a speaker as Pericles.—The dialogue upon the whole the *finest* part *of Cicero's works.—Of his treatise* De Senectute,—*not a dialogue, but a most pleasant little composition.—A translation of it into Greek by Theodorus Gaza.—Another little treatise of Cicero upon Friendship.—That comes nearer dialogue than the former.—Some general observations upon Cicero's dialogues.— Cicero more happy in the choice of the personages of his dialogues than Plato.— Also much greater politeness in Cicero's dialogues than in Plato's.—The best school of politeness to be found, is in Cicero's dialogues.—Cicero's dedication of his works to some friend, much to be approved of.— Those dedications show, that he had a heart capable of friendship.—The advantages of philosophy, friendship, and the society of such men as he lived with in those days, and in these.*

DIALOGUE writing is nothing elfe but converfation in writing, not converfation however upon the ordinary

Ch. VII. PROGRESS OF LANGUAGE. 309

affairs of life, but upon matters of art or science. It was by converfation among men of leifure collected together in colleges, fuch as the priefts of Egypt were, that, I believe, arts and fciences were invented: And I am fure, that, at this day, they are beft taught in that way; for the fcholar both learns and remembers beft, when, in the way of queftion and anfwer, he is made to teach himfelf *.

But dialogue writing muft not be a mere catechifm of art and fcience. There muft be character and manners in it, and fomething of a fable or ftory. It is therefore a kind of poetry; and though it may be founded in fact, as moft of the fables in poetry are, there muft likewife be a great deal of invention in it, otherwife it will be a forry dialogue. I hold therefore, that the converfations of Socrates recorded

---

* There is a fine example of this in the *Meno* of Plato, where an illiterate flave is by Socrates made to teach himfelf a curious problem of geometry.

by Xenophon, being real conversations, are not dialogues properly so called, any more than a real story, that has happened in life, is a tragedy or a comedy; for in every thing of the poetical kind, there must be what the painters call ideal beauty, and which is not to be found in nature, but only in the works of artists.

The most famous writer of dialogues in antient times, is Plato; and his dialogues are undoubtedly fictions, sometimes even as to the matter: For he has put into the mouth of Socrates a great deal of that τερατώδης σοφια of Pythagoras, as Xenophon calls it, meaning no doubt, that abstruse metaphysical philosophy which Plato had learned in Egypt, or from the Pythagoreans[*]. There is a story or fable in all of them, with circumstances of time and place as well as of persons. And in some of them, such as *the Gorgias* and *Protagoras*,

---

[*] See Xenophon's epistle to Eschines, preserved to us by Stobaeus, and printed at the end of Stephen's edition of Xenophon.

the characters and manners are so well painted, and such turns and incidents, and what may be called *peripeteias* contrived, that I think them very compleat dramatical pieces. In such dialogues I think he is admirable; but when he comes to deliver whole systems of polity and government, as he does in his *books of polity and laws*, where the same converfation is carried on through ten books in the one, and twelve in the other, the dialogue is lost, such a fiction being out of all bounds of probability: Nor are the characters preserved; for even the irony of Socrates is laid afide, and in the books I have mentioned, instead of pretending to know nothing, he becomes a dogmatical teacher. In such long works, I think it must be allowed, that the plain didactic manner of his scholar Aristotle is better.

As dialogue is conversation, the stile of it should be simple; but as the subject of it is much above the subject of ordinary conversation, so the stile of it may be more raised. Plato's stile, says the Halicarnasfian, while he keeps to the Socratic dialogue, is admirable; but when he becomes rhetorical as in *the Menexenus*, or enthufiaftical as in *the Phaedrus*, he becomes much worfe than himfelf, to ufe an expreffion of the Halicarnaffian. His fcholar Ariftotle faid of his ftile, as Diogenes Laertius reports, that is was neither verfe nor profe. This I do not underftand to relate to the words and phrafes, which, except in the fingle dialogue of *the Phaedrus*, are all, as far as I am able to judge, fufficiently profaical, but to the numbers and rhythms which he ftudied fo much, as appears from the ftory of his pocket-book, found about him when he died *; and for the purpofe of pleafing the ear in that way, he often ufes a very extraordinary arrangement of his words, of which I have given elfewhere an example †.

The next moft famous dialogift of antiquity is Cicero: His manner in his philofophical dialogues, is entirely different

---

* See Vol. ii. of this work, p. 567.

† Ibid. p. 569. in the note.

from Plato's. In the firſt place, his diſputations are not in the Socratic way of queſtion and anſwer, but in what may be called Orations, as in the treatiſe *De Natura Deorum*, *De Finibus*, and his *Academic Queſtions*, alſo his books *De Divinatione*, *De Fato*, *De Legibus*. But they ſo far reſemble Plato's dialogues, that the perſonages are real, and of different characters and opinions. They have alſo the circumſtances of time and place; and further I believe they are as much fiction as Plato's dialogues; at leaſt, with reſpect to the academic queſtions, he has expreſsly ſaid ſo. 2*do*, His five books of *Tuſculan Queſtions* cannot be ſaid to be dialogue at all, according to my definition of dialogue; for there are neither fable, character, or manners in them, only a converſation betwixt Cicero and a ſcholar whom he inſtructs, and who propoſes to him the queſtion about which he deſires to be ſatisfied. So that it reſembles more the manner of the ſophiſts, who at the Olympic games, or any other panegyric of Greece, uſed to deſire any body to propoſe a ſubject to them, and they would give a diſcourſe upon it. And, *laftly*, Plato never appears himself in any of his dialogues, whereas Cicero appears in all his, either in the beginning, the end, or through the whole.

I will speak first of Cicero's philosophical dialogues, (if the reader is pleased to give them that name), in which the manner is not only very different from that of Plato, but the stile; for it is of the rhetorical kind, and he professes to adorn philosophy with the flowers, or, as he calls them, the *lights* of eloquence. And indeed he practised speaking so much, not only in real causes but in fictitious, (for he declamed even when he was old and had retired from business, during Caesar's government,) that it is a wonder that any of his writings, even his familiar letters, are free of a taint of the declamatory stile, or that he could write in any other. His stile therefore is more copious than that of Plato, and much more ornamented: Nevertheless, it is not deficient in philosophical accuracy; and he has interspersed with it, here and there, the Stoical *spinosum genus dicendi*, as he calls it, which makes not only a variety, but is a perfect contrast to his

Ch. VII. PROGRESS OF LANGUAGE.

diffuse rhetorical stile of philosophy; for, if we may judge by the specimens we have of it, it hardly deserves the name of stile, any more than Euclid's Demonstrations. In his philosophical dialogues, there is a prodigious variety of argument upon every topic of philosophy, which Cicero was well able to furnish, having heard or conversed with all the famous philosophers of his time, and read the works of those who had gone before them, and he himself was of a sect, which held that nothing was certain, but only one thing more probable than another *; therefore he listened to the arguments of all the sects, and, in order to try the validity of their arguments, disputed against them all. In short, the dialogues of Cicero are most rich both in

* This sect was called the *New Academy*, the philosophers of which I think could not have been so good geometricians as those of the *old*; nor indeed does it appear to me, that they could have learned the elements of geometry, and, at the same time, have maintained that there was no such thing as certainty. And I should suspect that Cicero, who professed himself of that sect, had not studied geometry; for it is, I think, impossible, that, where the ideas are so simple, and expressed by such visible signs, and where the definitions and divisions are so clear, and the axioms, from whence the demonstrations are deduced, so perfectly evident,

words and arguments; and, when to that we join the many examples from the Greek and Roman hiftory, with which he fupports and illuftrates his arguments, I think we may pronounce them to be among the moft entertaining and inftructive works in the world, and which ought to be read by every man who would fill his mind with great ideas. His rhetorical ftile in them too I like much better than that of his orations, becaufe there is more variety in it; for it is not fo loaded with antithefes, nor with that kind of rhythm, which is made by a number of words and phrafes, of like form and ftructure, ftrung together, very different from the true *Numerus Oratorius*, but, which, no doubt, was applauded in the fchools of declamation at Rome, though it would not have been tolerated in Athens *. Neither is the compofition

there any man fhould have a doubt that there was certainty, at leaft in geometry. It was not therefore without reafon, that Pythagoras laid the foundation of his philofophy in geometry and arithmetic, as his fcholars thereby got the idea of what fcience and certainty was.—See what I have faid upon this fubject, p. 7. of Preface to Vol. III. of *Antient Metaphyfics*.

* See Vol. III. of this work, p. 81.—87.—90. where I have given fundry examples of that kind of concinnity, or *prettinefs* as it may be called, in Cicero's ftile.

Ch. VII. Progress of Language. 317

so uniform by the periods and the several members of them almost always terminating in a verb, a fault to which all Latin composition is more or less liable, as I have elsewhere observed *.

But though I esteem very much his philosophical dialogues, I think his dialogues upon eloquence, and in general his writings upon that subject, the best part of his works: For to philosophy he only applied, when he had nothing else to do, which was hardly ever the case before the civil wars. But the tribunals, the senate, and the forum, where he could shew his eloquence, were the occupations he delighted in. He had the best education as a speaker, that the world could then afford; for he was taught both at home and abroad by the best masters, and he constantly practised at the bar from his early youth: Nor did he for that interrupt the practice of declamation, to which he had been accustomed under his masters, but declamed in public till he was praetor, and after he had gone through all the great offices of state, when the ci-

* Page 95. and following of this Volume.

vil wars and the domination of Caesar
had put an end to his business in the forum
and the senate, he continued still the practice among his friends in his Tusculan villa, where, as he tells us, he had two Gym-
nasia. In the upper one, which he called
Lyceum, (the name of the place where
Aristotle taught), he practised his rhetorical exercises in the forenoon; and in the
afternoon he descended to what he called
his Academy, (the name of Plato's school,)
and there he held his philosophical dispu-
tations *. What he has written therefore
upon philosophy I consider only as compilements from Greek books, and these
not always the best, (for it is evident,
that he had not studied the philosophical
works of Aristotle †, who, he tells us, was

---

* Lib. i. cap. 5. De Divinat.—Tuscul. Quaest. lib.
iii. cap. 3.—Ibid. lib. 2. cap. 3.

† We need no other proof of this, than his saying
somewhere that Aristotle believed the Deity to be material; the contrary of which must be well known to
every man who has read the metaphysics of Aristotle,
which, it appears to me, that Cicero never studied,
nor any of his esoteric works. He therefore ascribes
to Aristotle the opinion of the Stoics, who, no doubt,

at that time, but little read and esteemed in Rome), and he would no doubt set down what he remembered of the conversations he had had with Greek philosophers then living. But as to eloquence, I believe there is in his writings every thing valuable that was to be found in any Greek book, and, over and above that, many excellent observations, which so long experience in so many causes public and private, and in so much business both in the senate and forum, must have suggested to a man of so much genius as Cicero. And besides, in his rhetorical writings, we have a very complete history of eloquence, its beginning and progress both in Greece and Rome.

Of all that he has written upon the subject of rhetoric, there are only two pieces in the form of dialogue, namely, the three books *De Oratore*, and the single book

believed that God was a material Being, and who appear to me to have been so little learned in metaphysical philosophy, and so vulgar in their notions, (however paradoxical they may have been in other things), as not to have had so much as the idea of an immaterial Being.

De Claris Oratoribus, the others being differtations, fuch as the *Orator ad M. Brutum*. Of thefe two dialogues, the laft mentioned is for the greater part, as the title bears, hiftorical, giving an account of the Romans who before his time excelled in eloquence. But the other takes in the whole compafs of the art; and, for the variety of the matter, the diverfity of the characters of the fpeakers, the conduct of the piece, and the elegance of the compofition, is, in my opinion, the fineft thing Cicero has written; and I am not fure, but it is the beft of the dialogue kind that is extant.

The perfonages in this dialogue, are Lucius Craffus, and Marcus Antonius, the two moft famous orators at that time in Rome, and both confular and cenforian men; with them was Quintus Mucius Scaevola, a famous lawyer of thofe days, whofe houfe, like that of all the great lawyers, was an oracle in the city, reforted to by men of the higheft rank and dignity[*]. Neither was he unlearned in phi-

[*] Lib. i. *De Oratore*, cap. 45.

losophy, and he was reckoned the most eloquent of all the lawyers. He was the oldest man of the company, and the father-in-law of Crassus. Besides these, there were two young men, Cotta and Sulpicius; from the first of whom Cicero is supposed to have got his information of what passed in the company. Cotta was a professed admirer and follower of Crassus; and both he and Sulpicius were very promising young men, and coming on very well in the art of speaking; and Sulpicius is described by Crassus, as having peculiar advantages of person, action, and voice[*]. These were all the interlocutors of the first day. But, on the second day, they were joined by an old man, Quintus Catulus, an orator too, but none of the most eminent, and Caius Julius Caesar his brother, who excelled in one part of the art, namely pleasantry and jest. As nothing should happen by accident in a well conducted fable, Catulus informed Crassus, who seemed to be a lit-

[*] Ibid. cap. 29.

tle surprised at their coming, that the evening before, when Caesar was coming from his Tusculanum to that of Catulus, he met upon the way Scaevola, who was coming from the Tusculanum of Crassus, and informed him of the learned conversation they had had that day, and how Crassus had been prevailed upon to lecture upon eloquence, as if he had been in a Greek school *.

The scene therefore of this dialogue is Crassus's villa in the Tusculanum; and the time was when a violent dispute was going on between Philip the consul, and Drusus the tribune of the people, who took a part very unusual for a tribune, which was to defend the cause of the Patricians and of the senate against the consul. During this dispute, the *Ludi Romani* were celebrated, which making a vacation in business, Crassus during that festivity, retired to his Tusculanum, together with

* Ibid. lib. ii. cap. 3.

Marcus Antonius and Quintus Mucius Scaevola his father-in-law.[*]

As to the time of the endurance of the dialogue, it is not spun out to an immoderate length, as I have observed that Plato's two dialogues *De Republica et De Legibus* are, but is divided into two days. In the conversation of the first day, which makes the subject of Cicero's first book, Crassus in order to incite the two young men, Cotta and Sulpicius, to prosecute their oratorial studies, began a discourse in praise of eloquence, which he extolled as the art not only of the greatest dignity and splendor, but of the greatest use, and also of the greatest extent, comprehending in it all other arts and sciences. This occasioned a dispute between him and Scaevola, who maintained that the art was neither of such use nor such extent, as Crassus would make it to be. Crassus answers his arguments, and mentions several arts which the orator ought to understand, particularly the ci-

[*] Lib. i. cap. 7.

vil law *, or the *ars boni et acqui*, as the doctors of law define it. In this dispute, every one of the company takes a part more or less; for Cicero takes care that the dialogue shall never run into dissertation: Particularly Antonius declared his opinion, that Crassus measured the extent of the art by his own genius, not by its real bounds and limits, which confined it to the business of the forum †. Then, says Crassus, as you have confined the art within such narrow limits, you can the more easily deliver the precepts of it;—but to-morrow;—For as Scaevola has appointed to go to his villa this evening, and the heat of the day is now coming on, during which it will be proper for him to rest, it is proper now to part.

In this second day's conversation, Scaevola is not present; for he had gone the evening before to keep an appointment,

* Lib. I. cap. 36. et seq.
† Ibid. cap. 49.

as he said, with Laelius in his own villa *, and did not return next day. Antonius, in the forenoon, proceeds to execute the part which Crassus had assigned to him, and explains fully and distinctly all the matter of an oration, where he treats of the several *loci* or topics, from which the arguments are to be drawn in different causes; and shows how these arguments are to be disposed and arranged; shows also, what is to be done in the several parts of an oration, such as the prooemium, the narration, the confirmation, the refutation, and the peroration. Cicero here too, has avoided the appearance of differtation, or continued discourse; for, though Antonius is the chief speaker, the others break in very frequently, either asking questions or making observations, and particularly Julius Caesar entertains the company very agreeably upon a part of oratory, in which, as I have said, he excelled, viz. in pleasantry and facetiousness. This subject he explains methodically, and illustrates by many exam-

* Lib. i. cap. 62.

ples, which, I believe, are a collection of almost all the witty sayings of that age and the preceeding *.

The next conversation was in the afternoon of the same day, when, after having reposed a little, according to their custom, at mid-day, they met together in the middle of the wood, where it was cool and shady †, and there they sat down; for their manner was to converse walking in the forenoon, but sitting in the afternoon. And then Crassus began upon the subject which Antonius had assigned to him, viz. the manner of the orator, and the ornaments of diction, pronunciation, and action, with which the matter that Antonius had explained was to be clothed and dressed.

This is the subject of the third book, which Cicero begins with informing his brother Quintus Cicero, to whom the whole work is addressed, of the fate of Crassus,

* Lib. ii. cap. 58. et sequen.

† Lib. iii. cap. 5.

and of the other interlocutors in this day's debate. Craſſus, he ſays, died in a few days after, having over-heated himſelf by ſpeaking with great vehemence in the debate above mentioned, betwixt Philip the conſul and Druſus the tribune. While he was ſpeaking, he was ſeized, he ſays, with a pain in his ſide, and that ended in a fever, of which he died in a few days; a death, ſays Cicero, to be lamented by his friends, his country, and all good men: But, ſoon after, ſuch calamities befel the commonwealth, *ut mihi non erepta Lucio Craſſo a diis immortalibus vita, ſed donata mors eſſe, videatur.* Then he proceeds to relate how, in the contention betwixt Sylla and Marius, all the perſons who were preſent in that day's converſation, were either put to death or driven into exile. And, here we may obſerve, that by Cicero himſelf appearing in this work, by which, as I have obſerved, his dialogues are diſtinguiſhed from thoſe of Plato, this moſt beautiful and moving paſſage is introduced, which otherwiſe could not have been done with ſo much propriety.

Craſſus begins with obſerving, that Antonius, in dividing the taſk betwixt them two, had ſeparated two things, which in nature never can be ſeparated;—the things which are the ſubject of the oration, and the words. That, in ancient times, there was no ſuch ſeparation of the knowledge of things, from the art of words;—to think and act properly, and to ſpeak well, was one and the ſame ſcience, and that which Phoenix taught Achilles. The diviſion was firſt made in the ſchools of philoſophers, who reſerved to themſelves the knowledge of things, but aſſigned, to certain profeſſors they called Rhetoricians, the province of teaching words. But the two cannot be divided without great injury to both: For the knowledge of things cannot be uſeful, if they be not properly expreſſed in words; and nothing is more vain or inſignificant, than words without ſenſe or matter. The perfect orator, therefore, muſt join the knowledge of both: And he inſiſts, as he did in the preceeding day's converſation, that the orator ought to be learned in all arts and ſciences, that can be made the ſubject of public ſpeaking, and ſhould be like

Gorgias, who, at the olympic games, defired that any body would propofe a fubject to him, upon which he might fpeak, and who was fo much honoured by the Greeks, that to him only they erected in Delphi a golden ftatue, whereas on others they only beftowed a gilt one *. And, particularly, he muft be thoroughly learned in every thing concerning human life, laws, and government. Such, he fays, were the ancient fages of Greece, and fuch were the great men in Rome before his time. But the perfect orator muft be learned likewife in other things: He muft have ftudied the philofophy of nature as well as of *man*; and muft know fomething of thofe arts, which are ufeful and ageeeable in human life. And, as to the difficulty of acquiring fuch an universal knowledge, in a life fo occupied as that of a Roman of high rank then was; he fays, in the firft place, that, unlefs you can learn fuch things quickly, you can never learn them well; and, there-

* Lib. iii. cap. 32.

fore, you should not attempt to learn them at all: And, secondly, he makes a distinction betwixt those who learn sciences and arts for use, and those who learn them for the pleasure of the study, and therefore spend their whole lives in them *.

After this preamble, there was a short pause in the conversation, which was interrupted by Cotta putting Crassus in mind of the part he had undertaken, which was to explain to them the ornaments of speech, and how the things treated of by the orator were to be expressed copiously, elegantly, and properly †. Upon this admonition, Crassus proceeds to treat of tropes, and all the ornaments of single words: Then he goes on to the composition of them; and there he insists much upon numbers and rhythms, which he considers as essential to the stile of an orator. Of this, I have already spoken at pretty great length: And I shall only add here, that he observes what

* Ibid. cap. 23.

† Ibid. cap. 36.

is certainly true, that the rhythms, in the cadence or claufule of the fentence, affect the ear the moft *. From thence he proceeds to fpeak of what is decent, proper, and fuitable to the fubject; without which, there can be nothing excellent in eloquence, or any other art. Then he fpeaks of action and pronunciation, and with that concludes. After he had done, Catulus makes him a compliment, in which he tells him, that he had explained all thole things fo well, that he feemed to be able to teach them to the Greeks, not to have learned them from the Greeks: And he adds, that he rejoices to have been prefent himfelf at fuch a difcourfe, but wifhes that his fon-in-law Hortenfius had been prefent likewife. Upon this occafion, Cicero makes a compliment from the mouth of Craffus to his friend, though rival in eloquence, Hortenfius; and fo the dialogue ends.

It is to be obferved, that Craffus, in this part of the dialogue, fpeaks more in continued difcourfe, than any other of the

* Ibid. cap. 50.

interlocutors. Antonius, who had spoken so much in the preceding part of the day, hardly says any thing. The young men, Caesar and Sulpicius, only express their admiration of Crassus; and it is only the elderly man Catulus, who takes occasion now and then to speak at some length. Every thing, therefore, in this last conversation, as well as in the preceding, appears to be conducted with the greatest propriety and decorum.

As Crassus expresses Cicero's own idea of a perfect orator, we may observe, that his part is much more laboured than that of any other of the speakers. And, besides what he makes him say of eloquence, he throws in to his discourse a great deal of very good philosophy, particularly where he makes him say, speaking of the necessary union betwixt words and things, that all things in nature are one; that there is a bond of union, by which every thing is connected with every thing, so that nothing can be separated from the whole, and exist entirely by itself*.

* Ibid. cap. 5. and 6.

So that here Cicero shows to be true, what he says elsewhere, that he was formed an orator, not in the shops of Rhetoricians, but in the walks of the Academy. The stile too I admire very much, for it is exceedingly copious, yet not superabundant, as it often is in his orations; nor does he dwell so long upon the same form and figure of speech, as he frequently does in these.

As to Crassus's idea of an orator, I believe most people will be inclined to the opinion of Antonius, who would confine him to the business of the bar, the forum, or the senate; and not oblige him to take such a range through all the arts and sciences as Crassus thinks necessary. But, in the first place, we are to consider, that Crassus is speaking of the ornaments of diction. Now, I maintain, that to make a stile of speaking both copious and ornamented, the knowledge of very many things is absolutely necessary; and that no man can speak in such a stile, whose studies are confined to one particular thing, though it be supposed to be the very thing upon which he speaks, and though his knowledge of it be as perfect as possible. I say as perfect as possible; for I hold it to be true, what Crassus says, that there is such a connection and *consent*, as he calls it, of all things in this universe, that no man who understands only one thing, can understand it perfectly. And, *secundo*, I say, that a man whose knowledge is so confined, cannot have that elevation of mind, which a great speaker ought to have; he cannot thunder and lighten, and astonish all Greece, as Pericles did; nor could Pericles have done that, if he had not heard Anaxagoras the philosopher.

Upon the whole, therefore, I do not hesitate to pronounce, that those three books *De Oratore*, are not only the completest work of the dialogue kind which he has executed, but the finest of all his works.

Besides these dialogues upon philosophy and eloquence, there is a work of Cicero's, which he entitles *Cato Major, seu De Senectute*. It is not a dialogue, but a continued discourse, made by Cato the elder, at the defire of Scipio and Laelius; and, befides, there is neither time nor place, nor any thing like a fable. It is, neverthelefs, the pleafanteft little work I ever read, and I don't wonder that Cicero had fuch delight in writing it, that it not only, as he fays, made him forget the infirmities of old age, but made that time of life pleafant to him. Philofophy therefore, he adds, never can be fufficiently praifed, which makes every time of life agreeable*. There is in it a great deal of Greek learning, as well as of Roman: For, as he tells us in his introduction, Cato in his old age became ftudious of Greek learning. The ftile is very elegant, but not near fo much raifed as the ftile of Craffus upon the fubject of oratory: Nor indeed was it proper that it fhould have been fo. Theodorus Gaza, one of the great reftorers of Greek learning in Italy †, was fo charmed with it, that he has done it an honour,

* In initio.

† See what I have faid of him, in the preface to the III. Volume of Metaphyfics, p. 71.

which, I believe, he never did to any Latin book, that of tranflating it into Greek, though he underftood the Latin very well, as appears not only from this tranflation, but from other tranflations, he was employed by the Popes to make, of Greek authors into Latin*. In reading it, I was at the pains to compare it with the original, paragraph by paragraph ; and this led me to obferve, what I have mentioned before, the great advantage the Greek has over the Latin, by the ufe of fo many connecting particles, giving a roundnefs and a flow to the Greek compofition, which even the language of Cicero has not.

There is another very fine treatife of Cicero's, and which comes nearer to dia-

* This tranflation of Theodorus is a very rare book. I never fo much as heard of it, till I was favoured with the ufe of a copy of it, and the only copy, for any thing that I know, that is in Britain, by My Lord Stormont; who is an excellent fcholar, and very curious about every thing relating to Greek learning. He did not, like many of our travellers now-a-days, drop his claffical learning in his travels, but carried it with him all over Europe, and continued the ftudy of it even in the courts where he refided, and where he was employed in public bufinefs.

logue than the one laſt mentioned. It is entitled *Laelius, ſive de Amicitia* ; for there is there a Story, with the circumſtances of Perſons, Time, and Place. It is a converſation, which Scaevola the augur and Caius Fannius had with Laelius, the friend of Publius Scipio, a few days after the death of Scipio. Which converſation, Cicero ſays, Scaevola, ſitting upon a ſemicircular bench in his houſe, related to him when he was very young, and to ſome other of his intimates. But it is a continued diſcourſe of Laelius, with little or no interruption, and no diverſity of ſentiments. But, though no dialogue, it is very inſtructive, as well as pleaſant, having a great deal of good philoſophy in it, and much knowledge of human life, and of men and manners.

I will conclude what I have to ſay of Cicero's dialogues, with two or three obſervations. My firſt obſervation is, that I think Cicero has choſen very well the perſonages whom he introduces ſpeaking. They are all men of eminence in the ſtate, either then living or dead; and, though dead, the Romans had such a just veneration for their ancestors, that they would hear, with the greatest pleasure, such men as Scipio, Laelius, and Cato speaking: And, I think, it is true what Cicero says, that such illustrious men gave more gravity and dignity to what was said, than it could otherwise have had. And he adds, '*Ipse, mea legens, sic afficior interdum, ut* '*Catonem, non me, loqui existimem* *.' This appears to me to be a great advantage, which Cicero in his dialogues has over Plato; for, unless it be Socrates and Alcibiades, there is hardly any person of eminence who speaks in his dialogues. The rest are all burghers of Athens, of whom we know nothing, itinerant sophists, such as Gorgias and Protagoras, or nameless strangers.

My other observation is, that there is a politeness in Cicero's dialogues, which I do not find in those of Plato; for the iro-

---

* *Laelius* in initio.

Ch. VII. PROGRESS OF LANGUAGE. 339

nical manner of Socrates, though it muſt have been very pleaſant to the by-ſtanders, could not have been agreeable to thoſe with whom he converſed, as the tendency of it was to ſhow their vanity and ignorance, or, in other words, to make fools of them; whereas in Cicero the perſonages treat one another with the greateſt reſpect, however much they may differ in opinion. Craſſus, in the laſt book *De Oratore*, finds fault with ſome things in the manner of ſpeaking both of Cotta and Sulpicius; but does it in ſo gentle and ſo friendly a manner, that they both think themſelves obliged to him for his obſervation. The praiſes they beſtow upon one another ſeem to be all ſincere and to proceed from the heart, without the leaſt appearance of flattery or ſervility: And of themſelves they ſpeak with the moſt becoming modeſty. In ſhort, I do not know that there is any where to be found a better ſchool for politeneſs, than the dialogues of Cicero.

Another thing which pleaſes me very much in Cicero's writings upon eloquence and philoſophy is, that they are almoſt all

of them inscribed to some friend, such as
Brutus, Pomponius Atticus, Varro; and his
best work, as I think, of the dialogue kind,
the three books *De Oratore*, is dedicated
to his brother. To all these works there
are prefaces in which he converses with
these friends in the most friendly manner;
and which convinces me, that he had really
a heart capable of friendship, the greatest
gift that I think God and nature could
have bestowed upon him, especially in the
times in which he lived, the miseries of
which, he says himself, he could not have
supported without philosophy and friendship. And I would have those, who live
in the present times, consider, whether it
be possible to live a happy life without the
aid of philosophy, and the society and
friendship of men of worth and knowledge,
such as those with whom Cicero lived.

CHAP. VIII.

Of Lord Shaftsbury's dialogue, entitled The Moralists; —*this a compleat dramatical piece in all its parts;—better divided as to time, than some dialogues of Plato.—Of the different characters in it.—The first day's conversation a proper introduction to what is principal in the piece, viz. the conversion of a sceptic to theism.—The second day's conversation is divided into four parts:—The first is of Philocles with Theocles in the morning, alone;—The second at dinner, when two new characters are introduced;—The third is in the fields, when Theocles, in a long discourse, demonstrates the existence of God from his works.—Here the catastrophe of the piece begins.—The sequel of this conversation contains consequences from what had been before demonstrated.—The fourth conversation of the second day is upon the subject of mira-*

cles and prodigies.—*This conversation agreeably varied with respect to the speakers as well as the subject.—Of the third day's conversation of Philocles with Theocles alone.—The scene the same as where they met the first day.—Of the Rhapsodies of Theocles in this conversation, and the stile of them;—not incredible to those who have heard the Italian rhapsodists.—Subject of the* first *rhapsody is an invocation of* Divinity; —*of the* second, *a description of that vivifying power, which pervades all nature:—The* third *has for its subject the elements and minerals:—The* fourth *contains a description of the different countries of the earth, and the various appearances of nature in them.—Betwixt some of the rhapsodies, a great deal of cool reasoning and dialogue in the Socratic way of question and answer is interspersed.—Conclusion of the work suitable to the main design of it;—contains,* 1mo, *An account of Beauty, and the several kinds of it;—shows that all beauty is resolvable into the Supreme Beauty of the first Being.—Beauty produces admiration, and Admiration enthusiasm.—Of the seve-*

Ch. VIII. PROGRESS OF LANGUAGE. 343

ral kinds of enthusiasm.—The sense of beauty shown to be innate in man, and not acquired.—2do, The conclusion also shows the necessity of philosophising; and that, in fact, every man does philosophise more or less. —Observations upon this dialogue:—The fable of it excellent, with greater variety than in Cicero's dialogue De Oratore : —*The stile such as might be expected from a man like Lord Shaftesbury:—Politeness too, such as in Cicero's dialogues. —Observations on the philosophy of this piece.—The love, of which beauty is the object, made a fundamental principle both of virtue and religion.—This philosophy perfectly agreeable to Scripture.— From the same principle, Shaftesbury demonstrates the Being and Attributes of God.—This demonstration better than any demonstration of the same* a priori.—*Dr Clarke's demonstration examined, and shown not to be so compleat as that of Shaftesbury.—Shaftesbury's philosophy, however, not perfect in this dialogue.— The distinction betwixt the animal and intellectual parts of our nature, not explicitly laid down.—The consequences of this diſtinction;—it demonſtrates the beautiful to be good;—puts an end to the paradox of the Stoics concerning virtue;— their language more proper than that of the other philoſophers.—Praiſe of Lord Shafteſbury's writings.—They are now out of faſhion.—That the fate of other writings, which deſerve it as little.— Of Mr Harris's dialogues upon art and happineſs,—not properly dialogues, according to my definition.—They have, however, great merit, as all the writings of that author have.*

THE fineſt dialogue of modern times, ſo fine, that I think it may be compared with any thing of the kind we have got from antiquity, is My Lord Safteſbury's rhapſody, entitled *The Moraliſts*. It has every thing which a dialogue requires; for it has a fable, characters, manners, incidents, and ſcenery too, and in ſhort, every thing belonging to a dramatic piece. The ſubject of it is the converſion of a ſceptic to theiſm. This converſion is made by

Ch. VIII. PROGRESS OF LANGUAGE.

a philosopher, who is possessed of the noblest of all passions, an enthusiastical admiration of God and Nature. So here are two very different characters distinctly marked: And in the course of the action, which lasts three days, there are other characters introduced; for my Lord has not fallen into the error, which, I think, Plato has committed, of making but one conversation of his ten books of Polity, and likewise only one of his thirteen books of Laws, and so drawing out each of these dialogues to an immeasurable length, an error, which, as I have observed, Cicero has also avoided. In the first day's conversation, Philocles (so the sceptic is called, who is the narrator of the dialogue), recites a conversation which passed betwixt him and his friend Palemon, in the park at London, upon the subject of the miseries of human life, in which Philocles having thown out some things of the sceptical kind that gave offence to Palemon, as tending to show, that there is no distinction of right and wrong in actions, any more than of truth and falschood in arguments,—Philocles, using the privilege, as he says, of a sceptic, entertained him with a discourse of some length upon the order and beauty which appears in nature, the government of the universal mind, which we ought from thence to infer, and to conclude, that all those ills natural and moral, of which they had been speaking, were no more than ills in appearance, being only the necessary consequences of the universe being a system. This sudden change having surprised Palemon, he asked Philocles what had produced sentiments so different from those he had before expressed. In answer to this, Philocles informs him, that some days ago he had had a conversation with a friend in the country, whom he calls Theocles, who had made a perfect convert of him to the firm belief of theism, and the government of an universal mind of infinite goodness and wisdom. This conversation Palemon earnestly desired to hear; but, as it was then growing late, Philocles could not satisfy him at that time, but promised that he would become author for his sake, and set it down in writing.

This is the firſt day's converſation, and I think a very natural and proper introduction to what is principal in the piece, viz. the converſations with Theocles, which make the ſubject of the two other days. The ſcene of theſe is Theocles's country ſeat, where Philocles had gone upon a viſit to him. There he finds him in the forenoon, walking in the fields with a Virgil in his hand. This rural ſcene is very well deſcribed *. Here, after ſome diſcourſe, which the company, that Theocles had with him, naturally gave occaſion to, the converſation took a philoſophical turn; and they began to talk of pleaſure and happineſs, and of what was good or ill in human life. Upon this ſubject they at laſt agreed, that, what made perfect happineſs, was the love and admiration of what was perfectly beautiful and good. Such an object, Theocles ſaid, was to be found in the univerſe, and which he promiſed to diſcover to him the next morning; for, by this time, a ſervant had come from the houſe

* Part ii. ſect. i.

to let Theocles know, that company was come to dine with him.

And here we have an epifode very naturally introduced, in which we have two new characters that give an agreeable variety to the piece, and furnifh matter for converfation on different fubjects, but all having a relation to the principal fubject of the piece. One of thefe characters is an old gentleman, a religious bigot, and a man not at all of pleafant manners: The other is a modeft young gentleman, and more agreeable in converfation.

The dinner was fuch, as to give occafion to Theocles to fpeak in praife of the virtue of temperance; from which it appears to have been a dinner very different from what is now given by men of fafhion. From temperance in eating and drinking, they came to fpeak of temperance with refpect to wealth and honours, and of virtue in general. Upon this fubject it was obferved, that to exalt virtue and its happinefs, was underftood by fome religious men to be depreffing and undervaluing religion: For virtue, they said, was misery; and that there was no happiness in this life, nor any except what religion promised in our future state. By arguing in this way, Theocles observed it was impossible to convince an atheist, who, if he believed that there was so much disorder in the present state of things, would not be disposed to think better of the future, and never could be persuaded, that the world was under the government of a Wise and Good Being. This naturally led the conversation to speak of atheism, and of the common way of arguing against atheists; when it was observed, that if an author argued calmly against atheists, and stated the arguments fully and fairly, he was understood to be a friend to them. This, it was said, was the case of the learned and pious Dr Cudworth: And the same objection was made to a late author, viz. the author of the ‘*Inquiry concerning Virtue.*’ And here Lord Shaftesbury introduces, I think not improperly, a defence of his own work from the mouth of Theocles, who speaks of that author as his friend, and therefore very willingly undertakes his defence in a pretty long discourse, where he shows, that the only way to convince an atheist, is to treat him with good manners, and with calmness and moderation. That solidly to refute the arguments of the atheists, and to establish upon sound principles the existence of a Deity, must necessarily be previous to our belief in any revelation from that Deity. That genuine theism and just notions of the Divinity must necessarily produce that divine love, which is acknowledged to be the perfection of religion, arising from the high idea we have of the Being which is the object of it. This, he says, was what his friend recommended, maintaining that we were not truly religious, unless our devotion proceeded from such a principle, and not from the hopes of reward, or the fears of punishment; though such motives might be very properly used, with those who were by nature incapable of so liberal a devotion. This, says Theocles, I think is sufficient to defend the morality of my friend's Inquiry, and shew, that it is nowise inconsistent with religion, but quite the contrary. At the same time, as his work is entirely confined to morality, he has not proved that a Being exists worthy of that disinterested love and admiration, in which he makes the perfection of religion to consist: To supply this defect, says he, I must become preacher, and give you a system of theology agreeable to his principles *.

Here this conversation ended, by the coming in of some visitants, who took up

* Part ii. sect. 3. *in fine.*—I consider therefore the Rhapsody as a sequel or appendix to the Inquiry, exalting morality to theology, which ought to be considered, and is considered by our author, as the summit of human virtue and human knowledge. I have elsewhere said, that the *Inquiry* is the best book in English upon the subject of morals: And I am not at all disposed to retract that opinion, but, on the contrary, after having read it over again, on occasion of this commentary, which I have given upon the *Rhapsody*, I am fully convinced, that it is the best demonstration to be found in any book that I know, antient or modern, of that most important truth, the foundation, I think, of theism, That virtue is the greatest happiness, and vice the greatest misery of men; for we cannot otherwise be convinced ourselves, nor convince others, that the world is under the Government of Supreme Intelligence, Power, and Goodness.

the remaining part of the afternoon in other difcourfe. In the evening, the fcene is changed from the houfe to the fields, and all the reſt of the company being gone, Philocles, with the old gentleman and his young friend who remained, infifted with Theocles, that he fhould give them the fermon he had mentioned, which accordingly he did, taking occafion to begin it from obfervations made by Philocles upon the ſtructure and organization of the plants they faw in the fields.

And here begins what may be called the cataſtrophe or *denoument* of the piece, to which every thing preceding has a tendency more or lefs; I mean the demonſtration of the exiſtence of a Sovereign Mind and Supreme Intelligence, given by Theocles in language as beautiful and as much ornamented as fcience can be delivered in. Nor does Philocles forget his character of fceptic, and the part affigned to him of objecting to the arguments of Theocles, which part he acts exceedingly well; and thus the argument is fully laid before us, and according to the fair method in which even atheism, as Theocles thinks, should be treated, every thing is said in its behalf that can be said, but to which Theocles gives a sufficient answer. In this debate the old gentleman takes a part suitable to his character, answering or endeavouring to answer the objections of Philocles, but in an angry passionate way: Whereas the answers of Theocles are perfectly mild and good humoured; for he is a most amiable enthusiast, without any mixture of that passion, violence, and furious zeal, which we often see in religious enthusiasts.

What follows after this is to be considered as corollaries or consequences of Theocles's demonstration; tending at the same time to strengthen it, by shewing that his theory is agreeable to fact and observation. The last conversation of this second day is after supper, and the subject of it is prodigies, miracles, apparitions, and other things altogether out of the ordinary course of nature. By these the old gentleman would prove the existence of a Deity; but Philocles, taking up the argument of Theocles, shews that it is only from order, regularity, and uniformity in the operations of Nature, that we can infer the exiftence of a Supreme Intelligence; but from fuch violation of the laws of Nature, as thofe mentioned by the old gentleman, and the confufion in the fyftem thence refulting, nothing could be inferred except either the chaos and atoms of the atheifts, or the magic and demons of the polytheifts. This converfation is agreeably varied and diftinguifhed from the preceding converfations of the fame day, not only by the fubject, but by Theocles, who was the chief fpeaker in thofe, faying nothing in this, and likewife by the modeft young gentleman, who had been only a hearer before, now taking a very proper part in the converfation, and joining Philocles to the great offence of the old gentleman, who gave him a rebuke in fuch rough terms, that Philocles interpofed, and finifhed the argument, which the young gentleman had fo well begun, but his modefty would not allow him to finifh.—And thus ends the fecond day.

The third and last day begins with Theocles dismissing his two guests early in the morning, (such was the custom in those days) and going out to his morning walk in the fields, where Philocles finds him. It is the same beautiful rural scene, where these two met the preceding morning. Here Theocles, at the desire of Philocles, addressed that Universal Mind in a strain very different from that in which he had proved the existence of such a Mind. Before he reasoned as a philosopher, now he speaks as one inspired, not by the demon which inspired the Delphic priestess or the Sybil of Virgil, but by Divine Love, which is mild, gentle, and humane. There is nothing therefore in Theocles of the *os rabidum*, or the *fera corda*, though his language be so much elevated, that it may be said to be *nill mortale sonans*. It is of that kind which the antients called dithyrambic, but much less obscure than the dithyrambics of Pindar, nor indeed is it at all obscure. It has those *loose numbers*, of which, as we have seen, the antients speak so much *, as much as our

* Page 261. et seq.

language will admit; and the only fault I
find with it is, that the numbers are sometimes too much aftricted and altogether
verfe, though that happens but very rarely. But, upon the whole, I think it the
moft fplendid language we have in profe,
and the fineft ftile of the kind in Englifh,
but abfolutely unfit for any other purpofe,
except for that for which the author has
employed it.

There are, I know, who, now that infpiration has ceafed, will think fuch extatic effufions altogether unnatural. But
thofe men know not the powers of human
nature, and judge of other men by themfelves. Even now the *Improvifatoris* and
Improvifatrices of Italy will pour forth
extempore, upon any fubject affigned to
them, a great many of their *octavo rimo*
verfes, of more difficult compofition than
any verfe we now ufe in Englifh, and much
more difficult than the meafured profe of
Theocles *. And I have no doubt, but

---

* Of old there were fuch Improvifatoris. Cicero
mentions one of them, viz. Archias the Poet, who,

Ch. VIII. PROGRESS OF LANGUAGE. 357

one of thefe, if he was as great a philofopher as Theocles, could make verfes extempore upon the fame fubjects.

The firft Rhapfody of Theocles, is an invocation in very fublime language, but without any thing like what we call Fuftian or Bombaft, of that Sovereign Mind, the exiftence of which he had proved, praying for affiftance to enable him to trace, in the works of creation, the marks of Wifdom, Goodnefs, and Power.

In the fecond Rhapfody (or rant, as thofe who are not initiated into this Sublime Philofophy, would call it,) he, in a ftill higher ftrain, goes through the works of nature, obferving how the vital principle, diffufed through the whole, operates in fo many different ways, producing ftill new forms out of the ruins of the old, fo that,

he fays, could pour forth extempore a number of excellent verfes, upon any fubject that happened then to be agitated ; (*Pro Archia porta,*) cap. 8. and the *admirabilis* Crichtonus, as he was called, could, it is faid, have done the fame.

amidſt the greateſt ſeeming profuſion, nothing is loſt. Here a great deal is ſaid of matter and of mind, and of thoſe two entities ſo difficult to be apprehended, Time and Motion. Then he proceeds in the ſame rapturous ſtrain to ſurvey the heavens, deſcribing the ſun, the planets, and the fixed ſtars, in language equal, if poſſible, to the ſubject.

The ſubject of the third Rhapſody, is this our earth; where, in deſcribing the minerals and the four elements, and particularly fire diffuſed, as he ſays, through the whole globe, and animating every thing in it, he ſhows more of natural knowledge than I thought he had been poſſeſſed of.

In his fourth and laſt *tranſport*, he ſurveys the ſurface of this our globe, going through every climate and every country of it, where there is any thing very remarkable, and deſcribing with great accuracy, as well as great pomp of language, all the wonderful ſcenes which it preſents to us.

Betwixt thefe fallies there is interjected a great deal of clofe reafoning by way of queftion and anfwer in the Socratic manner, which was very proper in a converfation betwixt them two, but would, I think, not have been fo proper in the mixt company they weie in before. The tendency of this reafoning, is to ftrengthen ftill farther, the proof of the exiftence of a Mind in nature, which unites the whole, and makes *one* of the univerfe. For proof of this, he appeals to every plant and every animal, in every one of which it is evident, that there is fome one thing, which makes *a whole* of each of them. And, as every thing in nature is connected, as well as the parts of a plant or animal, for the fame reafon, there muft be fomething in nature which makes a whole of it. In this interlude, as it may be called, there is a moft fatisfactory anfwer given to an objection made before by Philocles, but which had not been anfwered, namely, that tho' there may be union, order, and regularity, in fo much of the fyftem of the univerfe as we fee, yet all might be diforder and confufion in the reft of the univerfe, which is infinite with respect to the small part of it that we can discover; for, if it were so, says Theocles, the infinite must prevail over the finite, and all be disorder and confusion.

Betwixt the second and third Rhapsodies there is nothing interposed, but an interruption which Theocles makes to himself, supposing that Philocles had something to object to what he had said; but Philocles saying that he had nothing to object, he proceeded to descant, as I have said, upon the elements and minerals.

Betwixt the third and fourth there is also nothing interposed except an admonition of Philocles, that he would not insist so much upon the power of the element of fire, which, though so friendly to life, Theocles had said, might, when let loose, destroy every thing, and bring on an universal conflagration. But, says he, describe to me the mass of nature as it appears upon this our earth; and accordingly Theocles proceeds to give that beautiful map of the earth above mentioned.

The conclusion of the work is very proper and suitable to the main design. The subject of this conclusion is, 1*mo*, Beauty, and the different kinds of it: 2*do*, The necessity of philosophizing in order to be happy. As to Beauty, he shows, that it is essential both to virtue and religion; for beauty is the object of love, and we love no person, no action, no thing, in which we do not perceive beauty. Now, there can be no virtue without the love of virtue, nor any religion without the love of God. We must therefore perceive beauty both in God and in Virtue. Then he proceeds to shew, that body has in itself no beauty, but that the beauty we admire in it is all from mind: So that what we admire in the works of art is the genius of the artist; and the beauty in the works of nature, where else can it be, but in the Mind of the Sovereign Artist, who therefore is the fountain of all Beauty, whether of body or of mind, as well as of all Intelligence. As there can be no love without admiration, and as admiration to a great degree is enthusiasm, he from thence derives the enthusiasms of poets, painters, musicians, and the nobler enthusiasm still of the truly virtuous man*, and the noblest of all enthusiasms, that arising from the love and admiration of the Supreme Beauty.

He next proceeds to show, that the sense of the *fair* and the *beautiful*, the *pulchrum* and *honestum*, the *graceful* and the *becoming*, not only in outward forms, but in sentiments and actions, is in man from nature, not from art or teaching, institution or habit. This is so clear a proposition, that I wonder it should be denied, or even doubted of by any: And yet I am told, that in a book lately published upon the subject of morality, it is at least doubted of, if not denied. I think the author might

---

* See what I have collected from the Pythagorean philosophers upon the subject of the enthusiasm of virtue, in the preface to vol. iii. of Antient Metaphysics p. 33. and 34. to which may be added what Aristotle says, (*Magna Moralia*, lib. ii. cap. 7. versus finem) That the ὁρμη προς το καλον, is more the principle of virtue than λογος, or *reason*; for, says he, in the practice of virtue, the ὁρμη must begin and carry on the practice, while reason only directs and approves; It is therefore the leading principle.

have as well doubted whether such a thing as virtue or religion existed; or indeed whether such an animal as man existed: For I hold that there is nothing, which more eminently distinguishes the man from the brute, than the sense of the fair and the beautiful.

The other thing he mentions in the conclusion of the dialogue, namely, the utility of philosophy, does also belong to the subject; for it was very proper, after having philosophized so much, to show that it was not to no purpose, but on the contrary, of the highest use. This he proves, not by a continued discourse, as he proves other things, but by close pungent interrogations and answers, which, at the same time that they are most convincing, make a beautiful variety in the stile: And he concludes the whole by showing, that, in fact, all men do philosophize right or wrong; for they deliberate about what is useful or hurtful, what contributes to their happiness or not; and, even if they should determine not to deliberate at all, but to follow every fancy or conceit that is uppermoſt, ſtill that will be in ſome ſort to philoſophize.

Thus I have analyzed this moſt beautiful piece; ſo beautiful in its ſtile and compoſition, that it ſhews the author well qualified to write upon the Beautiful, which indeed is the chief ſubject of the piece. I will conclude with ſome general obſervations upon it.

And, in the firſt place, as the principal thing, according to Ariſtotle, in every dramatical piece, ſuch as I hold this to be, is the fable, that principal part in the Moraliſts is, I think, admirable: For, at the ſame time that there is a perfect unity in it, there is a greater variety of characters and incidents, than in any dialogue of Plato, and more than even in Cicero's dialogue *De O-ratore*, where the two days are not near ſo well filled up as the three days of the Moraliſts; and there are ſeveral changes of the ſcene, beſides the introduction of new perſonages, which I think are very agreeable. It is therefore a fable of the kind which Ariſtotle calls complex; and

Ch. VIII. PROGRESS OF LANGUAGE. 365

which, if the unity of the action is preserved, he prefers to the simple.

The stile is such as might be expected from a thorough well bred gentleman, well acquainted with life and manners, at the same time an accomplished scholar, and who in his travels had acquired a very high taste for the fine arts, as appears from many passages of his writings. The stile of such a writer must needs be copious and rich in all the ornaments which the knowledge of mythology, antient history, and the fine arts can furnish. His stile is too luxuriant, as I have observed elsewhere [*], in some other of his writings; but I think it is chaste and sober enough in this piece. The stile of the rhapsodies of Theocles, is, as I have observed, very uncommon, excellent however of the kind, but very different, as it ought to be, from that of the dialogue, which is easy and natural, and a very good imitation of the conversation of gentlemen upon learned

---

[*] Vol. iii. p. 284.—and p. 206. and 207. of this volume.

subjects: And it has that politeness, which I have commended so much in Cicero's dialogue, particularly in what is said by the two principal personages Theocles and Philocles, and which has a contrast in Shaftesbury, that is not to be found in Cicero; I mean the roughness and ill-breeding of the old gentleman.

As to the philosophy of this work, tho' it do not belong to the subject of this volume, I cannot help making some observations upon it. It is plainly a supplement, as the author has told us, to the *Inquiry concerning Virtue*; and he has in it carried the philosophy of morals to theology, and, I think, the most sublime theology that is to be found in English: And he has very properly connected the doctrine of morals, that is, the knowledge of ourselves, with theology; for, as I have observed elsewhere*, we can know nothing of Divinity, without first knowing ourselves. He has therefore founded morality and

---

* Antient Metaphysics, vol. iii. p. 5.

theology upon the same principle, namely, that the beautiful and good are one and the same thing; and that what is beautiful and good in the characters of men, is beautiful and good, but in an infinitely higher degree, in the Divinity. This proposition, therefore, that the beautiful and the good are the same, and which is a fundamental proposition in this treatise, I hold to be the basis both of morality and theology, though it be not so laid down in any treatise of morality in modern times, nor explicitly in any antient work, as far as I know, upon that subject.

And, as beauty is the object of love, without which, as I have observed, love cannot be conceived, I find a wonderful agreement betwixt the philosophy of my Lord Shaftesbury upon this subject and the doctrine of our holy religion. The first and fundamental precept of the law, as our Saviour tells us[*], was 'to love the 'Lord thy God with all thy heart, and with 'all thy soul, and with all thy strength,

[*] Luke, chap. x. v. 27.

'and with all thy mind, and thy neighbour
'as thyself.'—Again, our Saviour says to
his Disciples, 'a new commandment I
'give unto you, that ye love one another;
'as I loved you, that ye also love another.'
—'By this shall all men know, that ye
'are my Disciples, if ye have love one to
'another*.' And St Paul, in that remarkable passage in II. Corinthians chap. 13.
where he commends love, makes it the
essential duty of every Christian, without
which nothing that he can do, neither
prophesying, understanding mysteries, nor
working miracles, nor even martyrdom,
will signify any thing †.

---

* St John's Gospel, chap. xiii. v. 34. and 35. See
also the same gospel, chap. xv. v. 12.

† St Paul bestows this whole chapter upon the
praise of charity: It is written in a stile, which has
more of the rhetorical cast than any thing that I remember to have read in Scripture. The word, which
we translate *charity*, is αγαπη or *love*; for that it is not
giving alms to the poor, which is commonly called
charity, is evident from the third verse, where it is
said, ' That although I bestow all my goods to feed
' the poor, and have not charity, it profiteth me no-
' thing:' So that here *love* is set above all the christian

virtues. Now, the object, as I have said, of love is *beauty*; and we must understand it here not to be the beauty of outward form, but of the mind, that is, of sentiments and actions. And tho' we may and ought to do good offices, even to those who have no such beauty of character, it must proceed, if not from love to the person, from love to mankind, and to God, whose will we obey in doing such offices of kindness. And, if the action be truly virtuous and religious, we must have a sense of the beauty of the action, abstracted from any consideration of the person, who is the object of the action. In the end of the chapter St Paul speaks of the love of God being but imperfect in this state, in which we see the Divine Beauty but darkly, and as through a glass; but, in our future state, we shall see it more perfectly, and as it were face to face: For then we shall enjoy the Beatific Vision, and see the Beauty of the Divinity without a cloud. And, as *the beautiful* is the object of love, the same Apostle, in the first epistle to the Thessalonians, after recommending prayer and thanksgiving, and desiring them not to quench the Spirit, and not to despise prophesying, concludes with saying, παντα δοκιμαζετε, το καλον κατιχετε; as if without it nothing in religion could be perfect. Where we may observe, that we have translated improperly the last part of the precept, by the words, *Hold fast that which is good*; for the καλον and the αγαθον are distinguished in Scripture language, as well as

both of virtue and religion, Shaftesbury has deduced a demonstration of the Being,

in other Greek writings, though, no doubt, they are nearly allied, *beauty* being the *good*, and the only good of our intellectual part.—See vol. ii. of Antient Metaphysics, p. 109. And accordingly the two words are frequently joined together by Greek writers, and also in Scripture language, as in the parable of the *sower* in Luke, speaking of the seed that falls into καλη γη, it is added ουτοι εισι οιτινες εν καρδια καλη και αγαθη ακουσαντες τον λογον, κατιχουσι, cap. vii. v. 15. where he have again mistranslated the word καλη by the English word *honest*. There is another text of the same Apostle Paul, which I will also quote: It is in the epistle to the Philippians, chap. 4. v. 8. where he sums up the whole duty of a Christian in these words, Το λοιπον, αδελφοι, οσα εστιν αληθη, οσα σεμνα, οσα δικαια, οσα 'αγνα, οσα προσφιλη, οσα ευφημα, ει τις αρετη, και ει τις επαινος, ταυτα λογιζεσθε. where the word σεμνα is likewise improperly translated by the word *honest*; for σεμνον not only denotes what is *beautiful*, but what is grave and dignified, that is, beauty of the highest and most respectable kind; and it ought rather to have been translated *venerable*. John the beloved Disciple is full of the praise of love, both in his gospel and his epistles, and particularly in his first epistle, chap. iv. v. 16. he says, ' *God is Love*;
' and he that dwelleth in Love dwelleth in God, and
' God in him.'—And he further says, that our love must be unmixed with fear; for he adds, v. 18. ' *There*
' *is no fear in love; but perfect love casteth out fear, be-*
' *cause fear hath torment; he that feareth is not made*
' *perfect in love*.' From these authorities, I think I

as well as the Attributes of God, better, I
think, than what is to be found in any
modern book: For he has proved, from the
order, regularity, and beauty we see in all
the works of Nature above, below, and
round about us, that Supreme Intelligence
governs in the universe *; and, as there
can be no beauty without an unity of design, and as such unity appears to be in
every particular work of Nature, and in
the whole, as far as falls under our observation, he from thence very justly, I think,
infers that there is but one Supreme Intelligence †.

may conclude, that pure *love* is of the very essence of
the Christian Religion; and, indeed, it is the religion of
love, more than any other religion is, or ever was in
the world: And, as we cannot conceive love without
beauty, we must also conclude it to be the most beautiful of all religions. Those therefore, who think that
Christians ought to serve God from the fear of punishment or hope of reward, without love of God or of
our neighbour, know nothing of the true spirit of
Christianity, nor do they worship the Lord as they are
directed by the Psalmist, *In the Beauty of Holiness*, Pf.
xcvi. v. 9. see also Pf. xxix. v. 2.—1 Chron. xvi. v. 29.
—2 Chron. xx. v. 21.

* Part ii. sect. 4.

† Part iii. sect. 1.

This way of reasoning I like much better than the demonstrations that are pretended to be given us of the Being, the Unity, and the Attributes of God, *a priori*, and without consideration of his works. For I hold that in morality, physics, and even metaphysics and theology †, we must reason from the effect to the cause, and not *vice versa* from the cause to the effect, which may do very well after the cause is discovered, but is not at all proper for the investigation of it. Neither do I approve, any more than my Lord Shaftesbury does, of arguing in this matter from the necessity of a first principle and beginning of

---

† The division of philosophy by Plato, and in general by all the antient philosophers, was threefold, into Logic, or Dialectic as it was called by Plato, Ethics or moral philosophy as we call it, and Physics. Now, under physics they comprehended what was afterwards called by Aristotle Metaphysics, and which was nothing else but the causes or first principles of physical effects, and therefore, as philosophy always inquires into the causes of things, was very properly comprehended under physics. See upon this subject *Laertius*, lib. vii. cap. 39. also Cicero *de Legibus*, lib. i. cap. 23. and his *Academics*, lib. i. cap. 5.

motion. For I hold, that the antient philosophers were in the right, who maintained that there was no beginning of motion, nor consequently any First Principle, if by first principle is meant a principle prior to the existence of the effects produced by it. The material world, therefore, I hold to be an eternal emanation of the first cause, such as we believe the Second and Third Persons of the Trinity to be, which, tho' in dignity and excellence, they be far superior to the material world, are not prior in time. And this I will shew to be agreeable not only to philosophy but to Scripture, if I shall live to publish my fourth volume of Metaphysics [*].

Dr Clarke, in his Demonstration of the Being and Attributes of God, has acknowledged that the *Intelligence* of the Divinity cannot be demonstrated except *a posteriori*, that is, from facts. But he pretends that the existence of a Supreme Being, Self-existent, eternal, and One, may be

[*] See what I have already said upon this subject, in Vol. I. of Ancient Metaphysics, p. 259.

demonstrated *a priori*; and accordingly he
has given a demonstration of it, with which,
I confess, I am not satisfied; nor do I think
it is possible in the nature of things. For,
let me suppose that there was a time when
no material world existed, which, I believe,
is the general opinion; and let me also
suppose, that besides the Supreme Being,
there existed an intellectual being such as
man, it is, I think, impossible that he could
have had any proof of the existence of a
Being superior to himself, or of any o-
ther being besides himself. All he could
know of any thing was from consciousness,
by which he could only learn that he himself existed; for, as to any thing without
us, it is only discovered by our sensations.
Now, our sensations are nothing else but
the actions of material objects upon our
organs of sense.

I think, therefore, that our author has
judged it much better, when he has only
attempted to prove from the works of
creation, that there is one Supreme Intelligence in the universe, and that this Intelligence is also supremely Powerful, Wise,

and Good; and that what seems to be ill in the universe, is nothing else but appearances, such as must necessarily be to us of capacities so limited, who can only see and comprehend but a small part of the vast system of the universe. This I hold to be a sufficient proof of the doctrine of theism, without entering into questions whether the material world be from all eternity or not, and whether or not from the Supreme Intelligence have proceeded not only inferior intelligences and minds of every kind, but also matter and space; so that God must be supposed to have produced not only the world, such as we see it, but also the materials of which it is made, and the space or room in which it is contained. These are questions of subtle disputation, with which the plain doctrine of theism ought not to be perplexed and embarrassed. And, accordingly, I think Lord Shaftesbury has done well to avoid them *. He has proved, that the Divini-

---

* Such questions belong to a Metaphysical work of the kind I am engaged in; and, if I shall ever publish the IV. Volume of my Metaphysics, I will endeavour

ty has that in a supreme degree, which undoubtedly is Chief and Principal in the universe, I mean Intelligence; and also that he is All-powerful, Wise, and Good. Now, whoever believes that such a Being exists, I say, is a complete theist.

I beg leave to add further upon this subject, that if, a man, from what he sees of Nature, is not convinced that there is an order and system of things in the universe, and consequently that there is a Principle of Intelligence which there governs, cannot believe even in miracles; for a miracle is nothing else but a dispensation with the general laws of Nature, and a deviation from the established order of things, in particular cases. So that all miracles necessarily suppose such general laws, and such an established order of things.

to show that matter is likewise an eternal emanation of the Divine Being, but the last in point of dignity and precedence. As to space, I think I have already shown that it is no more than a capacity of containing body, and therefore it is impossible to conceive that it could be created. See Metaphysics, Vol. II. cap. 5.

But, however high my opinion may be
of our author's philosophy in this dialogue,
I think it could have been still more perfect, if he had been more learned in the
antient philosophy *. What he has said,
for example, upon the subject of matter
and motion, time and space, would have
been much better if he had studied the
philosophy of Aristotle. Further, the distinction betwixt man and brute, or, in other words, betwixt our animal and intellectual part, he has not laid down so clearly and explicitly as he might have done,
though it be evident that he acknowledged
it; If he had done so, it would have been
demonstrable that the Beautiful was the only good of man, considered as man, that
is, as an intellectual creature: For nothing
else can be conceived to give pleasure or
delight to the intellect, other than the
beautiful; whereas many things give pleasure to our animal nature, and may be said
properly enough to be *good* to it, which
have not the least of beauty in them †. The

* Ancient Metaphysics, Vol. II. p. 117.

† Ibid. p. 104.—109. 110.

same things are *good* to the brute; but, as he is merely a senfitive animal, and not an intellectual, he has no other good, nor any perception, as our author tells us, of the beautiful.

If this diftinction be well underftood, there is an end of that famous paradox of the Stoics, and which was the foundation of their whole philofophy, that virtue (under which they included every quality and difpofition of the mind that was amiable and praife-worthy, and even fciences, fuch as dialectic and phyfics *,) was the only good of man. For it appears that, inftead of being a paradox, it is a clear and evident propofition; and that the difference betwixt them and the other philofophers, fuch as the Peripatetics and thofe of the Academy, was, as Cicero has obferved †, only in words and not in things. For, in the firft place, the Stoics agreed with the other two fects of philofophers, that the *pulchrum*

---

* Cicero *De Finibus*, lib. iii. *in fine*.

† Ibid. lib. 4.

and the *honeſtum*, that is, the beautiful, was eſſential to virtue, being part of its definition, and that, without which it could not exiſt. This was not only the doctrine of the three ſects above mentioned, but of an older, and I think a better ſchool of philoſophy than any of them, I mean the Pythagorean ſchool, as I think I have ſhown very clearly elſewhere *. And I will venture to affirm, that, whoever would ground virtue and morality upon any other principle, than a ſenſe of the fair and the beautiful in ſentiments and actions, however learned he may be in other ſpecieſes of animals, knows nothing of his own, being ignorant even of the difference betwixt himſelf and a brute, which confiſts chiefly in the perception of the pulchrum and honeſtum, not given as I have ſaid to the brute. 2*dly*, The Peripatetics and Academics did not, nor could not, diſpute that virtue, in the large ſenſe I have mentioned, was the good and the only good of the intellectual part of our compoſition.

* Preface to Vol. III. of Ancient Metaphyſics, p. 34.

But they said, that man was an animal compounded of body and mind, and of an animal and an intellectual nature: And they said, that there was a good belonging to each of these natures: That undoubtedly virtue was the good of the intellectual, that is, the principal part of our nature: And that a virtuous life was a life according to Nature. But then we had another nature, viz. the animal; and we must live also according to that nature. We ought therefore to pursue what is agreeable to it, such as health, the perfect use of our senses, integrity of members, and what external things may be conducive to these ends, such as money, reputation, and friends. These therefore, though infinitely inferior to the goods of the mind, were still good and desirable things; and therefore, if we would live fully and completely according to our nature, as it is compounded of mind and body, we ought to labour to obtain these things, but in due subordination to our pursuit of the good of the principal part of our nature. Such things, therefore, the Peripatetics and Academics called good; and the contrary of these, such as

Ch. VIII. PROGRESS OF LANGUAGE.

pain, difeafe, mutilation, poverty, and the like, they faid were ills. But fuch things, the Stoics faid, were neither good nor ill. Yet they made a difference among them: For what the other philofophers called *good*, they faid were *things preferable*, and *to be chofen*; whereas the contrary of thefe were to be rejected, and avoided, as odious and contrary to nature, but not ill *.

It appears therefore, that it is true what Cicero fays, that, though the Stoics pretended to introduce a new philofophy, they did no more than give new names to old things, making philofophy fpeak a language, which they thought grander and more magnificent, than what it had for-

---

* For expreffing thefe nice diftinctions among things indifferent, which according to them were neither good nor ill, the Stoics invented the words *προηγμένα*, and *αποπροηγμένα*, which Cicero has rendered into Latin, by the words *præpofita* and *rejecta* vel *rejectanea*; Lib. iii. De Finibus, cap. 15. et 16. et lib. iv. cap. 26. or, as he has expreffed it at more length, he fays the things of the firft kind are *Res aptae, habiles, et ad naturam accommodatae;* ibid. lib. iv. cap. 20. the other he fays are *Res afperae, moleftae, odiofae, contra naturam, difficiles toleratu;* ibid cap. 19.

merly spoken under Plato and Aristotle, and the successors of their school. At the same time, I am so far disposed to adopt the language of the Stoics, and of this dialogue of Lord Shaftesbury, that I would give only to the good things of the mind the name of *good* by way of eminence; and would say that the beautiful, being the only object of love, was *good* and *good only*, and that the other things above mentioned, which are commonly said to be good, ought only to be called *useful*, and this only in so far as they contribute to what is *good*: And the fact is certain, that health, strength, vigour of body, and external things, such as wealth and reputation, if they be not used for the purposes of virtue, and of what is truly good and beautiful, are not to be considered as good or even useful, but, on the contrary, as pernicious. I think, therefore, those other philosophers did not speak so properly as the Stoics, when they dignified with the name of *good*, things of nature so ambiguous, and which were either good or ill according to the use made of them. But, I think, that the Stoics went much too far on the other hand, when they denied that health, wealth, and friends, though made the proper use of, were any addition to virtue, or made the possessor more happy, than he would be without them. I am therefore of opinion, that the Peripatetics, and before them the Pythagoreans, were perfectly in the right, who defined happiness to be the exercise of virtue in a perfect life, that is, in a life enjoying those advantages I have mentioned.

These are the things, and the only things which occur to me at present that may be observed as defects in the philosophy of this dialogue: For, as to his not defining what the beautiful is, though he has talked so much of it, it is a defect, which he has in common, as I have observed elsewhere*, with all the philosophers of antiquity, whose writings have come down to us: And, upon the whole, I am not afraid to pronounce the Rhapsody, not only the best dialogue in English, out of all degree of

* Ancient Metaphysics, Vol. II. p. 105. 106.

comparison, but the sublimest philosophy; and, if we will join with it the Inquiry, of which, as I have said, it is to be considered as a supplement, the completest system both of morality and theology that we have in our language, and at the same time, of the greatest beauty and elegance for the stile and composition.

Whatever may be said against other writings of Lord Shaftesbury, I never heard any serious objection made against this piece of his, though I know Mr Pope has endeavoured to ridicule the *rapturous visions of Theocles*. And I know very well that in my younger days, that is, about 50 years ago, all his writings, and particularly his Rhapsody, were much esteemed. But I do not know how it has happened, none of his writings at present appear to be in any estimation. I should wonder the more at this, if I did not know some other fine writings that appear to be forgot in much less time, such as the Art of Health by Dr Armstrong, as fine a didactic poem as in any language, and for diction and versification not exceeded by any thing in English;

and the Castle of Indolence, written by his friend Mr Thomson, is the best allegorical and descriptive poem that I know in any language, and the richest and best rhyming versification, for so long a work, that is to be found in English.

As to my Lord Shaftesbury's works, they are now so much out of fashion, that I have no doubt that I shall give offence to several readers, by endeavouring to bring them again into vogue. But I do not write to flatter the prejudices of any man or set of men, but to do justice to all authors, both antient and modern, dead or living, as far as I am able. The faults of Lord Shaftesbury I have censured pretty freely elsewhere *, and particularly the too great freedom which he has used with religion upon some occasions, to which he appears to have been provoked by the arrogance and high stile of authority, which was assumed by some churchmen of those days †.

* Vol. III. p. 284.—p. 206. and 207. of this Vol.

† See what he has said upon this subject, in the end of his last Miscellany.

But in this work, at the same time that he has established the truth of natural religion, better than any other writer in English, there is not a word in the whole work that carries the least insinuation against the Christian religion; but, on the contrary, he makes Palemon, in the end of the second section of the first part, speak of Christianity in the most respectful terms *.

And what have we got to put down such an author as Lord Shaftesbury? Writings, which for the honour of the nation

---

* His words are, ' As averse as I am to the cause of *theism* or name of *deist*, when taken in a sense exclusive of revelation, I consider still, that in strictness, the root of all is *theism*; and that to be a settled Christian, it is necessary to be first of all a *good theist*. For *theism* can only be opposed to *polytheism* or *atheism*; nor have I patience to hear the name of *deist* (the highest of all names) denied, and set in opposition to Christianity. As if our religion was a kind of magic, which depended not upon the belief of a single Supreme Being; or as if the firm and rational belief of such a Being on philosophical grounds, was an improper qualification for believing any thing further.—Excellent presumption, for those who naturally incline to the disbelief of revelation, or who through vanity affect a freedom of this kind.'

ought not to be mentioned. Original works of genius and learning we have hardly any, good or bad. It is all occasional publications to serve the purpose of the day, or it is editions of classics, that have been better published many years ago, or translations of them of no use to the scholar; or it is, at best, compilements of antient or modern history; but even these, for the greater part, written in such a stile, that they can hardly be read, for information of facts, by those who have formed their taste in writing upon the study of the antient authors. As to philosophy or science, we can expect nothing of that kind of the least value, now that the antient philosophy is laid aside. But what our writings want in beauty and excellence, they make up in number; for not only of annual productions, but of monthly, weekly, and, I may say, daily, the multitude is such, that if a man were to read them all, he could read nothing else, and hardly do any thing else. I would have those writers of the day, who affect to despise such an author as Lord Shaftesbury, try to produce a dialogue like the Moralists; or, if they say that they have not time or leisure to compose a work of such length, (for I am sure they will not think that they want. genius and learning,) let them try to write but a letter of such elegance of stile, and politeness of compliment, as the Letter on enthusiasm.

A kinsman of my Lord Shaftesbury, the late Mr Harris, has written two dialogues, one upon Art and another upon Happiness. But neither of them is a dialogue, according to my definition of that kind of writing; for they have no story or fable worth mentioning, nor characters, or manners. They want too entirely those incidents and turns, with which a dialogue ought to be varied. They are, therefore, truly no more than an analysis by way of question and answer, the one of a complex idea, viz. that of *art*, the other of a more complex idea still, and of much greater importance in human life; I mean the idea of *happiness*. They are therefore no more dialogues than an analysis of a geometrical proposition, carried on in the same way. They are, however, works of a great deal of merit, particularly the last mentioned, in which there is much excellent philosophy. The stile too is chaste and correct, but not near so much adorned and animated as that of his kinsman; and, particularly, he falls very much short in his attempt to imitate my Lord's high stile in the rhapsodies of Theocles; and tho' his rhapsodies were as good of the kind, they are not so well suited to the personages he introduces. I would recommend, however, to every student of ancient philosophy, to begin rather with his dialogues, particularly that upon happiness, than with my Lord's dialogue; for, he appears to have studied the antient books of philosophy, more than my Lord, and he abounds in quotations from them, the most of which he has taken the trouble to translate. And, upon the whole, I think him, next to my Lord Shaftesbury, the best writer of this age upon the subject of philosophy, both for matter and stile. I will only further add, that I am very glad of this opportunity of doing justice to an author, whom I had the pleasure of knowing intimately, and esteemed very much not only as an excellent scholar, and a good writer, but as a man of worth. He first began, as I have elsewhere acknowledged, the attempt, which I have endeavoured to carry on, of reviving the ancient philosophy, of which I got the first taste from his writings; and I made considerable advances in it, both by his conversation and by corresponding with him. And I have several letters of his in my possession, upon which I set a great value, as memorials of his esteem and regard for me.

And here I conclude the subject of dialogue-writing, upon which I have enlarged the more, that I think it the finest of all writing in prose: And it has the greatest beauty of poetry, namely a fable and manners. Even in a narrative poem, such as Homer's Iliad and Odyssey, dialogue is one of the greatest beauties; and, I think, it is not without reason that Aristotle commends Homer for speaking so little himself, and making others speak so much *.

---

* His commendation of Homer in this respect is very high; for he says, that Homer alone, of all poets, understood what he himself ought to do. Ὁμηρος δε αλλα τι πολλα αξιος επαινεισθαι, και δη και ότι μονος των ποιητων ουκ

Ch. VIII. Progress of Language. 391

Nor indeed do I think that any kind of writing can be perfectly fine without dia-

αγμοι ὁ δυ ποιειν αυτον. Αυτοι γαρ δι τον ποιητην ελαχιστα λιγειν. Ου γαρ ιστι κατα ταυτα μιμητης. Οι μεν ουν αλλοι, αυτοι μεν δι᾽ ὁλου αγονιζονται, μιμουνται δι ολιγα και ολιγακις. Ὁ δι ολιγα φροιμιασαμενος, ιυθυς εισαγει ανδρα ἢ γυναικα, ἢ αλλο τι ηθος, και ουδιν ανθις, αλλ᾽ ιχον ηθος. (περι Ποιητικης, Cap. 24.) The praise, which Aristotle here bestows upon Homer, may seem extravagant; but the meaning of it I take to be, 'That, of all the poets, who imitated 'as Homer does, partly by narrative and partly by dia- 'logue, he alone divided the two parts properly, and 'did not give too much to the narrative.' And here I cannot help stopping to correct a text in the *Poetics* upon this subject, which, as it stands in all the editions, and likewise, as I suppose, in the MSS. is altogether unintelligible; nor is it corrected in a late edition of the *Poetics* from Cambridge, which I have seen. It is, when speaking of the different manners of imitation in poetry, (for all poetry, according to Aristotle, is imitation), he says, Ετι δι τουτων τριτη διαφορα· τι, ὡς ἑκαστα τουτων μιμησαιτο αν τις. Και γαρ ἱν τοις αυτοις και τα αυτα μιμεισθαι ιστιν, ὁτι μιν απαγγιλλοντα, ἡ ἑτερον τι γιγνομινον, ὡσπερ Ομηρος ποιει· ἡ ὡς τον αυτον και μη μεταβαλλοντα, ἡ παντας ὡς πραττοντας και ινεργουντας τους μιμουμινους. (Cap. 3.) Here, in order to make the passage intelligible, you must make two corrections, first after ὁτι μιν απαγγιλλοντα, you must read ὁτι δι (in place of ἡ) ἑτερον τι γιγνομινον; otherwise it is not sense; nor is there any thing answering to the μιν in the first part of that member of the sentence: And in

logue, more or less. I have chosen for my text on this subject, two of the finest dialogues I know, that of Cicero *De Oratore*, and my Lord Shaftesbury's Rhapsody, both, I think, very fine, and the last without dispute the finest in English; for his Lordship appears to me to have had a genius, which fitted him peculiarly for this kind of writing: And accordingly, not only in the Rhapsody, where he is a professed dialogist, but in his other works, he has intermixed a great deal of excellent dialogue*, imitating in that respect, as I

---

the last member, in place of τους μιμουμενους, which has no sense at all, you must read μιμουμενοι. And then the whole sentence will be perfectly intelligible, expressing, clearly, and distinctly, the three different ways of imitation, either by narrative only, or by dialogue only, that is, by introducing all the persons acting and speaking, or in both ways as Homer imitates. See a passage from Plato, which I have quoted in Vol. III. of this work, p. 126. where the reader will find explained, what Aristotle means by ἑτερον τι γιγνομενον.

* There is a very short dialogue, which he has thrown into his *Soliloquy, or Advice to an Author*, sect. 3. in the beginning. It is so pretty and natural, that I cannot help transcribing it; it is where speaking of

Ch. VIII. Progress of Language.

have elsewhere observed, Horace, the chief beauty of whose satires and epistles is the dialogue in them: And I am not sure but his best ode is the dialogue betwixt him and Lydia *. My Lord Shaftesbury, in his dialogues, has avoided that fault in his stile of being too copious, and sometimes overloaded with epithets; for his dialogue is altogether in the stile of conversation, which does not admit

the justness and truth of workmanship, he makes a poor mechanic say to a rich customer, ' Sir, you are ' mistaken for coming to me for such a piece of work-' manship: Let who will make it for you, as you fan-' cy; I know it to be *wrong*: Whatever I have made ' hitherto, has been *true work*; and neither for your ' fake or any body's else, shall I put my hand to any ' other.' Here he has imitated the stile of a common mechanic; but he has in the same piece, sect. ii. a longer dialogue, in the form of a soliloquy, in a higher stile and upon a much nobler subject: It is too long to be here inserted; but I call again upon the fashionable wits and critics of this age, who think meanly of my Lord Shaftesbury's stile, to try whether they can do any thing better upon the subject.

* Book iii. ode 9.

of an exuberance of words, or multitude of epithets: And where he introduces gentlemen speaking, it is altogether the conversation of gentlemen. And, in general, there runs through his whole writings a certain liberal air, and gentleman-like manner*, without which, I think, nothing can be agreeably either spoken or written. The greatest learning and science, without it, cannot please though it may instruct.

* See Vol. III. p. 284. and 285.

CHAP. IX.

Of the stile of Hiſtory.—*Of the difference betwixt* Hiſtory *and* Biography.—*The ſubject of hiſtory is narrative.*—*Whatever is not narrative in hiſtory is epiſodical.*—*What epiſodes are proper for hiſtory,*—*not political or philoſophical reflections upon human nature, ſuch as thoſe of Salluſt in the beginning of* Cataline's conſpiracy, *and of the* Jugurthine war.—*Explanations of particular cuſtoms and manners of a nation, a proper epiſode in hiſtory.* —*Difference in this reſpect betwixt the Greek hiſtorians of Roman affairs, and their own.*—*Of the* rhetorical ſtile *in hiſtory.*—Speeches *in it, not digreſſions or epiſodes but matters of fact, and parts of the ſtory.*—Speeches *make political and philoſophical reflections not improper in hiſtory.*—*Hiſtory therefore a moſt pleaſant and various compoſition ;*—*but the* poetical *ſtile, a variety which hiſtory does* not admit.—*Of the peculiarities of the poetical stile which history does not admit, such as* Epithets, Similies, Metaphors, *and* Minute Descriptions.—*Of the* painting *in* Homer, *and the difference in that respect betwixt his stile, and the stile of history.*—*Of the choice of words in the historical stile.*—*Difference, in that respect, betwixt the stile of Homer and of history.*—*Of the* Composition *in history, by which the stile of it is chiefly to be distinguished from common speech ;—not to be distinguished in that way by* variety of arrangement, *as in Greek and Latin, but only by* Periods.—*Of the great beauty of* Periods.—*Quotation upon that subject from Aristotle, showing, that he thought there could be no beauty, without* 'a System and a Whole.—*There is nothing that can be properly called* Composition *without periods.*—*Of the defect of Sallust and Tacitus in this respect.*—*The stile of Tacitus worse than that of Sallust.*—*One example of a Greek author, who writes like Sallust.*—*Such compositions still more inexcusable in Greek than in Latin.*

Ch. IX. Progress of Language.

I AM now to treat of the ſtile of Hiſtory, according to the order I propoſed to follow in this work *. By hiſtory I mean not the hiſtory of flies or reptiles or of other animals, commonly called natural hiſtory; but the hiſtory of *man*, and not of particular men, but of nations: For I diſtinguiſh betwixt biography and hiſtory, as I diſtinguiſh betwixt an individual and the nation of which he makes a part.

That the ſtile of hiſtory ought to be different from the ſtile of converſation or dialogue, of which I have already treated, or from the didactic, the rhetorical, and poetical, of which I am to treat, muſt be evident at firſt ſight: And I am now to ſhow wherein that difference conſiſts.

As the ſubject, or matter treated of, is principal in every work, the ſtile ought to be ſuitable to it †. Now, the ſubject of

* Page 291.
† Page 291.

history, is the narrative of the tranfactions of a nation. Whatever therefore in hiftory is not narrative, muft be confidered as not principal, but only epifodical; and if the epifodes are too long, or not belonging to the principal fubject, and arifing naturally out of it, the work is in that refpect faulty. The queftion therefore is, what epifodes are proper for hiftory? How frequent! And how long continued?

In the firft place, I think it is evident, that philofophical reflections upon government, or political differtations, are not the proper bufinefs of hiftory, which, no doubt, furnifhes a text for them; but it is not the bufinefs of the hiftorian to be the commentator upon that text. This he ought to leave to the reader; and all that he has to do, is to give him a text exact and correct. I therefore take upon me to condemn all digreffions of that kind, efpecially when they run out to any length, fuch as the political reflections of Salluft upon the Roman ftate, in his introduction to *Cataline's confpiracy*, or his philofophical obfervations on human nature, in his preface to his *Jugurthine*

Ch. IX. Progress of Language. 399

war; both which might have been proper, if he had been writing a syſtem of morals or politics, or might have been more excuſable, if he had been writing a general hiſtory of the Roman ſtate, but, I think, are very foreign to the hiſtory of ſingle events in a nation, ſuch as the conſpiracy of Cataline, or the war of Jugurtha *.

But by what I have ſaid, I would not be underſtood to mean, that the explanation of particular cuſtoms and manners of the nation whoſe hiſtory you write, is improper in hiſtory; but, on the contrary, I think it is extremely proper; and I regret very much, that the Roman hiſtorians have not been at more pains to explain ſeveral things of that kind.—Their excuſe is, that ſuch explications were quite unneceſſary to thoſe for whom they wrote. But they ſhould have conſidered, that they were writing for poſterity, and for men of other nations, who knew nothing of the Roman cuſtoms

---

* This is the judgment of Quintilian, *Salluſtius, in bello Catalinario et Jugurthino, nihil ad hiſtoriam pertinentibus principiis orſus eſt*; Lib. iii. cap. 10.

and manners. And, indeed, this defect in
them would have made the Roman hiſtory hardly intelligible to us, if it had not
been ſupplied by the Greek hiſtorians, particularly by the Halicarnaſſian and Polybius; who, writing for their own countrymen,
have been at pains to inform us of many
things concerning the cuſtoms of the Romans both in peace and war, and the nature of their government, which otherwiſe we could not have underſtood. It
appears, therefore, that hiſtory may have
ſomething of the didactic ſtile in it.

But what ſhall we ſay of the rhetorical
ſtile, I mean the ſtile of the ſpeeches in
the antient hiſtories? Are they foreign to
the ſubject? And I ſay they are not, but,
on the contrary, very proper; for they
not only vary the ſtile moſt agreeably, and
relieve the reader from the diſguſt of hearing nothing but facts, without reaſon or
argument; but they are a part, and a material part of the hiſtory of nations, where
the public buſineſs was carried on chiefly
by ſpeaking; for, in ſuch a nation, the
ſpeeches are to be conſidered as matters of

fact: And accordingly Thucydides tells us, that the speeches he has given us, many and long as they are, were really spoken, at least in substance, he himself having heard them, or being informed by them who heard them [*]. And, even where the historian could have no such knowledge, which is the case of Livy and the Halicarnassian, with respect to the speeches which they put into the mouths of the personages of the first ages of the Roman state; yet, as we are sure that public business was then carried on by speaking, as well as in later times, they are not at all improper, more especially as they give the historian an opportunity of explaining the counsels and motives of actions, without digressing or letting his story stand still. Such speeches, therefore, are not to be considered as episodes, but as parts, not ornamental merely, but very useful, of the history.

And here the author has an opportunity of bringing into his work, without violating the rules of history, political, and even philosophical reflections, and likewise

VOL. IV.   3 E

[*] Lib. i. cap. 22.

a good deal of the history of other nations, by way of example, and of the same nation in more antient times.

And thus it appears, that history is a most pleasant and various composition, taking in not only the narrative but the didactic and rhetorical stiles, and even something of the philosophy of morals and politics, together with examples from the history of other nations and of other times.

It remains therefore only to be inquired, whether history does not partake of the poetical stile, as well as of the other stiles I have mentioned: And I say it does not; and that history is as different from poetry, as it is from painting; for, as Horace says, *uti pictura poesis*. And the chief difference betwixt poetry and painting is the instrument of imitation, painting imitating by lines and colours, poetry by words. And hence comes the difference betwixt the stile of poetry and history. One of the chief characteristics of the poetical stile is epithets, by which the object is represented to the imagination, as it is by painting to the eyes; and it is for this reason, that

Homer abounds so very much in epithets, bestowing them not only on persons, but on things; and even the most common things, such as earth and water, which in that manner may be painted or represented to the imagination in poetry, as to the eye in painting. But in history, even persons the most illustrious, ought not to be described in that way; I condemn therefore in history the designing persons by epithets, such as *the brave Prince, the gallant warrior, the philosophic sage,* and the like; though I know such expressions are reckoned ornaments of the historical stile by those who cannot make the proper distinction betwixt the stile of poetry and of history. And as to *things,* I say there ought never an adjective to be applied to any substantive, merely for the sake of adorning it, or exciting any passion in us, which is the proper definition of an epithet, but only for the purpose of narrative or argument. Then there is the use of similies, by which a thing that may not be so conspicuous in itself, is made more conspicuous by comparison with another thing. This figure very much ornaments the stile, by descriptions of beautiful things in nature, or art; and accordingly the similies of Homer are the most ornamented parts of his poems. Then there is the frequent use of metaphors in poetry, which are short similies: and, lastly, there is a particular and a minute description of things, called by the antient critics διατυπωσις *, by which things are so circumstantially and accurately described, that a painter may represent them in colours, by exactly copying the description given of them. Of this kind are many descriptions in Homer, and particularly one in the Odyssey, where he paints as much, as is possible for words to do, an event most interesting, as all of the kind in poetry are; I mean the discovery of Ulysses by his old nurse, when she was washing his feet, an event upon which his whole fortune and the catastrophe of the poem depended †. Now, such

* See what I have said on this *Figure*, Vol. III. p. 117.

† I do not know any so good a subject of painting, as this discovery; and, I am glad that so eminent a painter as Sir Joshua Reynolds has chosen it for the subject of a picture, which he is to paint for the Russian Prince Potemkin.

painting does not belong even to oratory, as I have elſewhere ſhown *, but much leſs to hiſtory. The reaſon of which is, that the chief end of poetry is to move the paſſions; whereas, the buſineſs of hiſtory is to inſtruct by a faithful narrative, accurate and circumſtantial enough to make the things be perceived by the underſtanding, but not ſo minute, or ſo much coloured, as to make them an object of the imagination. Such being therefore the difference betwixt poetry and hiſtory, I blame the ſtile of every hiſtory which abounds with epithets and ſimilies, or makes much uſe of metaphors that are not common in the language, or which, by a particular deſcription of things, applies itſelf to the imagination and paſſions.

The ſtile of hiſtory, as well as every other ſtile, conſiſts of two things, the choice of words, and the compoſition of theſe words: The laſt of which is acknowledged by all the maſters of the art to be the moſt difficult part, as well as that which gives

* Vol. III. p. 118.

the greateſt beauty to ſtile, when well executed. As to the choice of words in hiſtory, they ſhould be all the common words of the language, but of the beſt kind, that is, ſuch as are uſed by the politeſt and beſt educated men, ſpeaking or writing with gravity and dignity upon ſubjects of importance. Of metaphors and other tropes none ſhould be uſed but ſuch as are common and familiar, nor any words that are obſolete and antiquated. In this particular, Salluſt, as I have obſerved elſewhere*, is very faulty; for he abounds with obſolete words and phraſes, which are an ornament to poetry, if judiciouſly employed; and, accordingly, they are much uſed by Homer, in whom it is not difficult to diſcern two languages, the language of his own time, and that of times much more antient. And, I think, it is a very great beauty in the beſt rhyming poetry we have in Engliſh, I mean Mr Thomſon's *Caſtle of Indolence*. But I hold them to be improper both in hiſtory and rhetoric, or in any other kind of writing or ſpeaking, the ſubject of which is the ordinary affairs of life.

* Vol. III. p. 200.

The compofition, therefore, is that by which the hiftorical ftile is chiefly to be diftiguifhed from any other. How much the ftile in Greek and Latin may be varied and diftinguifhed from common fpeech by a different arrangement of the words, I have more than once obferved in the courfe of this work. But I have alfo obferved, that the ftinted genius of our language, fo defective in its grammar, and wanting that variety of flection, and thofe numbers and genders, by which words, at a diftance from one another in pofition, are joined together in fyntax, does not admit of that beautiful variety of arrangement, which, at the fame time that it pleafes the ear, conveys the fenfe more emphatically *. Neither does the fimple fyntax of our language admit of all that variety of figures of conftruction, with which Thucydides has adorned his ftile fo much, that, as the Halicarnaffian has obferved, the grammarians have not names for them all. Thefe figures, though they be what the antient critics call σολοικοφα-

* See what I have faid upon this fubject, in my Differtation upon the compofition of the ancients, annexed to Vol. II.

rus, that is, *having the appearance of so-lecisms*, yet, if they be not intemperately used, or so as to produce an obscurity in the sense, which is often the case in Thucydides, are a beauty of stile, but such as our language does not admit. The only way therefore remaining, by which our historical stile in English can be distinguished from common speech, is by composition in periods. And, indeed, it is the greatest beauty of all composition, whether in learned or unlearned languages, in prose or in verse. I have said a good deal upon this subject elsewhere in this volume *, which I will not here repeat. In volume third †, I have given definitions of a period from Aristotle and Cicero, and have shown how much better the philosopher has defined it than the orator; I have also illustrated what I have said upon the subject by examples from Demosthenes, Cicero, and Milton. I will only add here, that whoever is not sensible of the beauty of a period, does not appear to me to know

---

* Page 238. and following.

† Chapter 5.

what beauty is, which cannot be, as I have shown elsewhere *, without a system and

* Metaphysics, vol. II. p. 111. Aristotle speaking of the fable of a tragedy, says, (*Poetics*, cap. 7.) that it must not only be a whole, having a beginning, middle, and end; but it must have a certain size or extent: For, says he, a beautiful animal, or whatever else is beautiful, consisting of parts, must not only have these properly arranged, but must likewise have a certain magnitude; for the beautiful consists in order and magnitude. Therefore, says he, a very small animal is not beautiful, because we do not distinctly perceive the relation of the whole to its parts, nor is a very great animal beautiful, because we cannot comprehend it, so that we do not perceive *the one* in *the whole*. Such, says he, would be an animal of 10,000 stadia. I will subjoin the words of the original, as I think the passage very remarkable: Ετι δε επει το καλον, και ζωον και ἁπαν πραγμα ὁ συνεστηκεν εκ τινων, ου μονον ταυτα τεταγμενα δει εχειν, αλλα και μεγεθος ὑπαρχειν μη το τυχον· το γαρ καλον, εν μεγεθει και ταξει εστι. Διο ουτε παμμικρον αν τι γινοιτο καλον ζωον· συγχειται γαρ 'η θεωρια εγγυς του αναισθητου χρονου γινομενη· ουτε παμμεγεθες. Ου γαρ 'αμα 'η θεωρια γινεται, αλλ' οιχεται τοις θεωρουσι το 'εν και το 'ολον εκ της θεωριας· οιον ει μυριων σταδιων ειη ζωον.—This passage I had not before me, when I wrote the chapter of Metaphysics above quoted; but it gives me very great pleasure to find, that my notions upon a subject, which has been so little considered by any author ancient or

a whole, of a certain extent, having beginning, middle, and end.

Not only is a period one of the greateſt beauties of ſpeaking or writing, but it is ſo eſſential to compoſition, that nothing deſerves the name of *compoſition*, which has not periods longer or ſhorter, but conſiſts altogether of ſhort ſentences, eſpecially if theſe ſentences are unconnected; yet this is the ſtile of Salluſt, which is ſo uniform in that reſpect, that I hardly remem-

---

modern, I mean the definition of the τι ϛαλοι, and where I had ſo little light to guide me, none at all indeed, when I wrote that chapter, coincides ſo perfectly with Ariſtotle. Now, a period is a whole, as well as a fable of a tragedy: And, accordingly, Ariſtotle has defined it to be *that which has a beginning and an end* (he might have added *a middle too*) *in itſelf, and a ſufficient extent.* See the words of Ariſtotle quoted in vol. III. of this work, p. 57. The meaning of its having a beginning and end in itſelf is, that it muſt not be terminated by the ſenſe only, but by the ſound, ſo that the ear expects an end; which is not the caſe in the λεξις ειρομενη, as he calls it, in which the ear perceives neither beginning nor end; and therefore has not the pleaſure which a runner has, who ſees the goal before him.

ber any thing in him, which deserves the name of a period. So that, supposing this kind of stile were in itself beautiful, it has not variety enough to make it fine writing; and from this so great uniformity, it is evident that it was studied and affected. Now, an author may not have skill enough, or may not bestow pains sufficient to compose good periods. But, if he is at pains to make his sentences short, abrupt, and unconnected, he shows a very bad taste, and labours to write ill. I will not here repeat what I have said of the stile of Sallust and of Tacitus in Vol. III. of this work, where I have bestowed upon these two stiles the best part of three chapters *. I will only add here, that though Sallust very well deserves the censure which Seneca bestows on him, of *amputatae sententiae*, and *verba ante expectatum cadentia*, he does not deserve to be charged with the third fault which Seneca imputes to him, viz. *obscura brevitas* †; for I do not re-

* Chap. 11. 12. and 13.

† Seneca, epist. 114.

collect at present any passage in Sallust that I think is obscure. But as to Tacitus, he is most justly chargeable with all the three, and especially an *obscure brevity*, which has made notes upon Tacitus more necessary, I think, than upon any one Roman author; he has, besides, much more of point and affectation of wit, than Sallust. And, upon the whole, I reckon his stile much worse than that of Sallust, and among the worst stiles that is to be found even in modern times.

In my observations upon his stile and that of Sallust, I have said *, that I know no author in Greek who wrote in that stile; but there has fallen lately into my hands a Greek author of the fourth century, Achilles Tatius, who has written a kind of romance or novel upon the subject of the loves of Clitaphon and Leucippe. His cut of stile is, if possible, shorter and more unconnected than that of Sallust or Taci-

* Vol. III. p. 201.

tus*. Such a manner of writing is, I think, still more inexcusable in a Greek author than in a Latin, because one of the greatest beauties of the Greek is, as I have observed elsewhere †, that it abounds much more than the Latin in connecting particles, by which not only the words in the same sentence, but sentences themselves, are connected together, so that there is no stop or gap in the composition.

* I will give the reader a specimen of this author's stile; in the beginning of any work, one naturally expects some kind of composition; but this author's exordium is what follows: Σιδων ιστι θαλαττη πολις. Αστυρ:- οι 'η θαλασσα. Ματαρ Φοινικων 'η πολις. Θηβαιων 'ο δημος εστηρ. Διδυμος λιμην εν κολπω πλατυς. Ηρεμα κλυων τι πελαγος. A little after, going on in the same stile, he says, Περιων ουν και την αλλην πολιν, και τηρισκεπει τα οικηματα, 'ιρω γραφει ανακειμενον γης 'αμα και θαλαττης. Ερχονται 'η γραφη. Φοινικων 'η θαλαττη. Σιδωνις 'ε γη. Εν τη γη λιμην, και χορος περιων.

† Page 63.—66. of this Volume.

CHAP. X.

The history of Herodotus most various both in matter and stile.—The matter takes in the whole history of the world, as far as it was known, before his time.—Yet there is an unity in his work, such as there is in Homer's poems.—He begins his work, as Homer does, with the cause of the wars betwixt the Greeks and Barbarians, which are the subject of his work.—Other things he has introduced as episodes. —Of the truth of the facts in Herodotus. —These not credible to a man, who believes that men have always been the same in all ages and nations.—No lies in Herodotus.—Of the variety of his stile.— Not poetical, though like the stile of Homer;—very much figured, and yet neither rhetorical nor poetical.—It is composed in periods, but not rhetorical periods.— Examples of the periods in Herodotus.— Cicero mistaken in saying, that there are no numbers in Herodotus.—Of the speeches in Herodotus;—there are but few, but these upon proper occasions;—the matter of them excellent.—Not many reflections, nor philosophical and political observations; but these to the purpose.—One example of them.—The dialect, in which he writes, Ionic.—He uses much the terminations of the datives plural in that dialect.—No epithets, similes, or picturesque descriptions in his stile, nor any of the strong figures used by Homer.—One figure of Homer, much used by him, viz. dialogue.—Examples of Herodotus's dialogue.—His stile distinguished in that way from that of every other historian.—Herodotus a religious historian.—All historians, as well as poets of the higher order, ought to be religious.—Herodotus not superstitious, or over credulous, in matters of religion.

BUT, leaving such authors as Sallust and Tacitus to their admirers, without a rival, at least for me;—I proceed to speak of the first Greek historian, and, I think, the best both for matter and stile, the father of history, as he is called, and whose nine books are very properly named after the nine Muses. The first excellence of every history is, as the Halicarnassian has observed *, a proper choice of a subject: And indeed, it is the chief thing to be considered in all the works of art; for, let the execution be ever so good, if the subject be mean and contemptible or in any other respect ill chosen, the piece cannot be fine. Now, the subject of Herodotus's history is the grandest and noblest that can well be imagined, concluding with the greatest event which the history of man furnishes, (I mean the expedition of Xerxes into Greece), whether we consider the number of men employed in it, amounting, according to Herodotus's account, to above 5,000,000, the greatest collection, I believe, that ever was made of the human race;—the prodigious works preparatory to it, in which the power of men

* Epist. ad Cn. Pompeium, cap. iii.

seems to have triumphed even over nature; or, whether we confider the virtue of the Greeks oppofed to fuch a wonderful power, and which may be truly faid to have exhibited *Dignum Deo Spectaculum*; for never was fo manifefted, not even in the fictions of poets,

―― *Quid virtus et quid fapientia poffit* ;

or, laftly, the confequences which would have happened, if Xerxes had fucceeded in that expedition, and which make it not only the greateft war that ever exifted in the refpects I have mentioned, but alfo of the greateft importance to mankind. For, if the Perfians had prevailed, the Greeks, the fineft race of people that ever exifted, would have been fwallowed up and loft in the great empire of Perfia, it being the cuftom of the Perfians, as Plato informs us, to mix and confound the races of men, by tranfplanting nations from one country to another; an example of which Herodotus gives, in the inftance of a Thracian nation, viz. the Paeonians, which Darius, the father of Xerxes, tranfplanted far into Afia*. With Greece would have been loft all learning, philofophy, and fine arts: For Egypt was conquered, and become a part of the empire; and, confequently, the learning and the arts there deep in their decline. A good deal of their learning, indeed, had been brought into Italy by Pythagoras, and was then ftill preferved among his fcholars: But we know, that foon after his fchool was difperfed; and what remains of his philofophy at this day, we owe to the curiofity and diligence of the Greeks. So that, if the Greeks had been at that time conquered, it appears to me, that the Weftern and Northern parts of Europe, which from them have got all their arts and learning, muft have remained, at leaft for many ages longer, in ignorance and barbarity, and, I believe, for ever; for it does not appear to me, that we ever could have invented any liberal art or fcience; particularly here in Britain, we fhould have been no better than the favages of North America,

* Herodotus, lib. v. cap. 14. et 15.

and in this respect worse, that we have got wealth and luxury, against which the only preservative is the learning and philosophy of the Greeks. And thus it appears, that the cause of learning as well as of liberty was at stake upon the success of Xerxes's expedition.

As the history of Herodotus, therefore, is the noblest, with respect to its matter *, that can well be imagined, so it is the most various and comprehensive; for it contains the history of all the nations then known, and of Greece among the rest, from the Trojan war, where Homer leaves off, down to the war with Xerxes, which happened

* See what further the Halicarnassian has said, upon the choice that Herodotus has made for the subject of his history and his manner of treating it, compared with Thucydides's choice of his subject and his manner of treating it, in his *Epistle to Pompey*, above quoted, cap. 3. *et sequen.* where, among other things, he has observed, that Herodotus's subject has in it a great deal of philanthropy, and must have been particularly agreeable to his countrymen the Greeks. And, I am persuaded, when he recited his history in the great national panegyric of the Olympic games, he must have been heard with the greatest pleasure and admiration.

only a generation before the author lived. To this so various history he has contrived to give an unity, (for the ancients esteemed no work of any kind unless it was a whole or piece, without which, they conceived no beauty in any thing,) such as Homer has given to each of his two poems. And what makes the unity of his work, is the same that makes the unity of Homer's poems, namely, the subject; which, he tells us, is the war betwixt the Greeks and Barbarians, concluded by the invasion of Greece by Xerxes, in so far at least, that the war ceased to be offensive upon the part of the Barbarians, who were contented after that to defend themselves, and at last could not even do that, but were conquered by the Greeks. This subject he has, like Homer, proposed in the beginning of his work, and as Homer has begun his Iliad with narrating the cause of the quarrel betwixt Agamemnon and Achilles, which is the subject of that poem, so Herodotus begins his history with narrating the cause of the war betwixt the Greeks and Barbarians, the subject, as I have said, of his work. Then, as Homer has contrived to bring into his

two poems, by way of epifodes, almoſt all
the hiſtory of Greece before his time, fo
Herodotus has introduced into his work
not only the hiſtory of the Greeks and
Perſians, but the hiſtory of the Lydians,
Aſſyrians, Medes, Scythians, and Egyptians; and, indeed, the whole hiſtory of
the world then known; fo that as to the
variety of the matter he far exceeds Homer, and yet with all that variety the u-
nity of the work is ſtill preſerved. For,
as the fubjeft of his hiſtory is the wars betwixt the Greeks and Barbarians, and as
all nations were divided at that time into
Greeks and Barbarians, the fubjeft is com-
prehenſive enough to take in all the hiſtories of the feveral nations, with which he
fills up his piece; and, indeed, every thing
he relates, prior to Xerxes's expedition,
may be faid to be preparatory of that grand
event, which concludes his hiſtory. All
the hiſtories, therefore, above mentioned
are to be confidered as epifodes which he
has introduced, not abruptly or unconnected with what goes before or follows; but
all of them, like thoſe of Homer, are fome
way or other conneted, not only with the

principal fubject, but with one another;
for he has the art of tacking ftories together, and inferting them one into another,
like fo many boxes in a cafe, more than any other author I know, without excepting even Homer; fo that we infenfibly
flip from one ftory to another, hardly
knowing that it is an epifode or a digreffion. And, in this refpect, as well as in
many others, the Halicarnaffian has very
juftly given the preference to Herodotus
before Thucydides, who, he fays, has contrived it fo, as to make of one fubject, viz.
the Peloponnefian war, many fubjects;
whereas, Herodotus has had the art, of
many fubjects to make one *. And, as

* *Epiftola ad Cn. Pemprium*, cap. 3. This whole epiftle I would advife the learned reader to perufe very
diligently, as one of the beft pieces of criticifm that is
any where to be found. I have obferved fome errors
in it, whether of the printed edition or the MS. I cannot fay; but fome of them may be very eafily corrected,
and, I hope, will be corrected in fome future edition
to be given at Oxford. I will only mention one, that
happens to be under my eye. It is in the third chapter
of the epiftle, where comparing the fubject of Thucydides with that of Herodotus, he wonders that Thucydides

that is the chief art of a poet, I don't wonder that the Halicarnaffian gives to Herodotus's hiftory, the name of a poem *, which, I think, it much better deferves than the hiftory of Thucydides, to which the Halicarnaffian alfo gives that name: But the truth is, that every artificial compofition, fuch as the hiftory of Thucydides undoubtedly is, may be faid in fome refpects to be a *poem*.

As to the truth of the facts related by Herodotus, and which no doubt is the chief excellence of every hiftory, I have' fpoken elfewhere †. A reader, who be-

---

fhould have taken for his fubject, a war fo unfortunate to the Greeks, and particularly to the Athenians, being himfelf a Greek and an Athenian. And he adds, Και ταυτα ον ται ιτι ιιςαμιινοι οντα, αλλα 'ον ιν ηςοντιις ηγοι Αθηναιοι, στςατνγιον και ται αλλοι τιμον αξιουντις; where it is evident, that the words ον ται ιτι ιιςαμιινοι, have no fenfe at all: And, therefore, it is plain, that in place of them, we fhould read ον των φανλον, (or fome fuch word) οντα. And accordingly, I obferve it is fo tranflated.

* Ibid. cap. iii. *in fine.*

† Ancient Metaphyfics, Vol. III. p. 149.

lieves that men have always been the same
in all ages and nations, that we now see
them, and that there was no more communication betwixt men in ancient times and
superior intelligences, than there is now,
will reject the greater part of the facts related by Herodotus, as altogether incredible; and, for the same reason, he will disbelieve all ancient history, sacred as well as
prophane. To such a reader I would give
the advice, which Lord Bolingbrocke gives
to the student of history; not to go farther
back in his reading, than the days of Charles
the Fifth, and so rest satisfied with modern men and modern manners. As to
Herodotus, it appears that no historian or
traveller was ever at more pains to inform
himself*. For the discovery of truth, and
no other motive, he travelled over a great
part of the world then known; and almost
all that he relates of the different countries,
was either what he saw himself, or learned
from people of the country. And, as to
his veracity, I do not believe that there is

* Ibidem.

a lye in the whole book; though no doubt he relates many things that are not true, and which he did not believe himself, as he tells us, even when he ought to have believed it, as we know now that they were certainly true *. There is only one other historian of antiquity, to whom we are as much obliged as to Herodotus for the pains he took to inform us concerning those ancient times, that is, Diodorus Siculus, who travelled, as he tells us †, thirty years, and was in almost all the countries of which he speaks. But even his history I think much inferior to that of Herodotus, both as to the matter and the stile.

As to the stile of Herodotus, it is almost as various as his matter; for he has diversified his composition with every figure of construction, and all the variety of phraseology, as well as of order and arrangement of the words, that can well be imagined ‡; and this, joined with the peculia-

---

* Ibidem.
† Lib. i. cap. 4.
‡ See Dionysius, De Thucydide, cap. 23.

rity of his dialect, makes his ſtile very obſcure, even to thoſe who are maſters of the Greek language, if they have not very diligently ſtudied his manner*. Yet

---

* I can excuſe the tranſlators and commentators, when, from the uſe of ſuch figures, and particularly the figure of ἀποσιώπησις, which is not unfrequent in him, and from the peculiarities of his dialect, they miſtake his meaning, as they do in ſeveral paſſages that I have obſerved. But I cannot ſo eaſily pardon them, when, merely for want of a proper punctuation, they give an abſurd ſenſe, or no ſenſe at all, to a paſſage, ſuch as that in the ſecond book, where there is no error in the words, but only in the punctuation, which the new editor Weſſelingius might have corrected, if he had underſtood a note of one Valkenarius that he quotes, but which, it is clear both from his punctuation of the text, and from his tranſlation, he did not underſtand. I ſhall give the paſſage, as I had pointed it in my copy ſeveral years before this new edition appeared; without adding, taking away, or altering a ſingle word. The paſſage is in the 11th chapter of the ſecond book, where ſpeaking of the Arabian gulf, or Red ſea as we call it, and the gulf which the Mediterranean formed in Egypt, as he ſuppoſes, before the *Delta* was created by the river, he proves the poſſibility of ſuch a creation, by ſuppoſing the Nile to be turned into the Arabian gulf. The words are; Εἰ ὠν ἐθέλοι ἐκτρέψαι τὸ ῥέεθρον ὁ Νεῖλος εἰς τοῦτον τὸν Ἀράβιον κόλπον, τί μιν κωλύει ῥέοντος τούτου ἐκχωσθῆναι ἐντός γε δισμυρίων ἐτέων; Ἐγὼ μὲν γὰρ ἔλπομαι γε καὶ

Ch. X. PROGRESS OF LANGUAGE. 427

with all this variety, he ſtill keeps within the bounds of the hiſtorical ſtile, and is neither rhetorical nor poetical: For, though many readers may think his ſtile poetical, becauſe he uſes many of the words and phraſes of Homer, I am perſuaded that thoſe words and phraſes were in common uſe among the Ionians in Aſia; and, indeed, it is very natural that it ſhould be ſo, when we conſider that Homer was of that country. If they had been eſteemed among the Ionians poetical or gloſſematical

μοριων ιστις χρηςτοι αν. Καν γε δι εν τῷ ασαισιμομειῳ προτερον ε ιμι γινεσθαι, ουκ αν χρονιη κολπος και πολλῳ μᾶζον ετι τουτο υπο τοιουτε γε ποταμου και 'ουτως εργατικου;

And the meaning of the paſſage, this way pointed, is plain; which is this: 'If the Nile ſhould run into the 'Arabian gulf, what ſhould hinder that gulf to be fill-'ed up in 20,000 years? For my part, I think it would 'be filled up in 10,000 years; and if ſo, how ſhould 'it have happened, that, in all the time which has 'paſſed before I was born, this gulf,' (meaning the Egyptian gulf,) 'or a much greater than this, ſhould not 'have been filled by ſo great and ſo operative a river?'
—I have only farther to obſerve, that this Valkenarius makes a fooliſh ſcruple about the phraſe προτερον ε ιμι γινεσθαι, of which, I am perſuaded, there are many examples to be found, if it were worth the while to look for them.

words, Herodotus was too well acquainted with the nature of the hiſtorical ſtile, to have uſed them; and, without their aid, he knew as well as any man a ſecret, that is but little known now-a-days,—that of making an uncommon ſtile of common words. It is for this purpoſe, and not from any confuſion of thought, or inaccuracy of language, (as modern vanity is apt to believe), that he uſes thoſe diſorderly conſtructions, as they ſeem to be, and thoſe prepoſterous arrangements, as it would ſeem, of the different members of the ſentence, which diſtinguiſh his ſtile very much from common language, and yet create no difficulty to a man well acquainted with the beauty and variety of the Greek language, and the manner of the author. The ſtile, therefore, of Herodotus is neither rhetorical nor poetical; for it has not thoſe antitheſes with which the rhetorical ſtile abounds ſo much, nor is it compoſed in rhetorical periods, though he compoſes very often in long periods, and, I think, the moſt beautiful periods of the hiſtoric kind: But they are not rounded and conſtricted, or contorted, as the ancient critics expreſs it, like thoſe of an oration, but loofer and of a more eafy and natural flow, according to the account which I have given of the hiftorical period in another part of this work*. To perceive the difference betwixt thefe two periods, is a matter of tafte and pretty nice difcernment, depending upon a fenfe of what is proper, becoming, and fuitable to the fubject, without which we can neither write well, nor judge of good writing of any kind. And yet, as I have elfewhere obferved †, it cannot be reduced to rules: But, if nature has beftowed it upon us, (for no art can give it), we fhall perceive, that a compofition proper to enforce an argument, or to excite paffion, muft be different from plain hiftorical narrative. Now, I think, there is no author who has better diftinguifhed thofe two compofitions, or whofe narrative has a more eafy natural flow, than that of Herodotus. Of a period of this kind the Halicarnaffian has given us a very fine example from the be-

* Vol. III. p. 368.

† Page 244. of this Volume.

ginning of his history, where he describes the boundaries of the kingdom of Croesus; and the very first sentence of his history, in which he proposes his subject, and informs us of his design in writing, is, I think, a very good historical period. In those periods of Herodotus, there are numbers which please even my ear, but must have pleased much more the learned ear of the Halicarnassian. I therefore hold, that Cicero is much mistaken, when he says, that there are no numbers in Herodotus. There are not, indeed, such numbers in his history as in Cicero's orations; but these numbers of Cicero do not please me even in the rhetorical stile, but they would be still more unsuitable to the historical.

Herodotus, however, has speeches in his history, as many as, I think, should be in such a general history as his: And they are excellent for the matter, and never introduced but upon a proper occasion, such as when Xerxes laid before his council the design he had formed of invading Greece; for, as there were different opinions given in that council, his method of dialogue, of which I shall speak by and by, would not have been there so proper. And, when the seven conspirators against the Magi deliberate what form of government they should establish after pulling them down, Herodotus puts into the mouth of three of them, three political speeches, one in favour of each of the three forms of government, such as, for the beauty and propriety of the sentiments, may be compared to any in Thucydides, or to the famous orations in Dion Cassius of Moecenas and Agrippa, upon occasion of Augustus's deliberation, about laying down the government, and restoring liberty to the people of Rome.

There are also very fine reflections interspersed here and there in his narration, but only sparingly and upon proper occasions: For he is not every where sententious like Tacitus, nor makes his history a lecture upon politics, but, contenting himself with relating the facts, leaves the reader at liberty to make his own commentary upon them. I shall give only one instance of a very short but pertinent obfervation of his, which fhews, that, from his travels and obfervations, he had acquired a very comprehenfive view of the hiftory of man. It is upon the occafion of his relating a very extraordinary fact indeed, that there was a people in the northern parts of Europe, beyond the Danube, who faid they were a colony of the Medes, and accordingly wore the Median drefs. How this fhould have happened, fays he, I do not know; but παν γενοιτο αν εν τῳ μαχρῳ χρονῳ*. 'Any thing may happen 'in a long fpace of time.' And, indeed, there is nothing that one can imagine and is poffible to have happened, but I believe actually has happened fome time or other to the human fpecies: And, particularly, it appears, that, by fome accident or another, the different races of men have been ftrangely jumbled together. Thus, befides this colony of a nation fo remote, found in the midft of nations quite different in every refpect, the fame author tells us, that in the ifland of Cyprus, there were people of

* Tefpfichore, cap. 8.

many different nations, such as Athenians, Salaminians, Arcadians, Cythnians, Phoenicians, and Æthiopians*. And this agrees with what travellers tell us of some of the countries they have discovered in the South Sea, where there are found people of all different colours and complexions, black, white, copper-coloured, red, brown, olive, and yellow.

Thus it appears, that the narrative of Herodotus, has nothing of the philosophical or political cast, any more than of the rhetorical. As to his speeches, they are but few, for a reason before mentioned †: Nor

---

* Lib. vii. cap. 90.

† Page 430.—That he was deficient in the Rhetorical stile, or the stile of debate and contention, is the judgment of the Halicarnassian ; (*De Thucydide Judicium*, cap. 23.) ; but he allows him every other virtue of stile. Diodorus Siculus has no speeches at all in his history; not only because his history was too general, more general still than that of Herodotus, but, I believe, for another reason, the same for which there are no speeches in our modern histories ; namely, that he was incapable of composing them.

is the compofition of them fo rhetorical as
I could have wifhed; for it does not appear that he ever practifed that ftile much,
either in writing or fpeaking. I therefore
think, that the ftile of his fpeeches is inferior to the ftile of thofe of Thucydides,
and ftill more to that of the orations of
Demofthenes.

The dialect Herodotus writes in is, as
as I have obferved, the Ionic; a dialect,
which I like better than any other in Greek,
as being more vocal than any other, and
coming nearer to the language of Homer
(which I hold to be the perfection of the
Greek language.) and to the ancient form
of language: For, I believe, that there has
been an abbreviation of words in all
languages after they were formed, and
particularly a contraction of vowels ftanding together, and of fyllables; and fome
languages have been in that way made
worfe, (as for example our own), and
none better. I like therefore that concourfe of vowels, which the Attic writers fhun fo much: And thofe Homeric
terminations of οισι and ησι I like very

Ch. X. PROGRESS OF LANGUAGE. 435

much, if there be not too many of them together, which sometimes happens in Herodotus *; but never in Homer. He has too a great many words and phrases peculiar to the dialect in which he writes; of which Henry Stephen and Camerarius have made a full collection, very useful to the young Greek scholar. Of these there are many to be found in Homer; but I do not for that believe them to be poetical words, but, as I have said †, the common language of the Ionians, though not used in the Attic dialect ‡. Besides all this, he

---

* See Herodotus, lib. iv. cap. 22. where we have the following words, speaking of a nation he calls Ιυρκαι, conterminous to another nation he calls Θυσσαγεται. Συνηραι δε τουτοισι οι Ιυρκαι αυτιοι τοιοιοι και οιεκμενοισι απο των δενδρων κατα την ιηραν.—Here there is a great deal too much jingle; but such examples are very rare. In Homer, we have only two such rhymes together, and never but in his similies, where he describes some very pleasurable object, and wants to make his verse very sweet and flowing; as in the simile of the nightingale, in the Odyssey, he has this line,

Δενδρεων εν πεταλοισι καθεζομενη πυκινοισι.

† Page 427.

‡ I recollect a passage in his third book, where, I am

uses many of those figures of construction above mentioned *, which, though they throw the stile quite out of common idiom, yet, as they are used by Herodotus, create no obscurity, but, on the contrary, serve very often to make the stile more perspicuous than it would otherwise be.

He uses too, as Homer does, frequent repetitions of the same word, and particularly of the pronoun αυτος, by which he connects very well the sense of his long periods. He also uses recapitulations, as Homer does, which gives a great perspicuity to his narrative. But, though he uses an arrangement of words artificial enough, he has not those violent hyperbatons which we find in Homer, and which

---

persuaded, he had Homer in view. It is where Homer describes Bellerophon going to Lycia, Θιει ευν αμυμονι πομπη. This he applies to the conspirators against the Magi, when they went to attack them in their palace. But he has not used the same words; if he had done so, it would have been poetry: but he has said, Θιη πομπη χρευμενοι.

* Page 407.

are very proper for the poetical ſtile, but not for proſe. Neither are the parentheſes, with which he diverſifies his ſtile, ſo long as ſome of Homer's. And, as to epithets, ſimiles, and picturefque deſcriptions, which are the proper ornaments of the poetical ſtile, and by which, more than by any thing elſe, it is diſtinguiſhed from proſe, he has nothing at all of the kind.

There is, however, one figure of compoſition which Homer has uſed very much, and in which Herodotus has imitated him more than any other hiſtorian; and indeed, it is the diſtinguiſhing characteriſtic of his hiſtorical ſtile, and makes his hiſtory, as the Halicarnaſſian obſerves*, as beautiful and pleaſant to read as any poem. The figure I mean is dialogue, by which he has made his compoſition in ſome ſort dramatical, and has given it one of the chief beauties of poetry, the imitation of characters and manners, though, as I

* *De Thucydide Judicium*, cap. 23.

have elsewhere observed *, it be one reason, besides the ignorance of ancient customs and manners, that makes the modern reader, not acquainted with this art of writing history, believe the stories in Herodotus to be no better than poetical fictions. But such readers should consider, that this is the most ancient way of writing history; and that the most authentic, as well as the most ancient history in the world, is written as much, or more in dialogue than the *Pages of Herodotus*.

To quote all the dialogues in Herodotus, would be to transcribe a great part of his history: I shall therefore mention only one or two of them, by way of example. In the very beginning of his history, where he relates the story of Candaules, King of Lydia, he introduces a dialogue betwixt him and his favourite Gyges, by which the folly of the King is better shown than it could have been by any reflections of the author, and much more properly

* Vol. III. of this work, p. 366.—Also Vol. III. of Anc. Metaph. p. 148.

than if he had interrupted his narrative by such reflections. And the story of Paris coming with Helen to Egypt, with what passed betwixt him and the Egyptian King, he has also related by way of dialogue; and a very fine dialogue I think it is, in which he has both aggravated the crime of Paris, much more properly than if he had let his story stand still to do it, and, at the same time, has given us the character of the Egyptian King, which is better done by introducing him speaking, than by any description. The longest dialogue in Herodotus, and, I think, the best, is the conversation betwixt Demaratus, the exiled Spartan King, and Xerxes just come from the review of his prodigious forces: For, upon the one side, the pride and insolence of a young monarch, who had armed and collected together a great part of the human race, and had covered the land with his armies and the sea with his fleets, his inexperience and ignorance of liberty and its effects upon the minds of men, and the sentiments naturally thence arising, are finely set forth: On the other hand, the wisdom, the experience, and the knowledge of Demaratus, particularly of that of which Xerxes was totally ignorant, I mean liberty, are very well reprefented.

Thus it appears, that Herodotus has with great propriety given to his hiftory one of the greateft beauties, as I have obferved *, of writing, and has diftinguifhed his ftile of hiftory in that way from every other hiftorical ftile. Nor do I know any other hiftorian, that has fo much as attempted to imitate his dialogue, except Thucydides, but very unfortunately in the judgment of the Halicarnaffian †.

I think, therefore, that the ftile of Herodotus is the moft agreeably diverfified,

---

* Page 390.—391.

† This dialogue of Thucydides is in the fifth book of his hiftory, beginning p. 400 of Harry Stephen's edition, and is continued for feveral pages, being very much longer than any of Herodotus; and is truly, as the Halicarnaffian obferves, departing intirely from the hiftorical ftile, and making a drama inftead of a hiftory. See his obfervations upon it, *De Thucydide Judicium*, cap. 38.

Ch. X. Progress of Language.

and, upon the whole, the moſt beautiful ſtile of hiſtory that ever was written.

I cannot conclude this eulogium of Herodotus, without obſerving what the Halicarnaſſian thinks deſerves to be noticed in every hiſtorian, and that is the diſpoſition and character of the writer; and he obſerves, that there is a great deal of philanthropy in the character of Herodotus, delighting, as he does, in the ſucceſs of the good, and grieved with their misfortunes. But he has not mentioned one thing in his character, which I admire very much, that he is a religious hiſtorian, ſhowing his firm belief, not only that there is a God, but that his providence directs the events of human life, as well as the operations of nature. Who has not this knowledge of divine and human things cannot write well of the affairs of men, any more than he could give a good hiſtory of a particular nation, without knowing how that nation is governed; nor can he promote that prime virtue, *piety*, without which no other virtue can be perfect, nor can there be any real happiness among men. To recommend this virtue, I hold to be the duty of the historian, as well as of poets of the higher kind, such as the heroic and tragic *. I therefore intirely dif-

---

* That the Gods govern the affairs of men, and direct the events of human life, is the moral of the Iliad, Odyssey, and Æneid; about which some modern critics have said so much to so little purpose. And as to the tragic poets, Euripides commonly concludes his tragedies in this manner;

Πολλα δ' αελπτως κραινουσι θεοι,
Και τα δοκηθεντ' ουκ ετελεσθη·
Των δ' αδοκητων πορον 'ευρε θεος·
Τοιος δ' απεβη τοδε πραγμα.

See what I have further said in Volume I. of Ancient Metaphysics, p. 498. of a governing providence and a present Deity, both in the works of nature and the affairs of men.——To which I will add a passage from Cicero, where, after enumerating several things in which other nations excelled his countrymen, he adds, ' Sed pietate ac religione atque hac una sapi-
' entia, quod Deorum immortalium numine omnia re-
' gi gubernarique perspeximus, omnes gentes nationef-
' que superavimus..'——*Oratio de Haruspicum. Responsa*
And, to this belief, I am persuaded, they owed chiefly their glory and the conquest of the world.

approve of such historians as Tacitus and his modern imitators, who either say nothing at all of providence, or, what is worse, profess to believe that human affairs are governed either by blind chance or fatal necessity*; which must put an end at once to all practical piety, as much as the Epicurean philosophy did of old.

Although Herodotus was religious, very religious, yet he does not appear to have been over credulous even in religious matters. The story told him by the Chaldeans, that Jupiter Belus came down and lay upon a couch prepared for him in

---

* See Tacitus's *Annals*, lib. vi. chap. 22. And in his book *De Moribus Germanorum*, cap. 46. speaking of a savage people in Germany, he says, that being ‘ Securi adversus homines, securi adversus Deos, rem ‘ difficillimam assecuti sunt, ut illis ne voto quidem o- ‘ pus sit.’ This is asserting in the strongest terms man's independency upon superior beings, even if those beings were disposed to middle with human affairs, which, in the passage above quoted from the *annals*, he says, it was believed by many, (and among these I number himself,) that they did not, but that human affairs, were governed, as I have said, either by blind chance or fatal necessity.

his temple in Babylon, attended by a woman consecrated to his service, he says he does not believe, though he was told the same story by the Egyptian priests of their Jupiter in Thebes *: And it is evident, that neither did he believe what the same Egyptian priests told him, of two wolves conducting a blind-folded priest to a temple of Ceres, at the distance of twenty stadia, and bringing him back again †.

That Herodotus believed in dreams and in oracles, is no doubt true: And, if on that account he is to be reckoned superstitious and credulous, we must make the same charge against the whole ancient world, both civilized and barbarous. For my own part, I believe that even now, in these degenerate days, though not so frequently as in ancient times, there is sometimes, upon particular occasions, and for wise and good purposes, a communication betwixt our minds and superior intelli-

* Lib. i. cap. ꝑ. π. A.
† Lib. ii. cap. ꝑ. π. A.

gences in our sleep; of which I have known, in my time instances, not only vouched by most credible testimonies, but verified by events of public notoriety: And I have not yet learned, that the ancient Greek oracles, which were universally understood to be the wisdom of the nation, directing them in all their affairs of moment, were mere imposture and priestcraft; but, on the contrary, I believe, as the ancient fathers of the church did, that they proceeded from superior intelligences, whether good or bad I determine not, but which were allowed to guide the councils of men, till the coming of our Saviour put an end to them.

CHAP. XI.

An account of the stile and manner of three other Greek historians: First, of Thucydides;—*his stile is prose, but made harsh and obscure, by the affectation of singularity;—by this affectation, the taste of other arts have been spoiled, as well as of writing.—The second Greek historian mentioned in this chapter, is* Xenophon; —*his stile perfectly different;—too simple and too little Attic;—more of the stile of the Socratic dialogue than of history;—abounds too much with characters;—some apology for that.—The last Greek historian mentioned in this chapter, is* Diodorus Siculus;—*in stile much inferior to either* Herodotus *or* Xenophon,—*and more still in point of matter;—his account of some great events mere fictions.—Other Greek historians, such as* Dion Cassius *and* Appian, *have used the same freedom with truth.—General observations.—Of the great excellency of contemporary historians above the compilers of history.*

HAVING been so full upon Herodotus, who, I must confess, is my favourite historian, being, in my opinion, the most instructive as well as the most pleasant of all historians, I will be very short upon the subject of other three Greek historians, of whom I am to treat in this chapter. The first of them is Thucydides, of whose stile I have spoken at some length, in the third volume of this work*. It is, as the Halicarnassian observes, a most extraodinary stile of history, such as no author before him wrote, nor has any since. Yet it is prose; for the words are not poetical, and the figures of composition are such as may be used in prose as well as in poetry: But there are too many of them, and some of them too far removed from common speech; nor is there enough of plain work, which is a fault

* Chap. xi. p. 198. 199.

in the writing art, as well as in any other.
He has shown, more, I think, than any other author, that those figures of words, by which the stile is distinguished from common speech, may be used to such excess, as to make the stile harsh and uncouth, and not at all natural or persuasive: For a stile so laboured and so artificial, does not dispose us to believe the truth of the facts related; and, in that respect, his stile is exceedingly different from that of Herodotus, which has all the appearance of truth and sincerity. His narrative, however, is intelligible enough to a good Greek scholar; but in his orations, in which he abounds, I think, more than any other historian, his arguments are so crowded and complicated together, that they are little better than a riddle. His numbers too are harsh and uncouth, and his cadences as abrupt, and such as cheat the ear almost as much, as those of Tacitus. In short, he is a most striking example of the danger of affecting singularity, and endeavouring to distinguish one's self in that way from all the other writers before you, which, as the Halicarnassian tells us, was

Thucydides's motive for writing so extraordinary a stile of history *; and, indeed, it is the way by which the taste of all the arts, poetry as well as prose writing, painting, statuary, and architecture, has been at different times corrupted. Thucydides thought, that, if he wrote a plain and perspicuous stile, it would not be new and singular; he therefore laboured to make it obscure, that is, he laboured to write ill, which is, as I have observed elsewhere †, one of the greatest faults that any stile can have, and which, more than any other, offends the judicious reader.

The second Greek historian I shall mention in this chapter, is Xenophon, whose stile is perfectly different, and goes, I think, to the other extreme; for it is rather too plain and simple, and is more the stile of the Socratic dialogue than of history. His expedition of Cyrus abounds too much with characters, and in that respect is too

---

* Dionysius, *De Thucydide Judicium*, cap. 24.

† Vol. III. lib. iv. chap. 10. p. 182. 183.

like to biography *. They are no doubt very inftructive and entertaining, and in fuch a work as *The life of Agefilaus*, or *The education of Cyrus*, are very proper: But, in a piece of hiftory, fuch as *The retreat of the* 10,000, I think they are not fo proper, and far lefs in the hiftory of a nation. Even in the hiftory of one war only, fuch as the Peloponnefian, Thucydides has been fo judicious as not to introduce them. But Xenophon, being bred in the fchool of morals under Socrates, has adorned even his hiftory with characters and manners, which he appears to have underftood perfectly well.

But, in defence of Xenophon, may be faid what cannot be faid in behalf of our modern hiftorians, that the *Anabafis* was the hiftory of the greateft event of the life of a fingle man; fo that it may be confidered as a kind of biography, in which it was very proper to give the character of Cyrus, and not improper to give alfo the characters of fome of the principal perfons concerned with him in that expedition; whereas, in his *Hellenica*, or *hiftory of*

* Page 397. of this Volume.

Greece, it would have been improper; and accordingly he has not done it.

The last Greek historian I shall mention in this chapter, is Diodorus Siculus, whose stile certainly deserves the eulogium that Photius gives it, *of not being too Attic*. But, I think, it is too little Attic, by which I mean that it is too little ornamented, and too like to common speech: And, though it have a great deal of the simplicity of Xenophon, it has not his sweetness, nor those Attic graces, which abound in his stile.

As to his *matter*, though his plan be more comprehensive than that of Herodotus, he is more inferior, both to Herodotus and Xenophon, in the *matter* than in point of *stile*. And he appears to me to have had a worse affectation than that of Thucydides, which was to distinguish himself from the authors that had written before him in the relation of facts, so as to appear quite new and original in that respect. This must be evident to every man, who compares his history of Xerxes's invasion of Greece, with the same history given us by Herodotus; and, particularly, his description of the two sea fights at Artemisium, of the battle of Plataea, but, above all, of the famous action at Thermopylae, of which he has made a most romantic story, by telling us, that the Spartans, in the night time, penetrated into the Persian camp, and got even to the tent of Xerxes, where they killed every body except Xerxes himself; and then, the day breaking, the whole Persian army was alarmed, and surrounding the Greeks, cut them to pieces in the middle of the camp. This is a fiction, which, though it had been more credible in itself, never could have passed for truth at the time, or near the time, when the action at Thermopylae happened; because the monument of the Spartans that fell there, was then standing upon a little rising ground, in the narrowest part of the pass, near to the wall which the Persians demolished, and tumbled the ruins of it upon the Greeks *.

* Herodotus, lib. vii. cap. 223. 225.

And he has given us a history of *The retreat of the* 10,000, very different from the account given by Xenophon, who was one of the commanders of that *retreat*.

Nor is Diodorus Siculus the only ancient author, who has indulged himself in the pleasure of telling wonderful stories at the expence of truth. Dion Cassius has given us a description of Caesar's battle with Ariovistus, very different from that which Caesar himself has given, yet not so different as a late editor and translator of this author has made it. The name of this editor is *Samuel Reimerus*, who has published an edition of Dion Cassius in folio at Hamburgh, in 1750, but, like several of the late German editors, appears not to have understood the language of his author: For he has made this author describe the Romans as doing a thing in this battle, which they certainly did not do, and which, indeed, it is impossible to suppose that they could have done. They came on, says he, to the attack before they were in perfect order, and with such velocity, that they deprived the barbarians of the use of their darts, in which they confided so much, and even of their long swords; so that they were obliged immediately to take to their short swords or daggers. Now, it is evident, both from the words of this particular passage, and from Dion's whole narrative of the battle, as well as from Caesar's account of it, that it was the Germans who came on in this barbarous and disorderly manner, not the Romans; and they made the attack with such velocity, (so great, that I should not have believed it was possible, if it had been related by any other author than Julius himself), that the Romans in a fair field, not surprised, but, on the contrary, prepared to receive the enemy, to whom they had offered battle some days before, and to whose camp they advanced that very day in order of battle, lost the use of their *pilum*, a weapon to which, as Dion says, they trusted very much. And indeed they had good reason: For it was the best missive that ever was used by heavy-armed men, at least since the heroic times; to which they owed, in a great measure, their victory over the *Helvetii*, according to the account Cæsar has given us of that battle; with which, in another described by Cæsar, they killed the whole first rank of the Gauls; and with which, as Livy tell us, they killed even elephants. But this is an error, not of Dion Caſſius, but of his editor and tranſlator, who has plainly aſcribed to the Romans, what Dion has ſaid of the Barbarians: But it is the error of the author to make the Germans not attack in a phalanx, as Julius Caeſar ſaid they did; but, after they were beat and were going off, then to form different phalanxes of about 300 men each, which ſtood like ſo many towers, with the men ſo cloſely joined together that they did not fall when they were killed by the Romans; which no doubt is told as a circumſtance of wonder, and, I believe, was the reaſon for contriving thoſe ſtrange tower-like phalanxes. Dion is the leſs to be excuſed for ſuch fictions, that he muſt have ſeen, or had an opportunity of ſeeing, Julius Ceaſar's own account of the battle. As he is very fond of ſpeech-making, as well as of ſuch romantic deſcrip-

tions, he has given us a speech of Julius
Cæsar, which was certainly made before
this battle, and indeed was very neceffary in order to animate his men, who
were so much discouraged by the frightful
accounts they had heard of Ariovistus and
his Germans, that he was in hazard of
being deserted by them. This speech in
Dion is among the longest we have in
history, consisting of near seven columns
in folio, as it is printed in the edition a-
bove mentioned; whereas the speech really made is, as Caesar has given it us, a
short speech, but very much more to the
purpose than the long one of Dion. And
he has not given us at all what passed in
the conference betwixt Julius and Ariovistus, though he has told us in general,
that there was such a conference; whereas, Caesar has related at some length, what
passed on both sides, from which we learn,
what the pretensions were, both of the
Romans and of Ariovistus, and by what
reasons they were supported; which, I
think, it was of importance that the reader
should know: And it is no doubt the busi-

ness of an historian to relate the causes and reasons of a war, as well as the events of it.

His account of the battle of Pharsalia is still more extraordinary than that of Ariovistus's battle. Caesar's description of this decisive action betwixt him and Pompey is the best I ever read of any battle; but Dion thought it below him to copy it, and has given us a battle of his own, very different indeed from that of Julius.. In the first place, he has endeavoured to make a pathetic tragedy of it, by telling us, that the legions, before they engaged, stood facing one another for some time, deeply affected with the thought that Romans were to fight against Romans, sons with their fathers, brothers with brothers, and friends with friends; and could not be persuaded to advance to the charge, even by the signals of battle given by the generals, but continued still to stand motionless, and, he adds, weeping and lamenting; neither did they begin the engagement, till

the foreign auxiliaries ſhowed them the way. Now, this is not only a fiction, but an abſurd and incredible fiction; for it is certain, that men fight with more animoſity in civil than in foreign wars; and it was particularly ſo in theſe civil wars among the Romans, called by Lucan *bella pluſquam civilia*; an expreſſion, which, if it has any good meaning, muſt denote that theſe wars were fiercer, and carried on with more animoſity than even civil wars commonly are. That there was no backwardneſs, at leaſt in Caeſar's army, but, on the contrary, the greateſt keenneſs to fight, is evident from the ſtory he tells us of Craſtinus the centurion, which nobody can believe to be a lye. 2d/y, In the deſcription of the battle he is as circumſtantial as any poet: But his circumſtances are not ſo well choſen as thoſe of Homer's battles; for they are trivial and common to all battles, ſuch as theſe;
—'Some were flying, ſome purſuing; ſome
' were vanquiſhed, ſome were victorious;
' ſome were wounded, and ſome killed thoſe
' that wounded them:' And the only remarkable circumſtance he mentions, but which I

think incredible, is, that some, who were killed by their friends and relations, did, when they were dying, send, in the middle of the battle, their laſt commands to their friends and families at home, by thoſe who had killed them. And, *laſtly*, he has omitted to relate that order and diſpoſition of the battle, by which Julius gained the victory; I mean the drafting out of his third line ſix cohorts, and making of them a fourth line, which, upon a ſignal given, attacked Pompey's cavalry, in which he was much ſuperior to Caeſar; and, accordingly, they had got the better of Caeſar's cavalry, when theſe ſix cohorts fell upon them, and, as Pompey had neglected to provide a corps de reſerve of infantry to ſupport them, drove them off the field; then cut to pieces Pompey's archers and ſlingers; and, laſt of all, flanked and ſurrounded Pompey's legions, who were ſtill making a ſtout reſiſtance, though Pompey, by fooliſhly, as I think, altering the Roman method of running on to the attack, and making his men ſtand motionleſs in the line to receive the enemies charge, had done a great deal to damp their spirit and resolution, as well as to lessen the force of their spears, which must have been thrown with much greater force when they were running, than when they were standing still. This battle, therefore, Caesar did not gain, as he modestly says he gained the most of his battles, ‘ by the valour of his ‘ soldiers,’ but by his own conduct, and his superiority in genius and military skill to his antagonist Pompey. In one particular, however, he gives great praise to his soldiers even in this battle; for he says, that they, perceiving Pompey's soldiers did not advance to meet them, stopped in the middle of the course, and took breath, not by any command from him, which there was no time to give, but taught, as he says, by their great experience in war; the consequence of which was, that Pompey's design, of taking them breathless and exhausted by so long a course, was not only disappointed, but turned against him.

Appian, in his history of the Roman civil wars, has given us much the same account of this battle, but not quite so poetical, nor fo much loaded with circumſtances, and in much better language, as he lived in a better age, and is a much more elegant writer than Dion, who, I think, is among the worſt writers of later times; and there is hardly any fo bad, till we come down to the decline of the Greek empire, when they wrote a language that was neither Greek nor Latin, but a mixture of both, and hardly intelligible. But he has a defcription of another battle, viz. the battle of Zama, which I think more extravagant and ridiculous than any thing to be found even in Dion Caſſius: For he has made quite a Homeric battle of it, the generals, as he tells us, fighting hand to hand with one another, Hannibal firſt with Scipio, whom he wounded and difmounted, and then with Mafiniſſa the Numidian King: And he has omitted to tell us, as Dion has done in the defcription of the battle of Pharfalia, how the victory was gained; namely, by Scipio's fuperiority in horfe, of which Polybius, the moſt judicious and authentic hiſtorian, has taken care to inform us.

And here I cannot help obferving, that almoft all thefe later hiftorians among the ancients, as well as Dion Caffius and Appian, have made their hiftories rather rhetorical and poetical exercifes, than authentic narratives, and have ftudied more to amufe and furprife their readers, than to inftruct them in the truth of facts.

I will fay nothing at prefent of modern hiftories, but will refer them to the conclufion of what I have further to add upon the fubject of the ftile of hiftory. I conclude therefore this chapter and this volume, with obferving in general, that the works of fuch hiftorians as Julius Caefar and Xenophon, who were not only contemporary with the facts they relate, but were principal actors in them, or of fuch an author as Herodotus, who lived in the next age after that great event of Xerxes's invafion of Greece, and converfed, as he tells us, with men who lived at that time, are of much greater value to a man who does not read merely for amufement but is ftudious of truth, than any compilements of hiſtory from hearſay, or from authors that had written before; for we are not only more aſſured of the facts related by the contemporary hiſtorians, but we learn what, I think, is of more value, the arts, manners, and opinions, of the age, which are almoſt wholly loſt in our modern compilements of hiſtory.

The next volume will begin with an account of the hiſtorians, Greek and Latin, who have written the hiſtory of the greateſt empire, and of the longeſt duration, that ever was in the world; I mean the Roman empire: After which, I will make ſome obſervations upon our modern hiſtorians; and then I will proceed, according to the method I have laid down, to treat of the didactic, the rhetorical, and the poetical ſtiles, with which, and ſome general obſervations upon the utility of ancient learning, I will conclude this work, OF THE ORIGIN AND PROGRESS OF LANGUAGE.

END OF VOLUME FOURTH.

www.ingramcontent.com/pod-product-compliance
Lightning Source LLC
Chambersburg PA
CBHW051158300426
44116CB00006B/362